Rock Star

ROCK STAR

The Making of Musical Icons from Elvis to Springsteen

DAVID R. SHUMWAY

Foreword by Anthony DeCurtis

JOHNS HOPKINS UNIVERSITY PRESS *Baltimore*

9 8 7 6 5 4 3 2 1

Johns Hopkins University Press
2715 North Charles Street
Baltimore, Maryland 21218-4363
www.press.jhu.edu

Library of Congress Cataloging-in-Publication Data
Shumway, David R.
    Rock star : the making of musical icons from Elvis to
Springsteen / David R. Shumway ; foreword by Anthony
DeCurtis.
    pages cm
    Includes bibliographical references and index.
    ISBN-13: 978-1-4214-1392-1 (hardcover : alk. paper)
    ISBN-13: 978-1-4214-1393-8 (electronic)
    ISBN-10: 1-4214-1392-2 (hardcover : alk. paper)
    ISBN-10: 1-4214-1393-0 (electronic)
    1. Rock musicians—United States.   2. Rock groups—United
States.   3. Popular culture—United States.   4. Fame—Social
aspects—United States.   5. Rock music—Social aspects—
United States.   I. Title.
    ML3918.R63.S58 2014
    306.4'8426—dc23   2013043622

A catalog record for this book is available from the British
Library.

*Special discounts are available for bulk purchases of this book. For
more information, please contact Special Sales at 410-516-6936 or
specialsales@press.jhu.edu.*

Johns Hopkins University Press uses environmentally friendly
book materials, including recycled text paper that is composed
of at least 30 percent post-consumer waste, whenever possible.

For Travis, future rock star—in whatever field he chooses

CONTENTS

THE ROCK STAR AS METAPHOR

Bill Clinton may have been the first person I ever heard referred to as a rock star in the metaphorical sense. That was partly due to his charisma and partly to do with the fact that his political rise corresponded to the period in the late eighties and early nineties when it became not merely acceptable but advantageous for politicians to consort with rock musicians. Jerry Brown had done that in California in the seventies, of course, even to the point of dating Linda Ronstadt. But those associations didn't seem to help him beyond his home state or, more exactly, beyond Los Angeles. They just reinforced whatever perceptions might have already existed of him in the general population as a marginal figure, certainly not someone to take seriously as a presidential candidate. (Using *Rolling Stone*'s offices as his New York campaign headquarters during his 1992 presidential run probably didn't help in that regard either.)

But by the time Clinton was making his successful run for the presidency, the boomer generation that had grown up with rock & roll now wielded real power in the country and, for better and worse, Clinton reflected their ideals, ambitions, tastes, and appetites. His choice of Fleetwood Mac's "Don't Stop Thinking about Tomorrow" as his campaign song and his willingness to meet with the members of U2 while then president George H.W. Bush was clumsily dodging the phone calls that Bono was making to him from the stages of packed stadiums across the United States during U2's Zoo TV tour both indicated that a generational shift had taken place. (Clinton also fit the rock-star suit. His own sexual proclivities conformed exactly to the long-standing rule of the road among musicians in supposedly monogamous relationships: Blow jobs don't count.) Suddenly politicians didn't need to distance themselves from rock stars. Quite the opposite: They actively courted them. We'd come a long way from the days when Jimmy Carter quoting Bob Dylan in his 1977 inaugural address seemed daring.

Of course the success of this new relationship depended entirely on the specific politician and rock star. As David Shumway points out, when Ronald Reagan spoke about Bruce Springsteen and attempted to use "Born in the

U.S.A." during his 1984 reelection campaign, the gesture blew up in his face. Similar efforts by conservative politicians to use rock songs in their campaigns have met with similar results since then. And the knife cuts both ways. Bono has spoken about how his meetings with the likes of George W. Bush and Jesse Helms about debt relief and AIDS policy in Africa have not only displeased some fans but disturbed his own band members.

Along those lines, it's quite possible that the level of respectability that has allowed rock stars to move comfortably with mainstream politicians has also dimmed the luster of their stardom. Sure, it was fun to watch President Barack Obama tease the members of Led Zeppelin about not trashing the White House when they came by for their Kennedy Center Honors ("So, guys, just settle down—these paintings are valuable!"), but what's the point of being a rock star if it requires responsible behavior?

And right around the time "rock star" became a ubiquitous metaphor, the meaning of stardom in popular music began to change. In 2000 I was hired to do some editing for *Vibe* magazine, and one piece I worked on was about the rapper Q-Tip from A Tribe Called Quest. One of the secondary interviews for the story was with a prominent black music executive who wearily described Q-Tip as a "rock star." It wasn't a compliment. Hip-hop had fully established itself as a cultural force by then, so the reference carried none of the hurt and bitterness that, say, accompanied the Public Enemy line in "Bring Tha Noize" less than a decade earlier: "Roll with the rock stars, still never get accepted as."

No, the executive was making a different point about Q-Tip. By that point Sean "Puffy" Combs had redefined the image of the successful rapper from a street thug to a mogul, the line entirely blurred, or perhaps just rendered meaningless, between the artist and the businessman. Jay-Z has traveled that same trajectory and beyond, to the point of declaring, only half-jokingly, that when (not if) he's voted into the Rock & Roll Hall of Fame, he wants Barack Obama to induct him. ("It'd be all right," he told Bill Maher. "He owes me a couple.") That Q-Tip was not aspiring to the role of businessman / power broker was precisely the point the executive was making about him. In his view the term "rock star" meant something like "aesthete brat." That is, not commercially minded; too undisciplined and self-involved to increase his potential sales; too pretentious and self-conscious about his role as an "artist" to realize that, as one industry powerhouse once pointedly explained to me, "They don't call it 'the music art.' They call it 'the music business.'"

From that vantage, rock stars' insistence on acting as if money was never a consideration for them, on still dressing from the thrift store after earning tens of millions of dollars, just seemed ridiculous, or maybe even a little nuts. To deliver a warning that you're "crazy like Kurt Cobain" became something of a trope in rap after the Nirvana lead singer killed himself at the height of his band's popularity. Now wait a minute, the reasoning behind those references seemed to run: You killed yourself *because* you were successful and made a ton of money? That is some really scary shit. To be "crazy like Kurt Cobain" meant that you could not be relied upon in any way to behave rationally—such as, in Q-Tip's case, refusing to maximize your earning power. It was the true, and perhaps final, blow to the stature of being a rock star.

Cobain, indeed, marked something like the end point of rock stardom, the point when even actual rock stars rejected the role. We'd had alternative rock stars like Lou Reed and Iggy Pop, who looked and sounded the part but missed the memo about selling millions of records. In the early days of R.E.M., Michael Stipe defined the role of reluctant rock star, acting as if, through no recollected actions of his own, he suddenly discovered himself onstage, in front of a camera or doing an interview, and consequently had no choice but to play along. But after Cobain's shocking, definitive refusal, it became highly undesirable to be perceived as chasing rock stardom.

Which may be fortunate, since it seems to be disappearing anyway, as Shumway argues in this smart, provocative, and emotionally charged book. I'd hate for that to be true, but in the worlds of media and culture we're in the grips of changes as profound as any since the invention of the printing press. In that enormous context, the loss of rock stardom may seem trivial. But, as the old prerock era Gershwin song says, not for me.

Anthony DeCurtis

At a time when the music scene is fragmented and many of the records that top the charts seem to have reverted to prerock pop, it may be hard to remember how much rock stars once mattered. This book will investigate what some of the more prominent stars meant—and continue to mean—not merely to their fans but in the context of the culture at large. Popular culture in general had long been treated as either ephemeral entertainment or a dangerous influence. Popular music in particular, epitomized by Tin Pan Alley love songs, hardly seemed capable of serious content, and only aficionados understood jazz as an exception. But rock changed all of that. By the end of the 1960s, the news media accepted rock stars as representatives of their generation and its role in what was perceived to be the remaking of America. Rock stars were not mere entertainers but politically charged cultural icons.[1] Music mattered in a way it never had before, as Matthew Weiner illustrates in a 2012 episode of *Mad Men* set around the time of the Beatles' *Revolver* release in 1966. Don Draper, a Depression era baby and successful advertising executive, wonders at the quickly changing cultural landscape: "When," he asks his colleagues, "did music become so important?"[2]

Music was newly important, I am arguing, not mainly because of how it changed, but because of how its leading performers presented themselves and were perceived. I am also arguing that stardom as a particular social phenomenon, distinct from fame or celebrity, also matters in ways that have eluded most scholars. Star personas are complex and meaningful texts that require the kind of interpretive exploration we devote to other works of art. Moreover, given stars' widespread popularity, they may more accurately reflect and more strongly impact the larger culture than most other works.

The goal of this book is to explain what the personas of seven rock icons meant to the culture, by examining those stars through their many representations: live performance, films, television, videos, cover art and photography, interviews and journalism, in addition to recorded music and lyrics. These star personas might be the most important of rock & roll's many products. My argument is that these stars represented a new kind of star, one defined by the embodiment of cultural controversies, which replaced the movie star in the popular imagination and helped popular music attain a new cultural centrality. While they inherited the power and prominence of their Hollywood forebearers, rock stars came to stand for many of the changes that caused conflict in post–World War II America.

Each of the major figures I consider illustrates a different aspect of the cultural impact of rock & roll and of the new form of stardom. My book is a narrative told in a series of tableaux, the discussion of each star not only advancing a general story about the development of rock stardom but also illustrating from a different perspective the means by which stars' personas were presented and were received by audiences. Each of the stars I discuss depended differently on media other than sound recording. Each chapter deals with a different social conflict that the star persona in question comes to embody, for example, civil rights and black power for James Brown, high versus low culture for Bob Dylan.

Please note that my argument is not that the rock stars I discuss are, in the main, intending to be political actors but that their personas were understood as having distinct political valences. According to Peter Wicke, by 1967 "rock music was now placed in a context in which it no longer defined itself merely in musical terms, but also in political terms."[3] Wicke is cognizant of the contradiction between rock's revolutionary ideology and its actual existence as an industrial commodity, and he associates stardom entirely with the latter. The argument I'm making is that rock stardom also has to be understood as political, differing not only from Wicke's position but also from arguments about rock politics made by Dick Hebdige and Lawrence Grossberg. These scholars persuasively argue that rock has been a form of resistance in particular subcultures (Hebdige) or for the youth of postwar American society (Grossberg).[4] Grossberg treats rock & roll as "strategic empowerment," emphasizing what the formation does in the everyday lives of its participants.[5] My claim here has to do with the broader cultural meaning and impact of rock stars, which requires that we understand them not as defined against the larger culture as a whole but as an element of that culture, its internal opposition. Hebdige and Grossberg are concerned mainly with rock's role in contemporary cultural struggles, and it is important to acknowledge that these struggles continue. My focus, however, is on rock stars' connection to historical struggles and the changes they produced. While I accept the idea that rock was a force for change, it was also an instance of it. In discussing stardom, I must necessarily deemphasize what Grossberg calls the "boundaries" constructed by the rock formation, the idea of rock as "a differentiating machine . . . [that] continually separated Us . . . from Them" and emphasize rock's inclusion in the dominant culture.[6]

That culture should be understood not as unitary and unchanging but as diverse, characterized by struggle and change. Arthur Marwick has argued persuasively that a cultural revolution took place between 1958 and 1974 not only in the United States but also in Britain, France, and Italy. Marwick lists sixteen distinct categories of significant change during this period, including the formation of new subcultures and movements, an upsurge of entrepreneurialism resulting in the founding of theaters, clubs, boutiques, and so on, and the rise of young people to unprecedented influence. For our purposes, however, the following is most important: "A participatory and uninhibited popular culture, whose central component was rock music, which in effect became a kind of universal language."[7] While one might find this last claim questionable, we have evidence such as Tom Stoppard's play "Rock 'n' Roll," about events in late-1960s Czechoslovakia, to support the notion that rock had a very broad reach and was widely understood to be disruptive of the status quo. It is not my claim that rock & roll is a self-sufficient cause of all of the cultural change with which it should be associated. Rather, in most instances rock contributed to and reflected changes that were being fueled by other sources.

Rock & roll was not a purely musical language. As Grossberg explains, "Most writing about rock and roll has failed to define the production of the apparatus, which includes not only the production of recorded music but also of concerts, of music that is never recorded . . . of art and dance, of writing and fashion styles, and so on."[8] My project is to show how the star personas of rock & roll's leading performers are one of the most significant elements of this "apparatus." The force of stardom helps explain rock's cultural reach, while it also is a major aspect of the recording industry's commercial success. I argue that while music and lyrics are elements that help define a star's persona, that persona is also indispensible to understanding the songs and other works the star produces.

This volume is a historical study. It aims to understand the personas of different stars through the cultural forces at work in specific historical moments, mainly from 1956 though the 1970s. While the stars I'm concerned with here remain iconic today, in each case their cultural meaning emerged at an earlier moment and persisted despite changes in form and popularity. But my historical frame is longer than the history of rock & roll. Stardom itself is a distinct historical phenomenon, and chapter 1 situates rock stardom within that larger history. It deals with the concept of stardom and its relation to fame and celebrity. It then continues with a focus on Hollywood in the 1930s and 1940s and explores how their different media make popular music stardom different from film stardom. I next examine how stardom changes after World War II, when certain leading film stars develop politicized personas, setting the stage for the emergence of the rock star. In the final section I introduce the chapters on individual rock stars that make up the body of this book.

This book would not exist if I had not met Anthony DeCurtis in graduate school at Indiana University in the 1970s. Anthony was the first person I knew who taught rock records and lyrics in a college course, and talking with Anthony about music turned my dim inkling that serious rock criticism might be possible into an ambition for me; it has been, of course, a reality for him, and I have continued to learn from him and his writing. The book itself can be traced back to 1980, to what was my second academic conference paper, written for a panel that included Anthony and film scholar and rock musician Robert B. Ray at the Popular Culture Association Convention in Detroit. A few pages of that paper are present here in chapter 5, but more important, the idea of reading performers rather than music or lyrics was its basis.

My book comes out of rock criticism and popular music studies on the one hand and film history and criticism on the other, and I am appreciative of many who came before me in both areas. I am especially indebted to the late Robert Palmer, from whom I learned a great deal when he served as a visiting professor at Carnegie Mellon University in the late 1980s. Other scholars and critics who have influenced me include Greil Marcus, Richard Dyer, Simon Frith, Robert Christgau, Lawrence Grossberg, and Dick Hebdige.

I'm grateful to those colleagues who have taken the time to read the manuscript in whole or in part at various stages of its creation: Fran Bartkowski, Anahid Kassabian, Kathy Newman, and Jeff Williams. Their suggestions and encouragement were invaluable. Thanks to two anonymous readers for Johns Hopkins University Press who contributed significantly to the book's improvement. Jean Tamarin's editorial work on the first version of the conclusion was most helpful. Thanks also to Greg Nicholl for his editorial acumen and expertise in shepherding the manuscript through the approval process.

I appreciate the insights gained from conversations and contact with Marian Aguiar, Lynne Barrett, Lauren Berlant, Lucy Fischer, Joel Foreman, Loren

Glass, Daniel Herwitz, Keir Keightley, Jon Klancher, Peggy Knapp, Brian McHale, John Mowitt, Robert Myers, James Naremore, Jeffrey Nealon, Scott Sandage, Barry Shank, Jean Sieper, Paul Smith, Kristina Straub, Steve Waksman, and Tom Young. Thank you to students in several seminars I taught on stardom, especially Jeff Hinkelman, Katie Bird, and Tara Covelens.

I have presented many bits of this book at meetings of the International Association for the Study of Popular Music and its U.S. chapter, and I have benefited greatly from comments and discussion at those sessions. Many people have invited me to give portions of this book at their institutions, and for this I am grateful to Celia Ferreira Alves, Tony Badger, Niels Bjerre-Poulsen, Craig Dionne, Anne Fillaudeau, Winfried Fluck, Loren Glass, Dick Hebdige, Jonathan Hope, Gerd Hurm, Anahid Kassabian, Robert Kerr, Henry Krips, Sonia Di Loreto, René Lysloff, Robert Myers, Andrew Preston, Andreas Rude, Andrew Weintraub, Kathleen Woodward, and Josh Zeitz.

I also want to thank Carnegie Mellon University, which supported my research on this project with a leave, and by providing me with research assistants. While I was working mainly on other projects at the Wesleyan University Center for the Humanities during two residencies in the 1990s, the interdisciplinary exchange I experienced there helped to advance this book as well.

I am most grateful to Heather Scarlett Arnet, who has lived with this project longer than anyone but me, for her love, insight, and support. I have been inspired by our son Travis and his love of music. This book is dedicated to him.

The usual disclaimers apply.

An earlier version of chapter 2 was previously published as "Watching Elvis: The Male Rock Star as Object of the Gaze," in *The Other Fifties: Interrogating Midcentury American Icons,* ed. Joel Foreman (Urbana, IL: University of Illinois Press, 1997), 124–43.

A shorter version of chapter 4 was published as "Bob Dylan as Cultural Icon," *The Cambridge Companion to Bob Dylan,* ed. Kevin J. H. Dettmar (Cambridge: Cambridge University Press, 2009), 110–21.

The conclusion is developed from a much shorter essay, "Where Have All the Rock Stars Gone?," *The Chronicle of Higher Education,* June 22, 2007, The Chronicle Review, 6.

Rock Star

CHAPTER ONE

REFLECTIONS ON STARDOM AND ITS TRAJECTORIES

With the golden days of Hollywood long gone, and the movies having given way to pop music and pro sports as America's prime fantasy obsessions, a new kind of star had come along. The rock star.

Robert Greenfield

By the time Robert Greenfield observed that "a new kind of star had come along," rock stars had replaced movie stars at the head of the pantheon of American popular culture.[1] Where Greta Garbo, Cary Grant, Katharine Hepburn, and Humphrey Bogart had once reigned supreme, now Mick Jagger, Elvis Presley, Bob Dylan, and numerous others held court. "Rock star" replaced "movie star" as the standard designation for someone possessed of great charisma, glamour, and sex appeal. Thus, Bill Clinton was a rock star, where a generation earlier President John F. Kennedy was likened to a movie star. This change may seem to be a trivial shift in fashion, explicable in terms of the buying power of adolescent baby boomers and the decline of the studio system but not of any importance in itself. The rock star, however, really was a new kind of star, not merely the successor to the movie star as the biggest celebrity, but having a new cultural role. One reason we have failed to understand this is that we have consistently confused stardom with celebrity, and, as a result, we have not treated stars and stardom with the seriousness they deserve.

Daniel Herwitz, in his insightful book *The Star as Icon,* takes Princess Diana as his central instance. Herwitz says much that is persuasive about stardom, but I want to argue that, regardless of what one thinks of the late wife of the heir to the British throne, she cannot be called a star. She was certainly a celebrity and, by Herwitz's definition, an icon, but she does not meet the criteria that distinguish stardom as a specific historical and cultural phenomenon.[2] In making this claim, I mean to make no comment on Diana's importance to history, contribution to human welfare, or degree of attraction and fascination. To say that she is not a star is not a criticism of her but a simple act of taxonomy necessary so that we can understand the different forms that fame and visibility have had in our culture. Diana was not a star, because she had not *achieved success in a skilled field or profession,* one of five defining characteristics of stardom. The other four attributes that distinguish stardom, which I will discuss in more detail below, are (2) the star is the object of imagined personal relationships by fans; (3) the star has a persona that represents more than an individual personality but works as a widely understood culturally specific sign or icon; (4) the persona is consistent and well developed; and, finally and most subjectively, (5) a star has the degree of personal attractiveness that we call "star quality."

It would be impossible in popular discourse to expect any distinction between *celebrity* and *stardom* to be regularly observed. Scholarly discourse, however, should be able to support such a distinction, but it has routinely failed to do so. In recent scholarship, film studies partially excepted, celebrity has been far more often the focus. This fact seems to me to stem from the power of Daniel Boorstin's notion that "the Celebrity is a person who is well known for his well-knownness."[3] By "power," I don't mean "influence," although Boorstin's treatment of celebrity has doubtless been influential. Rather, I mean that Boorstin's critique of celebrity captured something that many people feel to be a fundamental condition of contemporary life. We believe that many, if not most, celebrities do not deserve the interest they receive.

All stars are celebrities, but not all celebrities are stars. Boorstin fails to recognize this distinction, treating stars as pseudo-events and as creatures of the machinery of publicity and advertising: "The qualities which now commonly make a man or woman into a 'nationally advertised' brand are in fact a new category of human emptiness."[4] Boorstin's conflation of star and celebrity has become the norm, and even some otherwise careful theorists such as David Marshall and Chris Rojek fail to escape it. While not everyone who conflates stardom and celebrity is as dismissive of it as Boorstin was, they continue to accept his basic assumption that, as Marshall puts it, "the interchangeability of celebrities means that no celebrity possesses any meaning of consequence." Marshall observes that this thesis "identifies in outline the postmodern condition," and he connects Boorstin to Jean Baudrillard. Marshall doesn't give this position his unqualified endorsement, but neither does he repudiate it.[5]

We need to distinguish celebrity both from fame and from stardom. I want to use the word *fame* as a category for those who have gained the public eye through public action.[6] By this definition the famous—generals, politicians, and authors—were traditionally not celebrities. The phenomenon of celebrity emerges when the private lives of the famous become of major public interest, which as Fred Inglis shows, happened within the past 250 years.[7] Those people we identify as stars are, like the traditionally famous, distinguished from other celebrities because of valued achievements. They are thus the opposite of people who are well known merely for being well known. Most people we call stars have achieved success in a skilled field or profession. This is perhaps most clear of sports stars, whose performance is readily quantified, making stardom seem like a simple matter of statistics. Although it is true that even sports stardom involves more than statistics—Babe Ruth and Michael Jordan had recognizable public personas—we don't typically denigrate athletic stars in the same way we do many others. Of course, stars in entertainment are also partly defined in terms of box office or record sales, and thus to some extent stardom here is also quantifiable.

While in sports the almost unquestioned assumption is that the star's abilities are the source of this success, the economic success of entertainment personalities does not always lead to the same belief in their worthiness. Still, even bad actors or mediocre musicians must have performed relatively skilled labor. Conversely, the fact that those we feel to be the most talented sometimes do not become stars does not mean that those who do are uniformly lacking in talent. Clearly, the unreliability of stardom as a measure of talent or worth is one of the conditions that lead critics to view stars as mere celebrities in Boorstin's sense. Stars, however, are no different in this regard than authors, painters, politicians, or, indeed, people in any field of endeavor. Ever since Ecclesiastes, we have known that the fastest runner does not always win a race. While "the celebrity," as Boorstin observes, "is always a contemporary," great stars, like authors, painters, and some U.S. presidents, are distinguished by the longevity of their cultural presence.[8] John Wayne, for example, was America's favorite movie star in 1995, more than fifteen years after his death. Greta Garbo, Humphrey Bogart, and Cary Grant continue to be widely recognized and revered today, long after their careers and lives have ended.

Although sports stars are the most easily recognized and agreed upon, sports stardom is also quite thin. There is a limited range of characteristics revealed in the performance of a sport, though that range may be greater in an individual sport like tennis than in a team sport such as football. Those people who are the most multidimensional stars are to be found in the performing arts. Performance in that special sense in which it happens in film, theater, or concert—rather than the everyday performance that Judith Butler and others have discussed—is important to stardom because it is through performance that the star's persona can be most richly developed.[9]

The phenomenon of celebrity has been traced by Inglis as far back as London of the 1760s, when, he asserts, it "stood to fame as marketing to production" and where "the intimate life of actors is greedily pursued."[10] This desire for intimacy is also a defining characteristic of stardom, and Inglis's example suggests that theatrical stardom may have been the prototype for celebrity in general. There was a star system in British theater of the eighteenth century, making it probably the first. Marcel Proust's account of his response to stars suggests that the phenomenon of stardom was already well established in late nineteenth-century Paris: "But if the thought of actors preoccupied me so . . . how much more did the name of a 'star' blazing outside the doors of a theater, how much more, seen through the window of a brougham passing by in the street, its horses' headbands decked with roses, did the face of a woman whom I took to be an actress, leave me in a state of troubled excitement, impotently and painfully trying to form a picture of her private life."[11] Proust describes here precisely the relationship of fan to star that defines the phenomenon. The young Proust wants to know the private person behind the star image, a person whose life he can and must imagine.

Movie Stars

There were theatrical stars in the United States in the nineteenth century, but it is the motion picture industry that provides the basic model of stardom for the twentieth-century United States. For this reason, we can best approach the change with which rock & roll was associated by looking first at stardom in film. It is largely by analogy with the movies that *star* was applied to other areas of entertainment, including sports, radio, music, and television. More recently, it has been used of politicians, architects, and even English professors.[12] Unlike most other fields, in theater and film stars portray characters. This enables the development of stars' personas, since each character played can potentially add new qualities or attributes. Richard Dyer asserts that the duality of persona and person is the basic condition for film stardom, which depends upon the existence of a consistent persona.[13] While it is true that film actors do not necessarily have such consistent personas—and we can distinguish those who practice "impersonation" acting, wherein an actor transforms him- or herself into different characters, from "personification," where his or her persona is constant from film to film—even impersonation actors who are stars develop personas. The star's persona then becomes associated with the private individual, but the two are never identical, and only the most naïve fans experience them as such. As Marshall puts it, "the relationship that the audience builds with the film celebrity is configured through a tension between the possibility and impossibility of knowing the authentic individual."[14]

The movies had distinct advantages over theater in creating widely recognized stars. The most obvious is the vast increase in the size of the audience, but perhaps just as important was the increase in the size of the actor, and especially her or his face, on the screen. Roland Barthes in "The Face of Garbo," associated this star with "that moment in cinema when capturing the human face still plunged audiences into the deepest ecstasy."[15] This visual intimacy with the face enabled the illusion of an emotional intimacy with the performer greater than one produced by being in the same room with her or him. The studios also had much greater resources, allowing them to exploit other media in their effort to encourage belief in this intimacy.

Unlike the famous, or mere celebrities, stars are defined by attractiveness, usually experienced as sexual, but that may be a more general personal magnetism. Movie stars are often said to be different from the rest of us because of their "star quality," which screenwriter Budd Schulberg defines as a "mysterious amalgam of self-love, vivacity, style, and sexual promise."[16] The components of star quality correspond to two components of audience response: desire and identification. The star's attractiveness works both directly and vicariously in the minds of the fans, who want either to have the star or to be the star. Sexual promise, conveyed through the portrayal of romantic relationships, is at the heart of what the dream factory made and sold, yet it would be a mistake to treat stars merely as sex objects. As sociologist Joshua Gamson notes, fans took the Hollywood star as a model, someone to identify with and to imitate.[17] Film scholar Jackie Stacey has shown that identification is central to how women responded to stars of the 1940s and 1950s, both while watching movies and at other times. Self-love is important because an individual lacking self-love tends not to be regarded as worthy of imitation or identification.[18]

According to architect Denise Scott Brown, "stardom is something done to a star by others. Stars cannot create themselves."[19] It is the audience's

Greta Garbo, a star "when capturing the human face still plunged audiences into the deepest ecstasy," c. 1930. (publicity photo, MGM)

identification and desire that "create" the star. Stardom is an effect of a relation between the celebrity and the fans. This points to the second distinguishing attribute of stars: they are the objects of imagined personal relationships by fans. For Richard Schickel, modern celebrity, the model for which is film stardom, is "based on an imagined intimacy fostered by the media."[20] But while stars share this condition with some other celebrities, not all celebrities engender such fantasies. How do we know that fans typically imagine such relationships? The evidence lies in fan mail, in public reactions to stars' marriages and divorces, and especially in the mourning—sometimes on a vast scale—of them when they die. Adoring fans make the star adorable; thus studios staged premieres and other events for the display of public worship, made sure that fan mail received responses so that fans would send more mail, and helped build quasi-religious shrines such as the Walk of Fame.

In the United States, film stardom begins around 1910 with the emergence of the first "picture personalities," performers whose identities were "constructed through the films [they] had appeared in and the publicity for those films."[21] It was at this point that studios discovered the economic advantages of stars and began to promote them. One kind of publicity was particularly important in making film stars distinctive from other celebrities. Producer Carl Laemmle seems to have been the first in the industry to actively manipulate public perceptions of film actors outside of the films by trying to convince the public that an actor—King Baggot in 1912—was the sort of person he played on the screen.[22] As this example shows, stardom is best created out of the interrelation of different media. The invention of stars' public images needs to be understood as a collaborative project of the star and industry, but the success of that invention clearly depends on audience response. The studios built a publicity apparatus to ensure that the personality portrayed in the movies would be further developed in other media and that images of the star's offscreen life would continue the fans' relationship with the star between film releases. The star system became a successful marketing strategy rooted in part on the system of contract labor that tied actors to a single studio, typically for seven years. Even without the same labor contracts, the music industry adopted this strategy, partly because its biggest stars of the prerock era, Bing Crosby and Frank Sinatra, were also movie stars. By the time rock & roll came along, this "star-maker machinery" was familiar and available. Stardom increased record sales because it created a desire for new products that preexisted the actual products themselves.

The mention of the machinery of stardom raises the issue of authenticity, which is a problem for stardom, because stars are in several important senses artificial. The most obvious of these is the importance of publicity and the conscious manipulation of the media in which the movie studios, agents, managers, and record companies regularly engage. How can we trust that the star we perceive isn't the mere invention of advertising and public relations? The authenticity of stars is also made problematic by the way in which their primary media, that is, film and sound recording, are typically understood. These media seem particularly artificial. Walter Benjamin, who lamented the loss of the storyteller's authenticity in the literature of his own time, famously argued that the mechanical reproduction of art would render the question of authenticity moot. Benjamin welcomed this destruction of art's aura, and modern art of all kinds has often reveled in the wholesale disappearance of the old, as Chuck Berry suggested with "Roll Over Beethoven." According to Benjamin, the "aura" of a venerated work of art derives from its authenticity and "the presence of the original is the prerequisite to the concept of authenticity." But once mechanical reproduction becomes the norm, the need for an original, authentic object is lost. "To an ever greater degree the work of art reproduced becomes the work of art designed for reproducibility. From a photographic negative, for example, one can make any number of prints; to ask for the 'authentic' print makes no sense." This leads Benjamin to conclude that the criterion of authenticity has ceased to be applicable to artistic production, and, as a result, "the total function of art is reversed." Thus, "that which withers away in the age of mechanical reproduction is the aura of the work of art."[23]

If Benjamin's idea that mechanically reproduced art lacks a significant element of the authenticity of a great painting is irrefutable, Herwitz shows how film nonetheless produced its own aura, which surrounded its stars. He suggests that there *is* an original—the real Cary Grant or Greta Garbo—a point that restates Marshall's insight about the inherent tension between persona and person.[24] Of course, Herwitz's point holds for rock as well, but perhaps even more strongly, since we are more likely to accept a rock star's persona as an authentic expression of his or her self. This throws the problem of authenticity back to the question of the star's agency in his or her own stardom. The fact that the star functions within an industrial system seems to render him or her a mere object of manipulation, but that doubt is rooted in the ideology of individualism. What this book will show is that rock stars are best understood as collaborators in the creation of their personas. They could not have done it alone, but it could not have been done without them either.

Doubtless the star system in rock has tended to undermine the authenticity of the music. At least part of the inevitable rejection by younger musicians and fans of the dominant stars of the previous generation—or moment—is a result of the conviction that anyone so popular and so frequently represented in the media could not possibly be "real." But this is only part of the story. The greatest stars continue to personify authenticity—at least to their fans—in the face of almost any changes or revelations that might call it into question. Elvis Presley remained authentically the King to numerous fans

"Everybody wants to be Cary Grant. Even I want to be Cary Grant," c. 1940. (publicity photo)

even after his personal appearance had become self-parody. Indeed, even the most radical of all changes—death—for many did not diminish their belief in Elvis's real presence.[25] The Rolling Stones continue to fill stadiums by playing the rebellious adolescents they have not been for more than thirty years.

This suggests a qualification of Marshall's point that the very condition of stardom creates a division between the star and an imagined private individual: not every fan experiences this division. Consider movie stars John Wayne and Arnold Schwarzenegger, both of whom are perceived by their fans to be the person they typically played onscreen. Steven Ross shows how candidate Schwarzenegger often used the lines of his movie characters in his campaign for governor of California.[26] Authenticity, then, is also an effect of the star system. This effect enables the star to have a persona that represents more than an individual personality but works as a widely understood culturally specific sign or icon. To be a star is to be perceived as standing apart from the movies or music and to exist in the cultural imaginary at the same level as historical figures like George Washington, fictional characters like Sherlock Holmes, or well-known symbols such as the Statue of Liberty.

The movie stars of the studio era were icons of personality, but, as I will show below, after World War II, stars in both film and music often represent a politics or an ideology. To prepare for that discussion, it is necessary to discuss how rock stardom is formally distinct from film stardom. The rock star differs from the movie star by virtue of differences in their primary media. Because the rock star's performance is, with a few exceptions, as him- or herself, rather than as a fictional character, performance and persona are very closely associated. If the movie industry tried to convince us that stars were like the characters they portrayed, the music industry's task was simpler: it needed to convince the audience that the performing self was a genuine reflection of the real self. That this effort was largely persuasive is shown by the fact that we do not normally take, say, John Lennon or Bob Dylan to be playing a role. We may perceive a movie star's personality in all of the roles he or she plays, but a rock star like Mick Jagger only plays Mick Jagger. One can't imagine him saying, like Cary Grant, that even he *wants* to be Mick Jagger.

The movie star entails three distinct levels—the character portrayed, the public persona, and the private or "real" person—but the rock star, only the latter two. Yet rock stars do come to portray characters that exist with more or less consistency throughout the media in which they perform. "Lennon," "Dylan," and "Jagger" are roles that, unlike those in film, exist in no script. Rock stars do not transform or animate the creation of another; they make themselves up as they go along. But if rock stars are characters, one is entitled to ask in what dramatic or narrative form do they exist. One answer is that they inhabit preexisting social roles, each of which implies at least the outline of a narrative. Dylan has assumed a series of these social roles. He is perhaps most well known as the prophet of such diverse messages as "Blowin' in the Wind" and "You Gotta Serve Somebody," but he has also played the aesthete (*Highway 61 Revisited* and *Blonde on Blonde*), the down home balladeer (*John Wesley Harding* and *Nashville Skyline*), and the poet wounded in love (*Blood on the Tracks*). Another answer is the story of rock itself. This story has been told often in print and occasionally in televised documentaries, but I want to argue that rock's story was invented prior to any of these more or less professional versions. Indeed, the importance of this narrative context to the experience of rock is one of the things that distinguishes it from other popular musical practices: only classical music foregrounds its own history more than rock has. Film stars also inhabit a historical narrative, of course, but it is less salient in the public's experience of them, probably because movie stars are not so readily conceived as authors of self-expression.

Celestial Revolution

Probably the single word most associated with pre–World War II movie stars was *glamour*. Today the word is associated especially with still photographs, which portray actors as more than just beautiful or attractive, a mystical embodiment of the good life. They seem often in such photos to glow, like the heavenly bodies for which they are named, from the inside rather from mere reflected light. The word *glamour* originally meant a magic spell or charm, and these portraits cast spells over charmed viewers. But if the lighting of the photos implies some kind of otherworldly quality, the clothes worn reveal that the good life suggested here is a life full of goods. Glamour was associated not just with a look but with, as Joshua Gamson puts it, "extravagant consumption," which is also something that fans doubtless dreamed of enjoying.[27] That's why product tie-ins used movies and stars in advertising, offering consumers the chance to purchase a little bit of a star's glamour.

Dyer observes, "Stardom is an image of the way stars live. For the most part, this generalized lifestyle is the assumed backdrop for the specific personality of the star and the details and events of her/his life."[28] Other photographs make this explicit, putting the stars at home in the midst of luxury goods. If the level of consumption makes the stars different from you or me, their personalities and private lives make them look more like the rest of us, and some photographs depict the stars living "ordinary" family life. The studios worked hard to keep a balance between these two poles. Stars were meant to be like us, but more so. They were to be our ideal images of ourselves, and therefore the "mask" of glamour was not enough. It is hard to have an imaginary personal relationship with someone who is perfect, so a few private difficulties or eccentricities helped. This duality largely remained intact in the era of the rock star, though glamour became less significant than excess and transgression in distinguishing stars from the rest of us.

A glamour photo of Carole Lombard, c. 1930. (publicity photo, Paramount Pictures)

A second concept central to the cultural meaning of stardom in the studio era is personality, which was an innovation of the early twentieth century. According to Samantha Barbas, "Personality entered American culture during the first two decades of the century as part of an ongoing dialogue on the nature of self in a rapidly modernizing culture."[29] Where nineteenth-century self-help writers urged the virtues of "character," which was understood to be at least partly inherent and featured morality and sincerity, twentieth-century advisers touted "personality," defined as "charm, friendliness, and flawless self-presentation." Studio era stars illustrate the triumph of personality over character: "by the 1920s, stars were more than just actors. To many Americans, they had become models of modern selfhood."[30] But stars were also models for a range of different personalities, distinct packages of attractive traits that might inspire imitation in some and desire in others but perhaps just as often provide a kind of illustrated taxonomy of human personalities. On this reading, the differences among movie stars, especially those who represented the same social types, were what made them interesting.

Through World War II, movie stars' cultural meanings tended to remain, at least overtly, at the level of personality, and exceptions such as Charlie Chaplin and Orson Welles merely prove the rule.[31] Early stars such as Mary Pickford and Douglas Fairbanks had explicitly political aspects of their identities, but these were not very elaborately developed.[32] This explicit politics would become less common after the studios began to manage the stars' images more closely in the wake of the scandals of the early 1920s. The enforcement of the production code in 1934 meant that films themselves would be political only in the sense that they were covertly ideological and that the studios would avoid political controversy. Popular entertainment during the Depression and World War II certainly served ideological ends, but it did so precisely by seeming not to be political. World War II era films that supported the war effort were not understood as political but patriotic.

After the war, the cultural function and perception of popular entertainment changed despite efforts to preserve the apolitical consensus of wartime, which as historian Lary May has shown, the studios tried to enforce by keeping class conflict out of their films.[33] The new head of the Motion Picture Association of America, Eric Johnston, sought to allow only movies that depicted America in a positive light: "We'll have no more *Grapes of Wrath*, we'll have no more *Tobacco Road*s, we'll have no more films that deal with the seamy side of American life. We'll have no more films that treat the banker as the villain."[34] Yet the consensus Johnston and the government hoped for failed to take hold. Instead, the very attempt to enforce consensus produced the opposite, and there emerged a more politicized cinema. The Cold War and the repression of the Left in the United States made people aware of the potential politics of the movies and other entertainment. Humphrey Bogart, who would not have been perceived as a political figure previously, suddenly found himself one when he stood up to and then backed down from the blacklisters. The personas of the greatest movie stars of the 1950s—John Wayne, James Dean, and Marilyn Monroe—are all overtly more political than those of the studio era stars.

Garry Wills asserts, "The year John Wayne became a superstar, 1948, was also the year he became a political activist."[35] Wayne had sat out the war and had not become interested in anticommunism until it was over. It was in 1948 that Howard Hawks released *Red River,* the film that, Wills argues, defined John Wayne for the rest of his career.[36] That year Wayne also made the first two of the three Seventh Cavalry films for John Ford, which associated the actor with the U.S. military. His appearance as Sergeant Stryker in *Sands of Iwo Jima* the following year "brought Wayne his first Oscar nomination and Stryker entered the mythology of right-wing America."[37] Wayne would spend the 1950s struggling to make *The Alamo* (1960), which he directed, and he began to plan that film in 1948, at the same time as he became an active anticommunist. According to Wills, Wayne became enduringly popular because he represented what his fans wanted an American to be. In other words, he became an icon for an ideology.

The case for Marilyn Monroe as a political figure is much less obvious, of course, but Richard Dyer's well-known essay on her can be read as making the case. Dyer argues that Monroe represented the condensation of 1950s discourses around sex, in particular, those of *Playboy* and of the problem of female sexuality. It is important to emphasize here that the 1950s were a period in which sex became much more visible in American culture and a much debated social problem. Monroe did more than merely reflect this change. Dyer notes that she was a "taboo breaker, from riding the scandal of the nude *Golden Dreams* calendar to showing her nipples in her last photo session with Bert Stern and doing a nude scene in the unfinished *Something's Got to Give,* unheard of for a major motion picture star."[38] Ever since the 1920s, Hollywood had guarded stars against such scandals, but Monroe's career was about pushing boundaries. In Dyer's view, she comes to represent the idea of the innocence of "natural sex." He quotes Diana Trilling saying, "None but Marilyn Monroe could suggest such a purity in sexual delight," and Monroe herself asserting, "I think that sexuality is only attractive when it is natural and spontaneous."[39] While actresses had long been sex objects, they had not previously been symbols of a particular ideology of sex.

For purposes of understanding rock stardom, however, the most important politicized movie star of the 1950s was James Dean. As cultural studies scholar Leerom Medovoi has shown, youth emerged in the 1950s as a new cultural identity. "Even as anticommunist ideology authorized the suppression of an Old Left rooted in radical class politics, the rise of the New Left,

John Wayne in his standard costume in *The Searchers,* 1956. (publicity photo, Warner Brothers)

animated by identity politics, was actually abetted by a different face of the Cold War imaginary that envisioned the young American rebel as guarantor of the nation's antiauthoritarian democratic character."[40] James Dean was the purest instance of that young American rebel, in part because he only made three movies and died at the height of his popularity. In the most popular of those films, *Rebel without a Cause,* he played the most iconic instance of the young American rebel, Jim Stark. Stark's blue jeans may have been borrowed from the working class, but Stark was middle class, and his rebellion was not motivated by economic or social oppression. Medovoi notes the sources of Jim Stark's delinquency in the failure of his father to live up to an older image

James Dean, middle-class youth in working-class garb, in *Rebel without a Cause,* 1955. (publicity photo, Warner Brothers)

of masculinity, and he correctly connects this to larger American anxieties around the Cold War and conformity.[41] Before youth-identity politics began to develop, James Dean became a leading image of resistance to the adults youth saw as their opponents.

These three stars are precursors of the rock star, because they embody explicit and controversial ideologies, and in Dean's case, one that rock stars will also embody. But it must be kept in mind that Wayne, Monroe, and Dean were exceptions, even in the 1950s. It is with the rock star that stardom became widely politicized. Rock stars were more political than any other previous genre of star. Let me be very clear, since this claim can be easily misunderstood. I am not asserting that rock stars as a group think of themselves as having an explicit politics—though it is true that rock stars have more often done this than have film stars. Still less am I claiming that rock stars' politics are necessarily, or even on the whole, progressive. Rather, my point is that rock stars from Elvis to Eminem have consistently figured politically in the cultural imagination, while movie stars, especially those of the studio era, generally have not.

The political edge that many rock stars had is an aspect of a broader characteristic of their personas, their adversarial stance. Previously, popular musicians were sometimes perceived as outsiders because of race or class, but they presented themselves as insiders, dressing like the bourgeoisie and keeping their drug use under wraps. But the rock star flaunted his or her differences from social norms. From Elvis on, rock stars' dress and hairstyles stood out from those of the entertainment world and ordinary, middle-class life. Also starting with Elvis, their performances deviated from the conventions that had governed popular musicians. By the mid-1960s, drug use had become associated with rock stardom, as had an image of virtually unlimited sexual behavior. Where movie stars' conduct was carefully monitored and publicity about it sanitized, rock stars became defined by their rejection of social propriety.

When rock & roll burst on the scene in the mid-1950s, it was doubtless not widely viewed as a political event. Yet there was an implicit politics from the moment that *Blackboard Jungle*'s use of "Rock Around the Clock" gave Bill Haley and His Comets rock's first number 1 hit. The song was blamed for theater riots, and it appeared to embody a celebration of the delinquents that the film's narrative avoids. It might be argued that this was the first musical salvo in what would become the "youth movement" of the 1960s. If Haley and his band did not seem to register politically, Elvis Presley's rise to unprecedented stardom a year later did. Elvis did not present himself politically. He didn't sing explicitly political lyrics or become personally involved in politics, but White Citizens' Councils in the South burned his records and vilified him as a "communist." If we combine his challenge to race, class, and, as I will show, gender boundaries to the fact that Elvis's fan base was almost exclusively teenage, we recognize his persona as outside the mainstream in four ways. Earlier pop singers like Frank Sinatra had been identified with teenage fans, and popular music since ragtime had succeeded by scandalizing the older generation, but there had never been a musical performer in whom so many pressing cultural conflicts were so widely displayed. Earlier pop stars may have helped to define generations, but there were no politics around these identities.

Chuck Berry helps to illustrate another reason why the rock & roll star would evolve into an increasingly political form. Berry was less controversial than Elvis because he did not achieve such enormous celebrity and because his onstage performance, while distinctive, was less suggestive. But Berry wrote his own songs, at least one of which, "Brown-Eyed Handsome Man," addressed racial politics using eye color as a metonymy for race. If most of his songs were not political, he established for rock & roll the paradigm of writing one's own songs, which would become dominant in the 1960s. From that point forward, the presumption was that rock musicians were expressing themselves, rather than interpreting the work of professional songwriters. This expectation meant that political statements coming from rock stars did not feel out of place but were rather of a piece with their larger work of self-expression.

Just as the studios had contained the nascent cultural power of movie stars by managing their public images, the record companies tried to groom docile, manageable artists to appeal to the rock audience. This resulted, on the one hand, in the post-Elvis "teen idols" and, on the other, in the industrial precision with which Motown created both acts and records. The British invasion, however, demonstrated the limitations of this approach. The record companies did not have the monopoly that the movie studios had had, and the rock audience was on the lookout for the kind of experience Elvis represented—a distinct break with the familiar, rather than the finely honed reproduction of tried and true formulas. While the Beatles didn't seem at all political in 1964, when they first made themselves heard in the United States, they and their hair became icons of youth-identity politics. As chapter 5 shows, the emergence of the Rolling Stones as the Beatles' dark other made it clear that there was now more at stake than mere style in their clashing identities. Another source of unfamiliar sounds and styles came from African American performers such as James Brown. As chapter 3 will show, Brown attracted a crossover audience by refusing to conform to the expectations that had defined popular music for previous generations. Bob Dylan paved the way for rockers to become explicitly political when he took up the form. Dylan had already rendered folk music more explicitly political by writing his own topical songs, but in becoming a rocker, he expanded his audience and the political reach of his songs even as his lyrics became less political. Rock stars were no longer like Elvis, symbols of youth in revolt, but rather articulate spokespeople for it.

Case Studies

The chapters that follow are seven case studies of rock stars and their cultural significance. Each chapter focuses on one individual or group and explores what they represented and how they helped to change stardom. My case studies are not intended to be comprehensive, as should be obvious from the fact there is no chapter focusing on the Beatles (who are nevertheless discussed at some length in chapter 5). Every reader will doubtless think of many stars who could have been represented here, but it was not my goal to produce an exhaustive treatment of this vast subject. In writing about these people, I make no claim that they are the best or the most significant or even the most interesting people in rock. Although there are bona fide stars whom I have not included here, there are many great performers discussed in this book who did not rise to the status of star. That's not a critique of their music or personal qualities, simply a judgment about the role the culture allotted them. As I argue in some detail in chapter 3, because of racism, African Americans had more trouble exploiting the possibilities of stardom than did white performers, and women of all races are underrepresented not only as stars but also as performers.

I chose artists of whom I have long been a fan, since, if stardom is inherently a relationship with fans, then it would be hard to write about stars with whom one did not have such a relationship. Within this group, I chose figures who could help me to explore the issues that I have raised in this chapter and to test out the theory that one can best understand stars by treating them not as one would historical figures, as subjects of biography, but as objects of interpretation, like works of art or literature.

In the service of that last consideration, I used another criterion, career longevity, which excluded important figures like Jimi Hendrix, Jim Morrison and the Doors, and Janis Joplin. These artists are all iconic but less complex because they did not live or perform long enough for their personas to significantly evolve. Indeed, Jimi, Jim, and Janis are in one sense more iconic, or at least more essential to the idea of a rock star, than the seven I discuss in depth. Their lives follow the pattern established by James Dean: they lived fast and died young, before they could become for us something other than the first, now indelible, image we had of them. Unlike Neil Young himself, they illustrate the creed that "it's better to burn out than to fade away." In tragic and spectacular fashion, they embodied the fate that the culture assigned to rock and rock stars, who were not supposed to last. And yet, while they did burn out, they have not faded away; neither has Young, or the stars I discuss here, whose careers give the lie to both the song's creed and to the prognostications of my parents' generation. There is doubtless more that one could say about each of them, but I'm convinced that Jimi, Janis, and Jim require less explication as rock icons than the stars I deal with in this book.

Readers may object that some of the stars I discuss didn't perform rock & roll, or that this or that one really isn't a star. In rebuttal, I would point out that all of my figures are members of the Rock & Roll Hall of Fame, and that fact is indicative of how most Americans would understand their musical affiliation and their preeminence. But more important, I understand "rock & roll" not as a particular kind of music but rather as what I call a "cultural practice."[42] Most people probably continue to think of rock & roll as a musical genre or style. While this popular conception requires no explicit definition, some critics have tried to give it one by resorting to a periodization of rock history. By reserving the name "rock 'n' roll" for music featuring the combination of R&B and country and western that emerged in the 1950s, these critics assert an original and genuine form of the music. In naming the dominant music of sixties "rock," they identify another period and in the process distinguish what must inevitably appear as a lesser genre, diluted or bastardized in its relation to the original.[43]

Aside from writing these critics' tastes into history, such periodization relies on a monolithic conception, which is nonetheless only vaguely specified, of 1950s rock & roll as a mixture of country and R&B.[44] Not only does the mixing of two previous genres tell us too little, but it also describes only some significant fifties rockers: preeminently Elvis, but not, for example, Little Richard, Fats Domino, or the Drifters. The point is that rock & roll had always been a stew of musical styles, and the music of the 1960s represents only a wider diversity of raw materials. Most importantly, the rock 'n' roll / rock periodization ignores the continuity of practices that existed from the 1950s through at least the early 1990s. The various activities associated with rock in the 1960s and later—radio programming, concerts, dances, festivals, and so on—all are impossible without the break in American popular culture that the emergence of rock & roll represents. My claim is illustrated by the observation that the Woodstock festival itself is best considered an instance of rock & roll, and, therefore, all of the music performed at the festival, regardless of its formal diversity, is properly identified as rock & roll.

As a cultural practice rock & roll includes, then, not just music but the other products, works, activities, and behavior of its performers and listeners. Rock & roll is not the only form that could be described this way. Jazz, classical, folk, country, and musical comedy could all be understood as cultural practices, each of which has been changed by the rise of the recording industry. Classical critics may still claim that recordings recall the memory of live performances, but to most listeners the recording has become the most common experience of classical music. Jazz and country music have undergone a much greater transformation than classical as the result of recording, but both remain more rooted than rock in music that preceded recording. When F. Scott Fitzgerald dubbed the 1920s the "jazz age," he almost certainly did not have recorded music in mind, but then he had more than just music in mind. He understood jazz as a cultural practice. Like "rock & roll," the name "jazz," conflates music, dancing, and sex. Jazz meant not just a certain musical form but also the speakeasies where it was performed and the manners that went with them. Jazz as a cultural practice of the 1920s was largely dead by the 1930s, however, and popular jazz music became increasingly adapted to the dominant tradition in Western music. By the 1930s, jazz was being performed by "orchestras" or big bands using music written or "arranged" in advance and principles any classically trained musician could comprehend.

Rock & roll had a different trajectory because it emerged in the context of the explosion of electronic media of the 1950s. Like jazz, rock's antecedents were folk forms, but they were transmuted in an entirely different way. Instead of being progressively tamed and assimilated, rock & roll took on a life of its own, not just as youth music but also as a way of life that youth live, and, more importantly, were represented as living. Rock developed as it did not because of its special musical properties but because of the conjuncture of particular social conditions and technological developments. The youth culture of the 1950s and later could not have happened without teenagers becoming a significant market, that is, without them having considerable disposable funds. Possessing money and an increased independence from family, teenagers began to identify themselves as a group, and they sought models by which to understand themselves as such. The media provided those models, which included the juvenile delinquent as "news" and as portrayed by James Dean and Marlon Brando in the movies. Businesses of all sorts were more than willing to provide the commodities teens would use to define themselves from others. Rock & roll records were one of these commodities, along with blue jeans and motorcycle jackets, but rock & roll combined these two structures of identity. Stars were both models and objects to be possessed and fetishized: millions of dollars' worth of Elvis paraphernalia were sold in 1956 alone.[45] In addition to cheaper, better recordings, television and films also disseminated rock & roll on a scale that far exceeded the jazz of Fitzgerald's era. Over four hundred rock & roll films were made between 1955 and 1986.[46]

In analyzing the various activities that make up the practice of rock & roll, we are led to the conclusion that stars might be the most important of the many objects produced by rock & roll. Music is a necessary but not sufficient condition for explaining rock stars and their meaning. Stars are represented by a great variety of products, their involvement in the production of which varies widely. A band or singer is identified not just with particular recordings but with music and lyrics, album covers, dress, films, videos, performing style, and concert staging. And whatever the involvement of the performer in producing these objects and behaviors, they remain as much collaborative productions as are feature films. Indeed, it might be argued that something like an auteur theory applies here, because rock stars since Elvis have always had auteur status regardless of who writes their songs. Even stars who do write their own songs do not work alone. To make a record or mount a tour, a performer typically needs a veritable army of collaborators, including producers, session musicians, promoters, roadies, and so on. Since the star is what gets represented on the record and onstage, the star is as much what is produced as any of the signs or products with which he or she is associated.

These products are what my case studies examine, rather than the actual lives of the stars. Biography and history play a role, of course, but only to the degree that they figure in the public persona of the star. My point is not to get at the truth of the individual life but the meaning of the star for the culture. That meaning is often at some remove from the actual life, and sometimes quite far removed. It is not my task to correct public perceptions. However, I am doing more than just tracking the representations of the stars in the media. In order to understand them in their complexity, media representations need to be complemented by an analysis of the way they have represented themselves in their music and by other means. In this sense, these studies go beyond historical recovery to reinterpretation, suggesting that to some extent each of the icons I discuss has heretofore been misunderstood. In some cases, I consider the star's meaning at a particular historical moment, as in the reaction to Elvis Presley in 1956. In most, however, I'm discussing meanings that are associated with the artist's entire career and that are still current and therefore also subject to change. Cultural icons are never mere artifacts; they continue to be part of everyday life, and they therefore can never be permanently fixed. Of necessity, I'm writing about what these stars mean now even if that meaning is often also dependent on a certain telling or remembering of history.

CHAPTER TWO

WATCHING ELVIS

You could make an argument that one of the most socially conscious artists in the second half of this century was Elvis Presley, even if he probably didn't start out with any set of political ideas he wanted to accomplish. He said, "I'm all shook up and I want to shake you up," and that's what happened.

Bruce Springsteen

Television was essential to the rise of rock & roll and its transformation of American popular music. Because TV could convey the visual excitement of rock & roll performances, popular music shifted from a primarily aural mass experience to one in which the visual field held equal primacy. Television had a profound impact on everyday life in America; its rapid penetration of American homes was unprecedented, the number of households with TV increasing from 0.66 percent in 1948, to 64 percent in 1955, and to 90 percent by the end of the decade.[1] Moreover, those TVs were fed by national networks, meaning that Americans of all regions experienced the same entertainment simultaneously, or nearly so. Television was thus the major factor in producing what Lynn Spigel has called "an odd sense of connection" in the disconnected new suburbia in which "people could keep their distance from the world but at the same time imagine that their domestic spheres were connected to a wider social fabric."[2] Television kept more people at home and out of taverns and movie theaters, but it gave them more or less the same experiences as their neighbors and counterparts across the nation.

The profound changes wrought by TV are part of a larger transformation of American culture that was occurring during the 1950s. While the decade has long been misunderstood as a period of normalcy from which the United States began to deviate in the 1960s, the idea that the 1950s were placid, or "tranquilized," to quote Robert Lowell, is no longer the standard assumption, and indeed is now considered part of the period's misrecognition of itself.[3] Television played a significant role in disseminating this ideology through situation comedies such as *The Adventures of Ozzie and Harriet* and *Leave It to Beaver*. Popular memory of the decade was later influenced by re-creations such as the film *American Graffiti* (directed by George Lucas, 1973) and the

1970s TV series *Happy Days*. But television was not only a reassuring diversion; it also brought political controversy and the dangers of the Cold War into the living room. I've already suggested in chapter 1 that movies became more controversial and politicized during the period, partly in response to the blandness of television entertainment. Television, however, was instrumental in spreading the threat of nuclear war and of a communist conspiracy, even as it was also instrumental in bringing down Senator Joseph McCarthy.[4] Television news brought pictures of the growing civil rights movement into homes throughout the land, helping to fracture the acquiescence of northern whites to segregation in the South. And it was television that made Elvis Presley a national star and the first rock icon.

No one benefited more from television than Elvis, who appeared on national programs at least twelve times from January 1956 to January 1957. This chapter looks at Elvis's televised performances and argues that the controversy he generated had much more to do with what people saw than what they heard. While it is well known that Elvis transgressed racial boundaries that still largely separated white and black culture in the 1950s, his appearance and behavior on the tube also threatened class hierarchies and reminded people that America's youth were defining themselves against adult norms. Elvis redefined popular music stardom by his failure to conform to accepted conventions of performance decorum, and the most threatening aspect of his performance was his violation of gender codes. Elvis crossed gender boundaries in several ways, but it is my contention that his most troubling transgression was to called attention to his body as a sexual object. In the history of mass culture, Elvis may be the first male star to display his body in this way overtly and consistently. In violating this taboo, Elvis became, like most women but unlike most men, sexualized. In adopting an explicitly sexualized self-representation, Elvis played out the implications of becoming the object of the gaze. In so doing, he both exploited and provoked cultural anxiety over the changing construction of gender.

The Fraught Fifties

The strong reactions to Elvis, both positive and negative, show that social divisions that had previously been taken for granted were now coming into question. The most fraught division in the 1950s was race. In 1954, the U.S. Supreme Court ruled in *Brown v. Board of Education* that segregated public schools were unconstitutional. That decision "marked the dawn of the modern civil rights movement and a new phase of mass black struggle in the southern states and beyond."[5] Elvis Presley famously was a white singer who sounded black, as Sam Phillips, the man who first recorded him, recognized. In the early 1950s, the popular music world was nearly as segregated as southern schools. "In 1950, for example, only three records which made the national Rhythm and Blues charts also crossed over into the pop field."[6] Beginning in 1954, however, R&B records began to have significant impact on the pop charts. So just as Jim Crow laws began to come under threat legally, musical apartheid also began to break down. Neither the Brown decision nor increased white interest in black music caused an immediate reaction, but by 1956, "throughout the South, opposition to black and black derived styles of music quickly escalated."[7] One factor in this was the "improved chart performance of original black recordings against white covers," while another "was the enormous commercial success of Elvis Presley."[8]

That whites would be troubled by the popularity of black entertainers is perhaps not surprising, but the long history of minstrelsy suggests that whites performing in black styles should not have been threatening. Yet as Eric Lott has observed in his study of blackface entertainment, "Certain kinds of cultural conquest—Jackie Robinson's entrance in major league baseball, Elvis Presley's explicit dismantling of 'racial' music—are far from harmless allowances on the part of white-supremacist capital."[9] And Elvis clearly did threaten—and not just southerners. One difference is that nothing in Elvis's performance suggests that he was mocking his black sources. Had he appeared in blackface and used an exaggerated African American dialect, his act would have been familiar and unthreatening. As it was, Elvis's performance seemed more like an homage to black music than a parody of it, largely because his approach was not mere imitation. The black songs he recorded he made his own, just as his vocal style was a distinctive reworking of black and white influences. Had white supremacy not appeared to be under attack, perhaps none of that would have mattered, but under the circumstances, Elvis stood for the "mongrel" culture that racists feared.

The threat posed by Elvis's transgression of the racial divide was exacerbated by his violation of the class divide. Although offspring of the white working class had long dominated American popular music, they seldom retained a distinct class identity. They adopted middle-class or even bourgeois dress and manners, reflecting the upward mobility of which their success became emblematic. Elvis, on the contrary, showed no inclination—or maybe lacked the ability—to hide his class origins. He all too clearly remained the son of a "common laborer" from Tupelo. While most other early rock & rollers, black and white, observed concert conventions of performance attire, wearing suits and ties, if not tuxedos, Elvis dressed somewhat but noticeably down. He typically sported tight pants and pointy-toed boots. He often did not wear a tie or suit, and when he did wear a suit it was not something you would expect to see on a banker. More important, his pompadour hairstyle, long sideburns, and pouty demeanor made him look like someone from the other side of the tracks. This was especially troubling because his music appealed to young people of all classes and America was then in the midst of a juvenile delinquency crisis that was blamed on, among other causes, the evil influence of the mass media.[10]

Like race and gender, the traditional class divisions were being challenged, as the working class benefited from the new power of labor unions. Where classes were once separated by neighborhoods, the large-scale exodus of workers to the suburbs produced the mixing of classes and seemed to portend the leveling of class distinctions. High schools, which once were safe havens for middle-class youth, became increasingly populated by working-class kids now encouraged—or forced—to stay in school, and the consequences were illustrated in the film *Blackboard Jungle* (1954), featuring the first rock & roll hit, Bill Haley and the Comets' "Rock Around the Clock." As another film, *Rebel without a Cause* (1955) revealed, the juvenile delinquency crisis represented the fear that middle-class youth were beginning to behave like those of the lower classes. The recently coined term *teenager* reveals the breakdown of previously assumed class distinctions. "The middle-class adolescent and the juvenile delinquent from the 'the other half' had once functioned as a normative binary, with clear class and ethnic lines separating them. The teenager, however, could not be so easily distinguished from the juvenile delinquent, for s/he had incorporated a degree of freedom from adult supervision previously associated with lower-class youth."[11] The very fact that teenagers bought Elvis's records was an indication to worried parents of the dangers of this new freedom.

Elvis's challenge to racial boundaries is well known, and his class associations are unlikely to come as a surprise. His challenge to gender norms, however, was largely unremarked at the time. The 1950s have traditionally been characterized by a reversion to prewar patterns, and they are sometimes said to have imposed even more rigid limits than had been typical of the 1920s and 1930s. But Beth Bailey, Barbara Ehrenreich, and others have observed important changes in the construction of sexuality and gender during the 1950s and noted the cultural tensions and anxieties that these changes produced. One change is the development of what has been called "a highly sexualized society," in which "the number of explicitly sexual references in the mass media doubled between 1950 and 1960." Yet it was a society that continued to demand that "teen and preteen girls . . . be not only 'good' and 'pure' but to be the enforcers of purity within their teen society."[12] Thus conditions were ripe for these girls to participate in communal fantasies that were at once sexually charged but not sexually explicit. Such fantasies are the stuff that fueled Elvis's rise.

It was not just teens who felt confusion, however. Changes in the social relations of the genders produced a crisis of gender roles. During the war a large number of women entered what had been a largely male workforce, threatening the definition of masculinity, which was also called into question because an increasing number of men found themselves in a job and in a home life that did not permit them to exhibit such masculine qualities as power, dominance, aggression, and ambition.[13] These changes permitted and were abetted by an increasing awareness that gender was not a natural expression of biology. The notion that gender is a cultural construction was spread in popularized form, at least partly as a result of equally popularized versions of Sigmund Freud. The result was a perception of the "fragility of gender," which was given expression in a deluge of articles about a "crisis of American masculinity" that in turn often seemed to be caused by a crisis in femininity.

The crisis—or crises—was attributed to two causes. The first had to do with the changing roles men played in American society. Previously, masculinity had been identified with independence and aggression, and it had been given its own spaces in society, the many forms of work and leisure that excluded women. According to Bailey, however, "In the postwar era Americans were coming to grips with changes in their economy and society that, they feared, had rendered 'traditional' masculinity obsolete and threatened the vitality of American culture. In the world of the corporation, the 'organization,' men needed different qualities to succeed. Teamwork, conformity, cooperation, the 'social ethic'—these were functional behaviors for corporate success. But they were traditional *feminine* behaviors—the antithesis of aggressive masculinity. To continue to provide well for his family, many feared, a man would have to act like a woman."[14] It was not just men's roles that were changing, however. In spite of the postwar ideological effort to return women to traditional roles, there were more married women in the labor force of the 1950s than before the war.[15] As more women entered the economy, critics charged "that women were robbing men of their masculinity by adopting masculine (aggressive) roles." These changes threatened three perquisites the American male had assumed as his right: his role as economic provider, his separate subculture of work and leisure, and aggressiveness, the definitive character of masculinity itself. As Bailey notes, there is a crisis of femininity implicit here: "The fragility of gender was the root of the trouble. The necessary barriers had broken down and women were exercising too much power—whether by stifling masculinity or by assuming masculine traits themselves."[16]

The Male Star as Object of the Gaze

The very perception that gender roles are fragile both made Elvis's transgressions all the more threatening and made them a cultural force that others would exploit. Elvis crossed gender boundaries in several ways, but it is my contention that his most troubling violation was to call attention to his body as a sexual object, which initiated a certain kind of visual presentation of male rock & roll stars that I call feminization. Not all rock stars exhibit themselves in this way, but enough have—and they represent a relatively wide spectrum of rock forms—that feminization cannot be regarded as merely an accident of individual expression. To say that rock stars have been feminized is to say that in their appearance and performance they have violated traditional male gender codes by adopting some that are normally female codes. But feminization does not, as Marjorie Garber contends, render Elvis a transvestite.[17] Transvestism, or female impersonation, might be seen as one extreme toward which feminization has developed, but the phenomenon on which I will focus here is not mainly a matter of cross-dressing. Elvis and other feminized rock stars retain many traditionally male characteristics in their appearance and behavior. They remain, for example, aggressive and even violent in their performances. Thus such cross-dressers as David Bowie or Boy George should not be understood primarily as examples of feminization, although the phenomenon might explain the conditions for their public acceptance. Transvestite rock has been more directly influenced by gay subcultures.

In describing Elvis's feminization, my aim is to try to account for the process in terms of a violation of a gender distinction that is at least as fundamental as dress but much more subtle: my claim is that Elvis becomes feminized because he displays his body as a sexualized object. The feminized rock star does not pretend to be a woman but rather takes up some of the markers usually reserved for women. As a result the rocker is perceived as feminine because of the rigidity of the gender system; were it not so rigid, he might be perceived as redefining masculinity. Moreover, unlike the transvestite, the rock star may or may not be aware that he is transgressing gender codes. Elvis, I think, was largely unaware that his performances violated a gender boundary. That may be because Elvis's violation was not so much his behavior but the relation of that behavior to the gaze, a relation that Elvis might not have comprehended, though later rock stars made explicit use of it.

Some of Garber's case for Elvis as a cross-dresser does refer to his costumes—his use of eye shadow, his 1950s gold-lamé suit, and his 1970s jumpsuit (though, of these, only eye shadow is unambiguously feminine). But much of it rests on the perception of Elvis's feminization. As she puts it, "Critic after critic notices that his sexuality is subject to reassignment. . . . This male sex symbol is insistently and paradoxically read by the culture as a boy, a eunuch, or a 'woman'—anything but a man."[18] The issue, as we will see, is even more complicated than Garber makes it, since Elvis is often perceived not merely as a man but as something of a superman. In spite of this, Elvis has been feminized. Biographer Albert Goldman offers the most extreme expression of this, providing Garber with an image of Elvis in his Las Vegas jumpsuit as a transvestite successor to Marlene Dietrich.[19] Goldman himself describes Elvis's postarmy appearance on a television program with Frank Sinatra as "queer. . . . When he confronts the smaller but more masculine Sinatra, Elvis's body language flashes, 'I surrender, dear.'"[20] Goldman's view is suspect, because he is an "Elvis debunker" and because his reading reflects the perceptions of 1981 far more than it does those of 1956. If few in the 1950s perceived Elvis as a "woman," he did seem in some odd way feminine.

I understand the gaze as a power relation or as a sign of that relation. One instantiation of male dominance exists in the unequal exchange of looks that men and women direct at each other. As many theorists have argued and empirical studies have demonstrated, men gaze at women far more often than the reverse.[21] This fact of social behavior is represented, enacted, and

reinforced in all forms of visual media. The propensity for male film characters to gaze at their female counterparts is well known, and feminist film
scholars since Laura Mulvey have argued persuasively that the camera's gaze
usually duplicates the male character's, so that the female is the object of the
viewer's gaze as well.[22] But we also have the history of painting and still photography, especially advertising, where women's bodies are displayed to sell
everything from women's clothing to motor oil. As John Berger puts it, "Men
look at women. Women watch themselves being looked at."[23] The power relations implied in this gaze are not a matter of voyeurism, at least as it has been
defined in the psychoanalytic tradition. It is not the illusion of a surrepti-
tious control that the gaze enacts; it is, rather, a direct assertion of dominance. The gaze is a gesture that, in modern American and European societies, is similar to gestures in animal social groups that mark and reinforce
their hierarchical relations.

The gaze does more than merely assert simple dominance, however. By
demarcating the female body as sexual, the gaze is central to the construction of sexuality. It is not just the one-way direction of the gaze that matters
but that the female body is gazed at precisely as a sexualized object. My point
here is that to be gazed at as a sexualized object is to be put into a role that
until recently only women have played in our culture. As Steve Neale has
observed, when males are presented as the object of an erotic look, as Rock
Hudson is in Sirk's melodramas, the male's "body is *feminized* . . . an indication of the strength of those conventions that dictate that only women can
function as objects of an explicitly erotic gaze."[24] The image or persona that
many male rock stars present in performance is the product of the same process of feminization. In other words, these stars have been constructed by
dominant relations of visibility.

The cinema, however, is a place where rupture in these relations could occur. Merely to be represented, to act in a film, is already to step to the other
side of the gaze. Most male stars in Hollywood cinema have avoided feminization by controlling the look within the filmic narrative. As Mulvey has explained, the camera's point of view is associated with the male hero, and the
audience is thereby made to identify with his gaze.[25] Moreover, male movie
stars typically played roles that conformed to ideas of traditional masculinity. Rudolph Valentino, however, does represent a rupture in visual relations.
His appeal, according to Miriam Hansen, depends "on the manner in which
he combines masculine control of the look with the feminine quality of

'to-be-looked-at-ness.' . . . To the extent that Valentino occupies the position of primary object of spectacle, this entails a systematic feminization of his persona."[26] Outside of his films, in photographs and performances as a dancer, Valentino was even more feminized, because in these he lacks the masculine control of the look and his body becomes solely the object of the gaze.[27] Like later rock stars, however, Valentino insisted on his masculinity, even to the point of challenging to fight anyone who questioned it.

Valentino, though, is the exception rather than the rule. We can find instances of male stars' bodies as objects of the gaze in the films of the classic period, but they are not common. Clark Gable, for example, does something of a striptease for Claudette Colbert in *It Happened One Night,* but this scene must be read against his dominance, in visual and all other relations, in the rest of the film. Only the faces of male stars are regularly the objects of the camera's gaze during the classic period of Hollywood, yet the convention dictates that a male face will appear to be watching someone else, revealing spiritual depth or intellectual activity. Cary Grant may have defined a certain image of the handsome male, and as such was certainly an object of desire, but seemingly without our noticing anything in particular about his body except his face.

Jon Savage points out that, after Valentino, James Dean is the next instance of a major male star who is presented as the object of the gaze and who, like Valentino, became the object of cult worship. In *Rebel without a Cause* Dean was the "uncanny enactment of 'the passivity of the adored object' that was the new condition of male stardom. Masculinity was now being defined by the female gaze."[28] But it is precisely "masculinity" that is put in question by this relationship. Savage describes Dean's sexuality in that film as "highly androgynous," which is to acknowledge Dean's feminization.[29] That both the Sal Mineo and the Natalie Wood characters appear to take Dean as an object of desire only reinforces this feminization. If being the object of the female gaze is feminizing, then a fortiori, so is being the object of the male gaze.

Valentino, Dean, and Elvis are routinely described as androgynous, but that problematic term deserves a bit of digression. A simple definition of the word is the combination of male and female in one being, and the dictionary gives *hermaphroditic* as a synonym. The latter term, however, is most often applied to the existence of both male and female genital organs in the same individual, whether such an arrangement is functional and biologically normal, as in earthworms, or is a nonfunctional defect, as in humans. Androgyny, on the other hand, is most often applied to the appearance and, less frequently, the behavior of people and thus concerns secondary sexual traits such as beards or breasts. Yet the term is often used as if physical features beyond these were also sexually differentiated. Thus Valentino is said to have a feminine face, while Elvis Presley and Mick Jagger are said to have female eyes or lips. In this conception, androgyny seems to be, like hermaphroditism, a kind of birth defect. Dean's androgyny, however, doesn't fit this model. His face and body are quite ordinary in their appearance and his blue jeans and T-shirts are usually markers of masculinity; nor is his behavior stereotypically feminine. It is, rather, that Dean's body is displayed for others, that it has "to-be-looked-at-ness," which leads us to experience him as androgynous. Similarly, a rock star's lips become a gender marker because of the way they are constituted in visual relations.

Valentino and Dean were cult objects of desire, but their onscreen sexualization is relatively subtle. Neither prepares us for Elvis Presley, who was a fan of both, nor does Frank Sinatra, who had a following of teenage girls in the 1940s. Because Elvis's androgyny, like Dean's, cannot be ascribed to dress or to what we would normally call feminine gestures, it can only be produced by his position within the structure of the gaze. Yet the passive/active opposition that has been held to structure the politics of looking in narrative films cannot operate in the same way in the concert setting. The singer is both active and passive, an object of adoration and at the same time someone engaged in demanding physical work. To be the object of mass adoration confers a sense of enormous power on the star. That power compensates to some extent for the lack of the control of the look, but it does so only ambiguously, for as Sue Wise has pointed out, the star is precisely an object to his fans and is thus in their power.[30] Moreover, "to be a performer is to be at one's most vulnerable."[31] Unlike most male stars, but like Valentino and Dean, Elvis consistently revealed that vulnerability.

Elvis on Television

The major factor in Elvis's feminization was the sexual suggestiveness of his dancing. This dancing was a source of shock when it was first presented on national TV. Yet it is important to keep in mind that when Elvis was performing in small clubs in the South, his dancing provoked no outrage. Even his first TV appearances on the Dorsey Brothers' *Stage Show*, which included some of his dancing, produced little outcry, perhaps because the shows were seen by smaller audiences or because Elvis's dancing was shot from a high angle, lasted for only a short time, and was relatively tame. But after Elvis's performance of "Hound Dog" on the *Milton Berle Show* in June 1956, things changed. One difference was that the TV cameras met Elvis head-on. Another is that he performed without a guitar, and as his biographer describes it,

> Perhaps to make up for its absence he seemed to have carefully worked out new moves, wrists splayed out almost limply in seeming contrast to the ferocity of his vocal attack, fingers fluttering, arms outspread. With Scotty's solo, he lurches backward in what might be interpreted as an upbeat adaptation of the shrugging, stuttering, existential hopelessness of a James Dean, there is a jittery fiddling with his mouth and nose, and as the song comes to an end he is dragging the microphone down to the floor, staggering almost to his knees. . . . He points at the audience and declares emphatically, *You* ain't nothin' but a hound dog, then goes into his patented half-time ending, gripping the mike, circling it sensuously, jackknifing his legs out as the audience half-scream, half laughs, and he laughs too—it is clearly all in good fun.[32]

Those in the TV studio that day may have experienced Elvis's performance as good fun, but many in the television audience did not. Elvis had given them a little peek at what they might have witnessed in a Beale Street club, and they were not amused. The reaction of both professional critics and of self-appointed guardians of morality was swift and harsh. According to *New York Times* critic Jack Gould, "He is a rock-and-roll variation on one of the most standard acts in show business: the virtuoso of the hootchy-kootchy. His one specialty is an accented movement of the body that heretofore has been primarily identified with the repertoire of the blonde bombshells of the burlesque runway."[33] *Life* called him "a disturbing kind of idol," and *Look* called him "vulgar."[34] The reaction went beyond Elvis to encompass all rock & roll, the live performance of which was banned by cities from Santa Cruz, California, to Jersey City.[35]

Although from a ratings point of view, "the broadcast was an unmitigated success," the negative reactions had an impact.[36] The public outcry nearly caused NBC to drop Elvis's next scheduled appearance on the *Steve Allen Show*. Rather than cancel the appearance, however, the network devised a plan to contain Elvis. Allen dressed him up in tails and had him sing "Hound

Elvis performs "Hound Dog" on the *Milton Berle Show,* with D. J. Fontana and Bill Black, 1956. (courtesy Photofest)

Dog" to a live basset hound—while standing more or less still. Later in the same year, Elvis was restrained by court order from making any offensive gyrations onstage in Jacksonville, Florida. Early in 1957, in what was Elvis's third appearance on his show, Ed Sullivan insisted that Elvis be photographed only from the waist up.

Why did Elvis's dancing cause such an outcry? People were not used to seeing such overt male self-display. Precursors, such as Valentino, whose dance performances and still photographs were read in much the same way, reached relatively few viewers when compared either to Valentino's more conventional film roles or Elvis's television performances. Fred Astaire, Gene Kelly, and other film dancers also bear comparison to Elvis, and Steven Cohan has argued that song-and-dance men were feminized as a result of the way they displayed their bodies before the camera.[37] Yet Astaire and his ilk never produced the cultural anxieties that Elvis did. While the dancer's body is much more the object of the gaze than that of the dramatic leading man,

Disciplined Elvis on Steve Allen with bassett hound, 1956. (courtesy Photofest)

he is not presented as the object of an explicitly sexual gaze. In part this is because a song-and-dance man like Astaire usually played a conventional male role in the films in which he danced. More important, however, the dancing itself is a highly conventionalized spectacle, the performance of which is understood as an art or craft of which the dancer is master. Moreover, the dancer's body is usually covered in formal wear or other conventional garb, making it much less the object of the gaze than is the male ballet dancer's. In fact, the song-and-dance man's dance diverts attention from his body as a sexual object, perhaps in the same way that athletic contests can display men's (and women's) bodies without such display being perceived as sexual.[38]

But if Elvis represents a break with male performance in mass culture, it does not mean that he invented the style of performance he displayed. On the contrary, there is good reason to believe that Elvis's dancing, like his singing, was an adaptation of black performers' styles. T-Bone Walker and

Wynonie Harris are often mentioned as precursors. Harris's producer, Henry Glover, said, "When you saw Elvis, you were seein' a mild version of Wynonie."[39] Some who knew Elvis in his prerecording days say that he learned his style from performers on Memphis's Beale Street: "He would watch the colored singers, understand me, and then got to doing it the same way as them. He got that shaking, that wiggle, from Charlie Burse . . . right there at the Gray Mule on Beale. Elvis, he wasn't doing nothing but what the colored people had been doing for the last hundred years."[40] The question of just what, if anything, Elvis did bring to this style can probably never be settled, because the black musicians whom he imitated were seldom filmed. But that is my point. Black blues musicians were part of a subculture; their music did reach a mass audience, but their live performances did not. What distinguished Elvis's performances was that they were televised, and, in the cases of the *Milton Berle Show* and *Ed Sullivan Show,* they were watched by enormous audiences consisting mainly of whites who had never seen R&B singers perform.

It was not just the size or racial composition of the audience that is significant here, however. The context in which Elvis performed gave the dancing he learned from black performers a new meaning, as did the persona he developed in collaboration with his manager, Colonel Tom Parker, and the entertainment industry. It is first worth considering what that persona was not. Elvis did not present himself as a typical blues or R&B figure. Elvis did not cultivate the image of a sexual athlete or lady-killer as Wynonie Harris, Robert Johnson, and Muddy Waters had in different ways. The lyrics to the latter's most famous songs—"Mannish Boy," "I'm Your Hoochie Coochie Man," "Rollin' Stone," "I'm Ready"—are celebrations of the singer's sexual prowess that brag about both his conquests and his abilities. There is not a hint in these songs of the vulnerability characteristic of many blues songs, including those of Johnson. Johnson's persona developed less in his lyrics than in his behavior and in the legends that spread after his death. By virtue of his reputed pact with the devil, Johnson *was* the hoochie coochie man whom Muddy Waters merely sang about. Elvis, on the other hand, was in his early years the antithesis of such Faustian characters. The lyrics of his major early hits almost invariably present a wounded or vulnerable lover—"Heartbreak Hotel," "Don't Be Cruel," "I Want You, I Need You, I Love You," "Love Me Tender." Big Mama Thornton's "Hound Dog" was, in her version, the female equivalent of a Muddy Waters song. Elvis's version of the Jerry Leiber and

Mike Stoller song, on the other hand, doesn't transform the material back into the male original (as Rufus Thomas had in "Bear Cat"). Elvis's "Hound Dog" is best understood as an inspired piece of scat singing or as a novelty song, sexual in attitude or presentation but not in content. The failure to occupy an unambiguous male subject position here corresponds to other, less subtle violations of the gender system we find in Elvis's visual presentation.

Elvis borrowed his performance style from another kind of blues—that of the singers and shouters who had fronted for bands—but he didn't imitate their personas, either. Wynonie Harris, for example, was explicit about the image he used to attract women: "I play to create impressions," Harris said, "women can get stirred up by a man who seems cruel, ornery, vulgar, and arrogant."[41] Charlie Gillett describes the performances of blues shouters, such as Harris and Joe Turner as "intimate, relaxed, loaded with sexual references and suggestive plays on words." "But it wasn't just the words—the whole character of the shouted blues was adult, in the tone of voice used by the singers, the assumptions behind the songs, and the sophistication of the musical arrangements."[42] Although Elvis may not have been at first understood mainly as a teen performer, it quickly became apparent that teenagers would be his major market. Cause and effect are hard to disentangle here, and we can't safely assert either that Elvis's persona was designed to attract his teen audience or that the audience was attracted to a persona that emerged without conscious design. In any case, some elements of Harris's style—orneriness, vulgarity—doubtless appealed to teens, and we find these in Elvis's performance. Nevertheless, Elvis does not act cruel in spite of the aggression of his performances, and he certainly doesn't come across as the sophisticated and insinuating adult. Innocence, rather, is the dominant characteristic of the Elvis of the 1950s. That quality has been apparent to many interpreters of his music, for example, Peter Guralnick on "That's All Right," Elvis's first release from Sun Records: "It sounds easy, unforced, joyous, spontaneous. It sounds as if the singer had broken free for the first time in his life. The voice soars with a purity and innocence."[43] In his seminal essay, "Elvis: Presliad," Greil Marcus describes Elvis in much the same terms that Richard Dyer would later apply to Marilyn Monroe: "Elvis embodies . . . a delight in sex that is sometimes simple, sometimes complex, but always open."[44]

This side of Elvis may have gotten lost in the late 1960s, when the first generation of rock critics described him as if he were the white incarnation of the bluesman's sexuality. This reading of Elvis ignores not only the image he presented in his music but his larger public persona as well. "The official El-vis," as Guralnick observes, is marked by "modesty, . . . deferential charm, [and] the soft-spoken assumption of commonsense virtues."[45] One sees this Elvis much in evidence in the TV appearances of the period, in the still pho-tos, and the interviews. And, there is a particular sense of vulnerability to Elvis, especially in the way he responds to various figures of authority, such as television host Steve Allen. On Allen's show, Elvis was being disciplined by being made to perform as a clown, and he responded to the humiliation with perfect submission. Compare Mick Jagger's mocking expression while sing-ing bowdlerized lyrics to "Let's Spend the Night Together" on the *Ed Sullivan Show* in 1967. Unlike the Rolling Stones or the Beatles, Elvis always seems to play the good son to the show business fathers, respecting their authority rather than mocking or challenging it.

Whether or not this official Elvis is a contrivance, it fit perfectly Tom Park-er's plans for the star. As various accounts of Elvis's career assert, Parker's goal was to make him a pop singer. It would, after all, have been impossible in 1955 for him to want to make Elvis a rock & roll star, since such a career path did not yet exist. Thus if the teen audience was to be Elvis's base, the peak he would try to reach would be a mass audience of the white middle class of all ages. His early, unsuccessful appearance in Las Vegas is a testimony to that plan, as is the mixture of material Elvis recorded, including an album of Christ-mas songs. Such a career plan precluded Elvis from producing a persona to match his R&B performance style, and may have contributed to perceptions of his feminization.

Elvis's performance style must be understood in terms of the social and cultural environment that would produce such a career plan. The mass audi-ence had a very narrow range of expectations about male sexuality, and it did not include any overt form of self-display; that mode was reserved for women. But television would also change the perception of the sort of performances a Wynonie Harris or a T-Bone Walker might perform in a nightclub. In a club setting, there is more interaction between the audience and the performer, and the performer is less the center of attention. The patrons may be more engaged in other activities than they are in watching the musicians, and their own dancing especially would render the performer more a part of an event than the event itself. Even in a concert setting—which was relatively rare for blues or R&B performances—a singer or bandleader is no more than the most important point of attention, and he or she never consumes the entire visual field. On television, however, the performer becomes not merely the center of attention but often its sole object. In other words, as a television performer, Elvis was the object of a much more focused and intense gaze than his predecessors had been. Elvis was not merely introducing a style with which whites were unfamiliar, he was using that style under conditions that transformed its cultural significance.

Contemporary commentators revealed by their descriptions of Elvis that they were aware that this display violated gender codes. The terms in which Elvis's performance was discussed are ones usually applied to striptease: for example, "bumping and grinding." By the middle of 1956, the time of the *Milton Berle Show* performance, he had already been given the nickname "the pelvis," a name that of course means what it doesn't say. What is it that is not being said? The standard answer is "the phallus," but unlike performances by some later male stars, in these TV performances at least the penis itself is not emphasized. Elvis's costume, which includes a jacket, hides, rather than displays, his genitals, and while there are stories about Elvis stuffing his pants to make himself look well endowed, the television performances reveal none of this. Rock critics in the late 1960s often celebrated what they saw as his prodigious endowment, and these claims at best reflect the way adolescent male fans of the 1950s might have interpreted Elvis. What contemporary adult audiences saw in Elvis's performance was not his parts but the whole. His motions suggested intercourse, and his performance was read as a public display of "sex." Elvis thus put the "sex" that the name "rock & roll" described explicitly into his performance. But in presenting himself as an object of sexual incitement or excitation, he violated not just Victorian morality—which was no longer hegemonic—but more importantly the taboo against male sexual display. In violating this taboo, Elvis became, like most women but unlike most men, sexualized. Women are routinely sexualized. Various parts of women's bodies—for example, hair, legs, breasts—become loci of sexualization; women's fashion always calls attention to these features, which are presented for the male gaze and thus mark the woman as a sexual object. While women are the most sexually marked group, some men are marked in different, lesser degrees. Gay men are perhaps the most marked, but black men are more sexually marked than white men. This last point suggests that if a black man had performed on television in the same way as Elvis, it might not have been met with the same response.

There is, however, one aspect of these early television performances that might have caused the largely white audience to be even more outraged had the performer been black: the pictures of white teenage girls losing control under the influence of the performer. Elvis's "effect" on young girls threatened those men who assumed that young girls needed to be protected, both from sex in general and from its expression in questionable characters like Elvis in particular. According to one narrative, Elvis made his "pelvic gyrations" a regular part of his act after female members of his audiences screamed and applauded at them.[46] Photos of one of these early performances already show young women in various states of rapture while watching Elvis perform. When Elvis is featured on major national TV programs, the audience becomes part of the show. In the *Milton Berle Show* performance, the film cuts between the stage and the audience, the latter presented not as a large mass of indistinguishable faces but of particular faces whose response tells us of the excitement the performer is generating. This editing also reinforces Elvis as the object of a specifically sexual gaze. It is not just an audience, of which each viewer is a member, that is watching Elvis. Rather, television or newsreel viewers experience Elvis as the object of the gaze of the (almost exclusively female) individuals who scream, faint, and otherwise enact ecstasy. This representation of Elvis is formally equivalent to the shot / reverse shot editing that structures the gaze in narrative cinema. It becomes a standard trope of the representation of rock and will be repeated numerous times during the British invasion of the '60s.

Now it may seem that the logic of my argument would lead inevitably to the claim that these girls who watch Elvis are masculinized by their place in the visual hierarchy, but the pictures themselves prohibit one from following this line of reasoning. The point is made clearer if we compare these screaming, ecstatic teenage girls to the familiar representations of male audiences watching striptease. The latter enact voyeurism; rather than expressing their desire, and thus their lack of control, these men sit impassively or they make jokes to relieve the embarrassment of experiencing sexual excitement in the company of other men. Thus the very expressiveness of these rock fans defines them as female, whatever they are read to be expressing. Often it was that most "female" of all emotions, hysteria.

The visual relation between fan and star under these conditions is ambiguous. The star remains an object of the fan's gaze and thus vulnerable to her, but the fan's visible response is apparently produced by the star and thus in his control. This ambiguity made Elvis all the more threatening, for he seemed, like alcohol, to cause girls to lose their proper inhibitions. This reading

Elvis was the object of the gaze of ecstatic female fans, 1956. (courtesy Photofest)

of Elvis and his fans can only come from the outside, for the fans themselves do not feel driven. But one might also argue that the girls who watched Elvis or the Beatles and screamed out their adoration were exercising agency, both in their choice of object and in their insistence on making themselves seen and heard. Sue Wise describes her Elvis as a "Teddy Bear" for whom she felt affection rather than desire.[47] She argues that Elvis was "an *object* of his fans," rather than the all-powerful subject that both adult opponents and male adolescent fans assumed him to be.[48] In fact, fans do behave as if Elvis and other rock stars are objects over which they exercise some control. Simon Frith argues that "the power struggle between stars and fans is what gives concerts their sexual charge."[49] The rock star becomes a fetish, not in the psychoanalytic sense, but in the root sense of an object believed to have magical power.

To the fan, the star as fetish has power for her, not over her. How else do we explain the enormous market for trinkets carrying names or likenesses of Elvis or other stars? In Elvis's case, the process has gone so far that he now seems quite literally to be deified.

Elvis was not the only rock star to violate gender codes in the 1950s. Little Richard emerged from gay subculture to be billed as the "queen of rock & roll," but Richard's race made him less threatening, not only because black men were already more sexualized, but also because the color line kept him out of the center of public attention. Furthermore, consciousness of Richard's sexual orientation was low among the white teen audience for his work. The gay themes of his lyrics were either expunged ("Tutti Frutti") or lost ("Long Tall Sally") on the straight audience.[50] Elvis's example created new possibilities for male performers, but it took a few years for these possibilities to be realized. Perhaps the first expressions were the teen idols, which the entertainment industry marketed as "safe Elvises." Performers such as Frankie Avalon, Bobby Rydell, and Fabian were essentially male pinups, that is, objects to be gazed at, but little in their behavior or appearance—except their passivity—realized the feminine position this placed them in. They were safe because their sexualization was relatively minor, and their appeal was explicitly likened to the "matinee idols" of the cinema. Yet this comparison does not adequately reflect the passivity that the role of teen idol entailed. Without fictional roles with which they could be identified, and even without great success making or selling records, the teen idols were little more than objects to be gazed at.

The Elvis Generation

If adults felt that Elvis threatened a social order built on racial, class, and gender hierarchies, Elvis's teenage fans were attracted to him both because they were less invested in them and because they liked the idea of upsetting their parents. Of course, they found Elvis appealing for other reasons as well. They certainly liked the music and the way he performed it. But Elvis also served as a symbol of what might be termed a new or newly significant social division, the generational one. The invention of the category "teenager" corresponded to a growing sense of age-group identity among those it named. While "youth" had first been named an identity group in the 1920s, it referred to an older group who belonged to a much narrower socioeconomic stratum. The typical twenties youth was a college student or recent graduate, and the image was defined by F. Scott Fitzgerald, both personally and in his novel about Princeton, *This Side of Paradise*. This group rejected some of the manners and morals of their parents, but they did not otherwise have a politics. Moreover, the "flaming youth" of the twenties burned out by the end of the decade, and the Depression and World War II would inhibit the formation of a significant new youth identity until the late 1940s.

Unlike the 1920s youth, the postwar teenager was invented for political reasons, and the concept had a political edge from the start. The term was first used in 1945 by Eliot Cohen in an article called "A Teen-Age Bill of Rights."[51] It was a response to the greater independence that the war had thrust upon teens, who, with dad off at war and mom working outside the home, had less parental supervision and who themselves joined the workforce in large numbers. The response of Cohen and other experts of the era was to urge parental and societal recognition of "the growing capacity for autonomy in the teen years." Leerom Medovoi argues that "the 'Teen-Age Bill of Rights' . . . petitions its readers to honor and respect youth as *the embodiment of emergent identity*," and he argues that the meaning of "teenager" was tied up with American ideology articulated against both fascism and communism.[52] The category of teenager then involved an identity politics right from the start.

It must be stipulated, however, that teenagers in the 1950s were unlikely to have been conscious of having a generational politics. The idea that the 1950s was a period of quietude and conformity is not without foundation. The Cold War, McCarthyism, and the ideology of domesticity all restricted the range of overt political activities among all age groups, but especially among the young. However, the cohort most aptly described as conformist were those who would have entered college in the 1950s, while younger teens—those whose identity would have been most strongly shaped by the idea of the teenager—went on to become the campus rebels of the 1960s. It is these younger teens who were Elvis's most devoted fans, and what they developed could be said to be an identity in search of a politics. This identity was shaped as much by the experience of being part of new consumer group, the target of specialized products and advertising aimed at attracting a new source of disposable income. It was in the 1950s that teenagers became the most reliable movie audience, and as media historian Thomas Doherty has shown, the industry responded to this change by producing teenpics, films designed to appeal especially to it. Such specialized marketing strengthened teenage identity.[53]

Elvis was arguably the single most important product marketed to 1950s teenagers, but he was also their most important figure of group identification. James Dean had preceded Elvis and had influenced him, but his brief career as a movie star meant that Dean would reach a much smaller audience. Moreover, since his character was mediated through film narrative, he would never have the immediate rapport with his fans that Elvis did when he performed. The adult reaction against Elvis meant that identifying with him was a marker of generational difference. Television brought Elvis into the living room and created immediate generational conflict where previously there had been agreement. In his history of the New Left, Todd Gitlin explains:

> For those of us who were ten or twelve when Elvis Presley came along, it was rock 'n' roll that named us a generation. The shift was abrupt and amazing. One moment parents and children were listening together to the easygoing likes of Dean Martin's "Memories Are Made of This," of Rosemary Clooney's "Hey There" ("you with the stars in your eyes"), and gathering together on Saturday night to watch the regulars of *Your Hit Parade* cover the week's hits; the next, the spectacle of crooners trying to simulate Elvis Presley and straddle the widening cultural chasm was too laughable to behold. . . . Popular music often serves to insulate young people against the authority of the previous generation, and the commercial search for the Latest makes generation tension over music virtually automatic. But in rock's heyday there was a special intensity on both sides. On one side, generational defiance: "Hail hail rock 'n' roll / Deliver me from days of old" (Chuck Berry); "Rock and Roll is here to stay" (Danny and the Juniors). On the other: Perry Como, Patti Page, Tony Bennett, adult fear and loathing.[54]

Elvis was the most important symbol of this divide, and one could argue that he was awarded the title "King of Rock & Roll" for that reason. In challenging the old social divisions, Elvis became the central figure in a newly important one. The generational chasm would only widen in the 1960s, as generational identity became the basis for a political movement. The iconicity of the other stars in this book is dependent on youth as a political and cultural identity.

CHAPTER THREE

JAMES BROWN
Self-Remade Man

My story is the Horatio Alger story. It's an American story, it's the kind America can be proud of, but yet if you tell it in detail, if you tell all the things I fought to make it, it's like the Satchel Paige story.

James Brown

Brown represented the political black man, the successful black man, the sexual black man, the relentless black warrior that was "Black and Proud," and as the song says, "ready to die on our feet, rather than be livin' on our knees." Brown grabbed hold of the jugular vein of black aspirations and would not let go.

Rickey Vincent

James Brown published two autobiographies, *James Brown: The Godfather of Soul* (1986) and *I Feel Good* (2005).[1] These books are in many respects quite different, but the narrative Brown tells remains largely the same. That story is, as Brown himself has called it, "the Horatio Alger story."[2] More accurately, it is what we misremember as the Horatio Alger story, since, unlike Alger's novels, Brown's narrative attributes nothing to luck or the kind intervention of a patron. Brown portrays himself as a self-made man, and the only real credit he gives to anyone else is to God, from whom he says he received directly all the education he needed. But Brown's story is also more complicated, because it is not the simple story of a rise out of poverty into wealth and success. He didn't just succeed but repeatedly reinvented himself, successfully remaking his persona at least three times. Thus Brown's story adds to the traditionally American bootstrap myth, a story of self-fashioning that goes back to Henry David Thoreau and Walt Whitman but that here entails a far more protean self that emerges in the repeated re-creations of his public persona.

Brown's success, as we will see, could be measured in many ways, but what may be most remarkable is that Brown made himself a star, a peer of Elvis, the Beatles, the Stones, and Dylan. This is a startling achievement, given the lack of precedence for black stardom. In the late 1950s, before Sidney Poitier made it to the top of the box office, there had not been a black movie star.

Louis Armstrong, Ella Fitzgerald, and other jazz performers had attained significant popularity, but their reputations were restricted to the realm of music. None had, like Frank Sinatra or Elvis, managed to become multimedia stars. Little Richard, Fats Domino, and Chuck Berry were genuine stars during the 1950s, but racism limited their ability to define and, especially, to redefine themselves. That's one reason, perhaps, why none of these performers developed significantly after the 1950s, even though Berry continued to have some hits and Richard remained a well-known figure. This chapter looks at the way in which James Brown managed to circumvent these limitations to produce successive reinventions of his persona. From "the Hardest Working Man in Show Business," to "Soul Brother No. 1," and "the Godfather of Soul," Brown successfully redefined himself to fit different musical and cultural moments. It would be a mistake to see these changes as mere adaptations to the market, for they enabled Brown to participate much more directly in political struggle than did most other black performers. Brown changed stardom not only by integrating it but also by becoming briefly a widely recognized African American leader. Brown thus made stardom political in a more direct way than Bob Dylan would.

Ray Charles and Sam Cooke are usually listed as black artists who attained pop stardom prior to Brown, but the key word here is "pop." Both of them existed on the margins of rock & roll as a cultural practice; Charles "emphasized adult passion" and attracted an older audience, while Cooke "gracefully walked the line between pop and schlock."[3] Both men would significantly influence rock and soul without ever being in the mainstream of either. What they shared with Brown was the use of gospel music as the basis for R&B and an unusual degree of economic and artistic control. Their careers entailed radical changes of direction, Charles moving with impunity among different genres and Cooke risking his gospel stardom to sing R&B. Cooke's career was tragically cut short, so we will never know how he might have made use of the greater freedom the 1960s would afford black artists. Charles continued to produce great records, but his persona was largely a complete work by the early 1960s. So, if Charles and Cooke did invent themselves, those inventions remained relatively safe; they did not challenge preconceived notions about what popular musicians should be. James Brown did challenge those conceptions, and he did so right from the start of his career. "Long after Ray Charles had left the parochial world of soul and Sam Cooke was on the verge of Las Vegas bookings and Hollywood success, James Brown alone, a contemporary of both Charles and Cooke, was still out there toiling in the vineyards, singing self-created music that increasingly left both the idea of accommodation and the old tired formulations of R&B behind."[4]

The common idea about stars is that they are industrial artifacts, the creations of movie studios or record companies. I've been arguing throughout this book that, especially in the case of rock stars, this is a misconception. But Brown is an extreme instance. While he certainly had many collaborators over the years—especially the musicians who gave his band the reputation as the best in the business—there is no figure like Tom Parker or Andrew Oldham who helped to shape his persona. Brown's managers were doubtless important factors in his success, but they do not seem to have played a role in defining his identity. His band members contributed much more musically than Brown gave them credit for, but they did it at his bidding. Brown was perceived as "the boss" long before Bruce Springsteen picked up that designation.

Brown's first record company, King, which released most of his hits, did nothing to develop his persona and even seemed to inhibit his own attempts to do so. This was not an uncommon situation for an R&B artist. Labels featuring African American artists in general did little to help produce star personas. Independent labels were important to the rise of soul music, because the majors were largely uninterested in reaching the black audience. While many independent labels serving the African American market were white owned, some, including Motown and Stax during the latter half of its existence, were black enterprises. So we cannot argue that black performers were denied star treatment because of the companies' racism, since we can assume that these black entrepreneurs were not overtly or consciously racist. Black-owned Motown chose musical assimilation as its strategy to expand beyond the "race" market. Although it was under white ownership, Stax distinguished itself by its distinctly black sound, and it had a distribution deal with Atlantic, itself an independent oriented to the black audience. Stax never imitated Motown's attempt to produce "the sound of young America," and founder James Stewart "wasn't the least bit interested in crossing over if crossing over meant compromising . . . the 'Stax sound.' "[5]

It is safe to say, however, that the crossover success of soul music in the mid-1960s affected both companies, reinforcing Motown's commitment to its strategy and making Stax imagine new goals and possibilities. But neither label offered its artists a chance to develop their own style, sounds, or personalities. Rather, the labels gave their artists a packaged sound and an audience that wanted to hear it. Motown artists in particular were supposed to fit the model the label prescribed. Like Hollywood of the studio era, Motown's performers were presented to the public carefully, allowing only the desired image to be visible. But Hollywood's strategy had been to invent backstage lives for its stars so that fans might continue to identify with them between their screen appearances. The major record companies followed this pattern, though typically on a smaller scale. Motown, however, presented its acts almost as if they had been literally, like robots, produced by the company. The differences among Diana Ross, Martha Reeves, and Gladys Knight were supposed to be perceived, but they were differences of style and perhaps talent, and not differences of personality. Indeed, they were ranked just as General Motors ranked Cadillacs, Buicks, and Chevrolets and came out of a process that "replicated the manufacturing techniques of the auto industry."[6]

It has been argued that the lack of individualized personas coming out of Stax and the Muscle Shoals studio, where many Atlantic artists recorded, resulted from an ethic of cooperation, also foreign to Brown. "Unlike nearly everyone else in the greater soul community for whom the success of any soul artist was another rung up the ladder, each step forward a step for mankind (Muscle Shoals and Stax are only two of the more prominent examples of this kind of cooperative enterprise), James Brown was a Solo Man who forged ahead on his own, who, far from negotiating any kind of compromise solution to reach a broader audience, demanded that that very audience sit up and listen to what he had to say."[7] Star personas did eventually emerge out of both labels, first at Stax with Otis Redding—though only at the very moment when he died in a plane crash—and later at Motown with Stevie Wonder, Marvin Gaye, and Michael Jackson. James Brown preceded all of them, and only the Michael Jackson of the early 1980s and later could be said to have developed a persona of equal complexity and recognition.

Even if Brown is not unambiguously the first black rock star, he was the first African American to be able to fully take advantage of the new star system that rock & roll produced. It's hard to think of any other popular musician who has been identified by so many different monikers, designations that reveal the various sides of Brown's persona. But, he also retained enough consistency of style and image that no one questioned his authenticity. This combination enabled Brown to participate much more effectively as a politically engaged intellectual than did most other black rock & rollers and to become, in his own perfectly accurate description, "a cultural force."[8] However, Brown's success, and especially his understanding of it, has rendered his political significance unclear. No other rock & roller has been more committed to the American Dream, a position that led Brown to support Richard Nixon.

The Hardest Working Man in Show Business

James Brown was born in Barnwell, South Carolina, in 1933, and according to his own telling, he began pulling himself up by his bootstraps that very day: "I wasn't supposed to be James. I wasn't supposed to be Brown. And I wasn't supposed to be alive. You see, I was a stillborn kid."[9] His mother left the family when he was four. He grew up poor, first living with his father in shacks in South Carolina and then with an aunt in a brothel in Augusta, Georgia. At night, he would "hit the streets, dancing for pennies and shining shoes for nickels, trying to earn enough money to put some food on our table. Earning money—now that excited me."[10] Brown says that he was often sent home from school for "insufficient clothes," and at the age of sixteen he was convicted of stealing clothing out of cars and served about three years in juvenile prison.[11]

Brown learned to sing in church, and in prison he formed a gospel quartet. He began working as a musician in 1953, after having a potential career in baseball ended by an injury. He joined a group fronted by Bobby Byrd, which soon became known as the Flames, with Brown quickly displacing Byrd. They played around Augusta and then Macon, Georgia, and got some of their earliest exposure filling in for Little Richard at venues that were suddenly too small to interest him. The Flames were signed to a recording contract with King Records, and in early 1956 released "Please, Please, Please." It could be argued that this early recording remains Brown's signature song—another of his monikers was Mr. Please, Please, Please—even though it lacks the innovations for which he would later be known. As Brown describes the song's genesis, "At the time, we were doing an Orioles song called 'Baby, Please Don't Go.' The background vocals for it included the word 'please' repeated several times. With that as a starting point, I wrote 'Please, Please, Please.'"[12] The song differs from the Orioles' version in the minimalism of its lyrics. As Peter Guralnick explains, "The Famous Flames took the chorus not simply as their theme but as virtually their only text. This sense of single-minded intensity was further enhanced by the effect of James's near-sobbing voice against the smooth gospel harmonies of the Flames . . . with each chorus mounting in a rising crescendo of emotion and simple repetition."[13] This early recording reveals Brown's talent for innovation, and its raw emotion and repetitive drive would become hallmarks of his great recordings of the 1960s.

"Please, Please, Please" reached number 5 on *Billboard*'s R&B chart. This record appeared just as Elvis Presley rose to become the King of something that most people had only known about since 1955, rock & roll. In 1956, segregation was the rule in popular music, as it was throughout the South and many other localities. (*Brown v. Board of Education,* the case in which the Supreme Court declared school segregation illegal, came from Kansas.) While a few black jazz or classical performers might have had significant white audiences, most African American musicians performed and recorded for what until recently had been officially known as the "race" market. As we observed in chapter 2, rock & roll emerged from the beginning of the breakdown of that separation, as white teenagers sought out black music. Still, in the mid-fifties, black musicians' ability to reach white audiences remained limited. Although Chuck Berry and Little Richard had records on the pop charts in 1955 and 1956, only Berry's "Maybellene" made it into the top 10. The less-threatening Fats Domino had four top 10 hits, including "Blueberry Hill," which made it to number 4. In 1956, the Platters, a doo-wop group, were the only African Americans to have a number 1 record. Performing venues were also largely segregated, with African American artists playing mainly in the South on what was known as the Chitlin Circuit, which included whites-only venues but tended to limit the ability of black artists to develop national interracial audiences.

These conditions meant that James Brown would be largely unknown to whites through nearly the first ten years of his career. Of his 1950s singles, only "Try Me" made it into the top 50 on the *Billboard* pop chart. But segregation also meant that he could develop his music and persona without reference to the white audience. As he put it, "Little Richard . . . geared his show to mostly White audiences. . . . I, on the other hand, was much more raw and stayed strictly within the confines of what I knew, soul."[14] His music was, as LeRoi Jones said of R&B in general, "an exclusive music. It was performed almost exclusively for, and had to satisfy, a Negro audience."[15] When Brown finally did begin to reach a white audience in the 1960s, it was on his terms, and a large part of his appeal was that he remained true to these roots.

James Brown putting on a show with the well-choreographed Famous Flames. (film still from the *T.A.M.I. Show,* 1964)

Between "Please, Please, Please" and his 1963 album *Live at the Apollo,* Brown's singles tended to be ballads, powerfully performed to be sure, but not especially innovative. What Brown did during this period was to establish himself as a great live performer. In the 1950s, he performed as many as 350 nights a year, and he became known as the King of One Nighters.[16] His stage show became increasingly distinctive. As one of his managers, Alan Leeds, observed, his theatrical style of presentation was inspired by vaudeville.[17] It became, in fact, a variety show in miniature, with several lead vocalists, its own dancers, a comedian, and an MC, Danny Ray, whose job it was to build up the star by reciting his hits and the long list of identities Brown had taken on. Moreover, Brown's musical choices were also distinguished by their variety. By the mid-1960s, the show would include standards made famous by Tony Bennett and Frank Sinatra and blues such as "Going to Kansas City." As Brown explained, "To me, putting on a show means exactly that—putting on a *show*. . . . I'm one of the very last acts that actually works his band in rehearsal until I'm confident they understand that they are not just playing some notes together, but putting on a spectacle: a James Brown performance!"[18]

Aesthetically, the show was defined by the tension between the band's disciplined precision and its leader's performance, seemingly on the edge of emotional and physical endurance. That's not to say that Brown himself was undisciplined; despite appearances, his show was carefully planned. Brown's power over the band through discipline was part of his star persona. As *Newsweek* put it in 1968, "One by one he has found the men he needs and he runs them like a militia, giving demerits for inadequacy and fines for mistakes."[19] The contrast with the ensemble's precision made the effect of his performance all the greater, both by creating tension between freedom and constraint and by providing a controlled sonic space within which Brown's extremity could seem musical.

Performing at the edge was itself a key to Brown's persona. As "Please, Please, Please" illustrates, Brown's songs often depict someone at the limit of emotional control. The singer of that song is someone who has become one with his plea, and one can't imagine how he could survive being turned down. In performance, Brown embodied that extremity of emotion, not only in the fervor of his singing, but also in his frequent screams and moans, which took his vocal performance to the very limit of song. His dancing, with its precise movements, might have seemed controlled by comparison to his vocalizing, but the frenetic energy he expended appeared to put Brown at the physical edge as well. Not only was it hard to believe that anyone could move that fast and flexibly but also that that amount of motion could be sustained for such a long time. What made Brown's moniker "the Hardest Working Man in Show Business" stick was not merely the number of shows he performed every year but, more important, the energy he expended on stage. In every aspect of his work, James Brown appeared like an athlete in an Olympic final who leaves nothing in reserve because there is no tomorrow. For Brown, there was always another show tomorrow, and yet he performed each as if it were his last.

The idea of giving everything to the audience lies behind a bit of theater that became part of Brown's show starting in the early 1960s. As rock critic Robert Palmer memorably described it,

As he wrenched out the pleading refrain to "Please, Please, Please" he would slowly sink to his knees, writhing with the tune's lugubrious rhythm until finally, still singing, he collapsed in a heap. Famous Flames Bobby Byrd, Bobby Bennett and Lloyd Stallworth would approach him hesitantly. One would produce a purple cape and, reverently draping it over the fallen singer's body, help him to his feet and slowly escort him offstage. Brown, still holding the microphone, would begin to drag his feet, struggle, and, after a dramatic pause, shake off the cape and walk deliberately back to stage center.[20]

The act would be repeated several times with different-colored capes, until finally Brown and band would leave the stage together. The point, of course, was that the performer would not quit until he had expended his last ounce of energy, regardless of the apparent cost to his health or well-being.

One question that might have been raised by such overt showmanship is that of authenticity. As rock & roll developed its own performance conventions during the 1960s, it rejected most of the trappings of popular music showmanship in favor of what was understood to be a more natural and direct presentation. Rock & roll acts in the early 1960s might well appear as part of television variety shows like Ed Sullivan's, but by the midsixties, they often seemed too strange to fit into that format, as revealed by the Rolling Stones' 1964 appearance on the *Hollywood Palace Show,* where host Dean Martin "vilified and degraded them."[21] Similarly, while the Beatles and most other British invasion groups performed in relatively conventional uniforms, after 1965, bands tended to follow the Rolling Stones' lead and dispense with them, or choose such outlandish ones that the very idea of the uniform was satirized.

Under these circumstances, had a white rock & roll band presented a James Brown–style show in 1967 or '68, they would have doubtless been met with derision. Audiences, however, continued to expect more traditional showmanship from soul acts. Motown groups, for example, performed carefully choreographed dances, while the convention of the MC—in practice, often a member of the band—was widely observed by southern soul acts. No other group, black or white, used a variety show model, however, and no other group made so much of performance attire. One of the offenses for which Brown fined his band members was having an unpressed uniform. As biographer Cynthia Rose observes, Brown discovered that "style . . . held the key to consistent success."[22] Thus, the uniforms themselves changed frequently and, until 1968, when African-style tunics were introduced in the wake of the release of "Say It Loud, I'm Black and I'm Proud," they were versions of the suit and tie. James himself would change costume more frequently than the band, and his dress would usually involve much more outlandish variations on the suit and tie theme. His dress conveyed extravagance, wealth, and power in a semiotics that was specific to African American culture. To white America, dressing in that way simply appeared consistent with that culture, and that, finally, was why James Brown could get away with putting on a show and still seem authentic. But he could carry it off only because his music always proclaimed its blackness. As he put it, he "turned racist minstrelsy into Black soul—and by doing so, became a cultural force."[23]

The first inkling of that force was felt with the success of the album *Live at the Apollo* (1963). The record was startling for more than just its success at capturing the sound of Brown's live performance. At that time, black artists sold mainly singles, and live albums were rare. Ray Charles had released a successful live album in 1959, *Ray Charles in Person,* but Charles's older and whiter audience did buy albums. Of Brown's seven albums released prior to *Live at the Apollo,* none had sold more than 10,000 copies.[24] The live album's success confounded expectations. According to Alan Leeds, "It took some time for sales to start building, but gradually more and more young blacks started buying it—for many it might have been the first LP they'd ever bought in their lives, it was one of those hip things that everybody had to have."[25] Brown had not had a single reach any higher than number 35 on the pop charts, but *Live at the Apollo* reached number 2 on *Billboard*'s pop album chart, and it stayed on the chart for sixty-six weeks. It earned Brown a gold record, signifying a million dollars in sales. According to rock historian Peter Guralnick, this was "an almost unprecedented accomplishment for a pure R&B record (and this was unquestionably pure R&B). It also established James Brown once and for all not only as the premier R&B box-office attraction of his time but as an artist with untapped potential for crossover success even without adulterating what he had to offer."[26]

The story of the making of *Live at the Apollo* has contributed to James Brown's image as a self-made man. Though it was not widely publicized at the time of the album's release, Sid Nathan, the owner of King Records, refused Brown's request to record a live album. Brown quotes him as saying, "You can't keep on recording the same songs over and over again. Nobody's going to buy that."[27] Brown financed the project himself, spending $5,700, a

James Brown at the start of the cape act in the *T.A.M.I. Show,* 1964. (film still)

lot of money to him at the time.[28] Moreover, he rented the Apollo for the recorded concerts and even put its employees in uniforms. These entrepreneurial efforts paid off so well that Brown increasingly charted his own career path, and his control of his own business affairs gave his hard work on stage a new resonance. He was working for his audience and himself but not for "the man."

Live at the Apollo let the world hear what a James Brown show sounded like, but it did not, of course, let them see it. That lack was filled in 1964, when James Brown and the Famous Flames appeared on the *T.A.M.I. Show.*[29] Originally a theater-only closed-circuit television offering, the show was filmed, and it later played on both broadcast TV and in movie houses. The lineup included a great many Motown acts, then riding a wave of crossover success, as well as first-generation rock & rollers like Chuck Berry and Bo Diddley, and popular white performers such as Lesley Gore, Jan and Dean, and Gerry and the Pacemakers. The show was to be closed by the Rolling Stones, suggesting that they were regarded as its biggest stars. The Stones had had a top 10 hit in 1964 ("Time Is on My Side"), but they were not yet the dominant group they would become after "Satisfaction." It was their misfortune to have to follow James Brown on the *T.A.M.I. Show.* According to all reports, the Stones were blown away by Brown's performance, and according to Stones' biographer Stephen Davis, "After that, Mick decided to *become* James Brown."[30] The film made Brown's performance of "Please, Please, Please" and the cape act available to millions who had not seen Brown in person. They could see for themselves that Brown was indeed the Hardest Working Man in Show Business. What that meant to the audience was that Brown would always deliver on the implicit contract between them. And that promise, in turn, defined a certain equality between the two parties. The hardest working man is, after all, a working man.

Soul Brother No. 1

In 1964 and 1965, James Brown also appeared for the first time on broadcast television, including the *Ed Sullivan Show* and *Shindig.* Together with the *T.A.M.I. Show,* these appearances enabled Brown to build a significant white audience. His performance of his new single "Papa's Got a Brand New Bag" on *Shindig* on September 1, 1965, helped it to become his first top 10 hit. What's especially remarkable about this success is that, far from being a retreat from R&B, the record was an advance into unfamiliar musical territory that sounded more like Africa than Detroit or Memphis. The song incorporated a new style that Brown had first experimented with on *Out of Sight* (1964) in which, as Palmer famously describes it,

> Rhythm became everything. Brown and his musicians and arrangers began to treat every instrument and voice in the group as if it were a drum. The horns played single-note bursts that were often sprung against the downbeats. The bass lines were broken up into choppy two- or three-note patterns, a procedure common in Latin music since the Forties but unusual in R&B. Brown's rhythm guitarist choked his guitar strings against the instrument's neck so hard that his playing began to sound like a jagged tin can being scraped with a pocket knife.

Only occasionally were the horns, organ, or backing vocalists allowed to provide a harmonic continuum by holding a chord.[31]

Palmer effectively explains the strangeness of "Brand New Bag," though he
exaggerates the degree to which Brown did away with harmony and other
nonrhythmic musical features. As musicologist David Brackett has argued,
"Brand New Bag" and other songs of its period are "actually based on I–IV–
I–V–IV–I blues progressions," and later songs, like "Cold Sweat," that do consist mainly of ostinati (very short repeated melodies), nevertheless "do feature harmonic shifts and more than one ostinato, thereby avoiding complete
harmonic stasis."[32] Brackett's point is not that Brown's music lacks innovation but that it is all the more inventive because it can be understood as a
form of musical signifying. In discussing "Superbad," he asserts, "The most
common harmonic progression in the common practice of Western art music
is present in 'Superbad,' but . . . in an almost unrecognizable form. . . . it belongs to, while simultaneously comments upon, the langue or 'norms' of
Western music of the past 250 years."[33] Another musicologist, Alexander
Stewart, shows how the influence of jazz distinguished Brown's music: "His
use of ninth cords, chromaticism, extended improvisation and 'modal' harmonies . . . confirm his interest in jazz."[34] This level of musical invention sets
Brown apart from everyone else making popular records at the time, and
only the Beatles, with "Yesterday" and *Revolver* the following year, would
soon be in his league.

Brown himself described the innovation as the "One," and he asserts, "I
can tell you the exact moment when I went from being a soul singer to a cultural icon. It happened with the 'One.'"[35] While Brown's various explana-
tions of the "One" range to the mystical, he describes its role in "Papa's Got a
Brand New Bag" with impressive clarity:

I made sure that the first word in the song, *Papa*, had an American style emphasis. From the opening beat there came a necessary shift in the rhythm of the
words, with the "One" emerging in the way *Papa* was pronounced. . . . Nevertheless, I can so clearly remember how no one—*no one*—got it when I first introduced the song to the band. The drummers couldn't move their sticks in their
hands to the *ONE two THREE four* progression I asked for as a replacement to the
one TWO three FOUR they had always played or, more precisely, the *one AND two
AND three AND four AND*—the basic rhythm of rock and roll that stretched back
to Chuck Berry.[36]

Stewart shows that Brown's development of funk was based on rhythms common in New Orleans R&B, which Brown learned from a drummer named Clayton Fillyau. Even before "Brand New Bag," Brown recorded songs such as "I've Got Money," in which we already find "Fillyau . . . landing on the beat only on 'one' of each measure." According to Stewart, "Brown's high level of artistic control (unique among soul artists of that time) enabled him to bring a virtuosic style of drumming to the forefront of his music. Musicians and listeners perceived African qualities and, especially during an era of rising black nationalism, the intricate, more 'in-your-face' style of drumming easily became identified as a funky celebratory march of ethnic difference."[37]

Even if his rhythmic innovations had been developing since 1962, it was "Papa's Got a Brand New Bag" that put these to work in a form that is recognizable as funk. Brown is right to include that record as one of the major events of 1965, that annus mirabilis of rock & roll, which, he notes, "was rife with fresh sounds," among them Sam Cooke's "A Change Is Gonna Come," the Stones' "(I Can't Get No) Satisfaction," Dylan's "Like a Rolling Stone," the Byrds' "Mr. Tambourine Man," and the Beatles' album *Rubber Soul*.[38] Of all of these innovative records, Brown's may be the most radical, and, according to Rickey Vincent, the one that had the greatest long-term impact on popular music: "It was a song that changed soul music forever. 'New Bag' paved the way for the funk era."[39] "Papa's Got a Brand New Bag" is cited as the beginning of funk for its rhythm and arrangement, and as providing the germ for the development of rap by virtue, not only of these same features, but also of the lyrics and near absence of melody. Michael Eric Dyson has called Brown "the primal progenitor of the beats and rhythms of hip-hop music."[40]

Yet, it is important to observe that in the midsixties none of this could have been predicted, much less known. Listeners then would have been aware that "Papa" sounded like nothing they were familiar with and judged it to be great or weird or weird and great at the same time. Clearly, more decided it was great than not, because "Papa" was James Brown's breakthrough record, the one that both gave him his first pop chart hit and initiated a period (between 1965 and 1968) in which he scored six top 10 records and became an international star, with a stature similar to that of the Rolling Stones. That stature was not mainly a matter of how many hits he had, however. Motown produced top 10 singles by the bushel, but no Motown artist in the 1960s came close to attaining Brown's authority.

If "Papa's Got a Brand New Bag" is indisputably the record that established James Brown as a star of the first rank, the claim that the record made him a "cultural icon" is also somewhat misleading. Even before "Brand New Bag," his live performances, especially his dancing, had established his distinctive cultural image. His refusal to compromise aesthetically, manifest in "New Bag" but already well known, was indispensable to his persona, and it gave him the authenticity necessary to become more than just a soul singer. As "Soul Brother No. 1," he became a representative figure for African American culture. Emerging and established black intellectuals recognized Brown's significance. LeRoi Jones called him "our number one black poet" and asserted, "James Brown's form and content identify an entire group of people in America. However these may be transmuted and reused, reappear in other areas, in other musics for different purposes in the society, the initial energy and image are about a specific grouping of people, Black People."[41] Historian David Levering Lewis agreed: "If there is any black man who symbolizes the vast differences between black and white cultural and aesthetic values, Soul Brother No. 1 . . . is that man."[42] Another contemporary judgment went, "The James Brown band represents the quintessence of an African-directed movement in black music."[43]

Brown's rise to become one of the first popular musicians to attain the status of public intellectual corresponded with the rise of black nationalism in the 1960s. While Sam Cooke's belated civil rights hymn "A Change Is Gonna Come" reflects the hopes and dreams of racial social justice and equality of that movement, Brown's music celebrated black culture. By the time he released his first explicitly political track, "Say It Loud, I'm Black and I'm Proud" in 1968, he was already celebrated by the black power movement. This is explained by African American studies scholar William Van Deburg, who asserts, "The Black Power movement was not exclusively cultural, but it was essentially cultural."[44] So even though Brown had not aligned himself either in lyrics or interviews with that movement—and specifically dissented from revolutionary ambitions of leaders such as H. Rap Brown—he already represented black power: he was a powerful black man who never denied his race or its culture.

James Brown became a living instance of black power, which also explains the perception of Brown as a leader of the black community. Before "Say It Loud," Brown's lyrics were not explicitly political. His closest thing to a protest song up to that point was "Don't Be a Dropout," which was hardly a controversial stand to take. The only other song that might be said to take a position of any sort was "It's a Man's Man's Man's World," and that position did not generate much controversy in 1966, when second-wave feminism had yet to make much of an impact. But these songs reveal two important aspects of Brown's persona as it developed in the mid-1960s. "Man's World" expresses an ideology of male dominance disguised as a condition of nature. Because racist ideology had for hundreds of years diminished black manhood, Brown's assertion of male dominance here needs to be understood as more than the mere affirmation of the sexist status quo. For if male dominance was the general rule in the culture, it was not so in the same sense for African American men. Black men certainly weren't dominant within the culture as a whole, and their position vis-à-vis women was much more ambiguous than that of white men. "Man's World" was a hit, presumably, not merely because it reaffirmed sexist stereotypes but because of its powerful expression of one of them, that woman's essential purpose is sex. The song positions Brown himself as an alpha male unthreatened by what has sometimes been described as the black matriarchy. He needs women, but for just one thing, which we are persuaded he always gets. This image of confident power is what allows Brown to make a record like "Don't Be a Dropout" and not lose face with his young male fans, who would not have accepted many others as the bearer of such a message. Whether many actually took the advice is beside the point. By making the record, Brown showed himself to be someone whom black youth accepted as a leader.

Brown's leadership proved itself a reality in the wake of the assassination of Dr. Martin Luther King Jr. in April of 1968. Brown had been scheduled to play a show at the Boston Garden on April 5th, the day after the murder. Boston did not experience much unrest on Thursday, but officials worried that things might get worse, and the mayor wanted to cancel the concert. But black city councilman Thomas Atkins pointed out that thousands of disappointed James Brown fans could make matters worse. Someone proposed that the concert be televised instead as a way of keeping people off the street. The local public television station, WGBH, agreed to broadcast the concert, and the city agreed to guarantee the gate to offset lost ticket sales. The plan worked better than anyone had hoped. According to Brown, "The police said the streets in Roxbury [Boston's largest black neighborhood] were almost empty. Not only was there no trouble, there were fewer people out than there would be ordinarily."[45]

Both Atkins and Boston mayor Kevin White appeared onstage at the event to urge calm and to eulogize King. They also praised Brown, and he in turn praised the politicians, identifying both of them as "young" and calling the mayor a "swinging cat." Brown's stature as a leader was enhanced because he was treated as a person of significance by these powerful men. The fact that he now had the influence and popularity to keep Boston quiet when many other major U.S. cities erupted in riots made national political leaders take notice.[46] He was invited to the White House for a state dinner, and his request to be allowed to entertain the troops in Vietnam was granted. That summer, he played to 45,000 in Yankee Stadium, and *Ebony* called him "the biggest draw in America," a claim hard to gainsay, with the Beatles having given up the road, Dylan hiding out in Woodstock, the Stones' first grand tour more than a year away, and the San Francisco bands not yet filling stadiums.[47]

In the wake of these events, *Newsweek* posed the rhetorical question, "Who speaks for the black man in the streets?" And immediately supplied the answer, "Above all, soul-singer James Brown." The article noted that Brown attracted 3 million in attendance to see 300 shows in 1967, sold 50 million records, and his "royal trappings include 500 suits and 300 pairs of shoes, a house like a castle, a fleet of six cars including a Rolls-Royce and a pair of Cadillacs, a $713,000 jet airplane, and a business empire that brings in $4 million a year." It depicted Brown as an entrepreneur who "has large Wall Street investments, two radio stations, music-publishing companies, extensive real-estate."[48] Becoming known as an entrepreneur at the time when there were relatively few among African Americans added another dimension to his persona. In his Horatio Alger narrative, his own success represented the possibility of power: "Do you know that I shined shoes in front of radio station WRDW in Augusta, Ga.? You know something? Now I own that station. That's black power."[49] According to historian Brian Ward, "It was this conspicuous material success, the Lear jets and limousines, the businesses and bulging bank account, which combined with the music to fix Brown's unique place in black American consciousness."[50]

In early 1969, *Look* magazine could put James Brown on its cover and ask, "Is he the most important black man in America?"[51] *Look* dealt more seriously with Brown's music than had *Newsweek,* calling Brown "another reminder of the world's debt to Afro-American music," and it also mentioned Brown's business success, calling him "a ranking black capitalist." Its focus, however, was on Brown the "popular leader. . . . In 1969, when millions of

Brown gets equal billing on the *Look* cover with former Democratic vice presidential nominee Senator Edmund Muskie, 1969. (courtesy Photofest)

hyper-aware young men and women wonder whether it is still possible to be both black and American, James Brown is a new important leader. His constituency dwarfs Stokely Carmichael's and the late Dr. Martin Luther King's."[52]

It is hard to imagine any popular musician, even Elvis Presley, being spoken of in this way just a few years earlier. If *Look* was correct in its judgment of Brown, one would have to say that he had transcended the category of star and become something new. But Brown's role as a leader was brief, and even if his popularity did exceed Dr. King's, it's misleading to call his fans "a constituency." Of course, racism meant that there were relatively few blacks who could compete to be "most important," especially after so many leaders had been cut down in their prime. Still, the fact that *Look* could present James Brown in the way that it did is powerful evidence of the increasingly political character of stardom and the increasing influence of popular music and musicians. It has been argued that even as late as 1975, "Brown carried more weight than any black politician and still commanded the moral authority of the Black nation."[53] Indeed, while Brown's status as a leader, however briefly he held it, distinguishes him from the other stars I'm dealing with here, the seriousness with which he was taken in the late sixties was made possible by Elvis, the Beatles, and especially Bob Dylan. They transformed popular music from mere entertainment into cutting-edge culture.

"Say It Loud" was recorded after the Boston broadcast, his visit to the White House, and his trip to Vietnam. Black power activists were especially unhappy about the last of these and also with Brown's record "America Is My Home," released in June of 1968. They wanted a more explicit political endorsement from Brown. According to Vincent, what he did in response, not only to this pressure but to the tenor of the times, "had perhaps the greatest impact on the black nation since the deaths of King and Malcolm. 'Say It Loud' was a turning point in black music. Never before had black popular music explicitly reflected the bitterness of blacks toward the white man—and here it was done with ferocious funk. Classic works such as Billie Holiday's 'Strange Fruit' and John Coltrane's 'Alabama' were powerful indictments of racism, and Martha and the Vandellas' 'Dancing in the Streets' may indeed have been a symbolic call to protest, but 'Say It Loud' was a call to *action*."[54] With the lyrics that said blacks were "ready to die on our feet, rather than be livin' on our knees," the song was unambiguous in its critique of the status quo.

"Say It Loud" confirmed Brown's identity as Soul Brother No. 1. If Brown was still being billed as the Hardest Working Man in Show Business, the cultural resonance of his persona had shifted. Most obviously, he moved from being a working man to being a race man. With "Say It Loud," he took up what became known as identity politics. By identifying himself as a "Soul Brother," Brown expressed solidarity with black people, both politically and culturally. Such solidarity entails a kind of equality but one that differs subtly from that attached to being the Hardest Working Man. To be Soul Brother No. 1 is to be one with all of the other brothers, but it is also to stand apart from them. In effect, Brown's identity claimed to be blacker than thou. That was an important statement to make at a time when the idea of embracing black identity and culture remained controversial even among many African Americans. But by insisting on his priority over his other brothers, Brown also started down the road away from political leadership.

The Fall and Rise and Fall Etc. of the Godfather

James Brown believed, and a number of influential commentators agree, that "Say It Loud" caused white listeners to turn off. It was his last top 10 pop chart single until 1985's "Living in America," but I don't find Brown's endorsement of black pride a good explanation for this drop-off in record sales. Whites who bought his records in the mid-1960s were in effect declaring their sympathy with black culture. R. J. Smith's explanation, that "white-owned radio stations and white programmers turned their backs on him en masse," is more plausible, but why they did so can't be blamed on racism alone.[55] Rather, changes in the industry and rapidly evolving tastes meant that the business and aesthetics that had brought Brown to prominence could no longer keep him near the top. In 1969, Brown performed at the Newport Jazz Festival. Other artists on the bill included acts ranging from Dave Brubeck and Miles Davis to the Mothers of Invention, Jeff Beck, and Sly and the Family Stone. Rowdy rock fans led producer George Wein to consider cancelling remaining performances by rock acts, and they would drive the festival from Newport after 1971. It wasn't James Brown's performance that caused all of the excitement, however, but Sly and the Family Stone's. At their performance fans without tickets crashed the gate to produce what was later exaggerated in the press as a riot.

The acts at this festival differed somewhat from those who would appear at Woodstock six weeks later, but both reflect the new significance of FM radio's "progressive rock" stations like WBCN in Boston, which played albums rather than singles and which sought serious rock listeners—roughly the same demographic that was also being targeted by the new music magazine *Rolling Stone*. These new FM stations were not overtly racist—they played black performers like Sly and the Family Stone and Jimi Hendrix—but they did not play much soul. The audience for these stations increasingly bought albums and did not buy singles. They sought out what they heard as new and innovative—Sly, Hendrix, Cream, the Grateful Dead—and shunned anything that sounded like it belonged on top 40 radio. James Brown's career was built on singles, and, as Robert Palmer has observed, his recordings suffered from "apparent monotony." As Palmer explains, "Attacking him for being repetitive is like attacking Africans for being overly fond of drumming. Where the European listener may hear monotonous beating, the African distinguishes subtle polyrhythmic interplay," but such subtleties were apparently lost on an audience that sought guitar heroes and psychedelically altered consciousness.[56] However, it is also true that the popular music business is defined by rapid shifts of style, and Brown's music was heard as soul and identified with top 40 radio. It is a testament to Brown's connection to his black listeners that they continued to make his records R&B hits through 1976, more than ten years after "Papa's Got a Brand New Bag."

There was also a political dimension to Brown's decline, however. It's not that he was too radical for white rock fans but that he didn't seem radical enough. He apparently got away with recording "America Is My Home," which appeared only a few months before "Say It Loud," because the latter record redeemed him. Although his appearing in photos with Vice President Hubert Humphrey or going to Vietnam to entertain the troops certainly did not endear him to rock fans or black radicals, such lapses probably would have been tolerated. But what called Brown's radical credentials irreparably into question was his cozying up to President Richard Nixon. Brown had supported Humphrey's campaign for the White House in 1968 (he says, only because Robert Kennedy was no longer an option), but in 1972 he endorsed Richard Nixon over the antiwar Democratic nominee, George McGovern. Brown says this decision was based on Nixon's support for black capitalism as a solution to black poverty, and we have good reasons to accept that Brown really did believe in this idea. Not only was he a successful capitalist who believed that his success was largely the result of his own efforts, but in 1969, he had recorded what might be called an anthem for this position, "I Don't Want Nobody to Give Me Nothing (Open Up the Door, I'll Get It Myself)."

What doesn't seem to fit here, however, is the idea that the Democrats and George McGovern were opponents of black capitalism. In fact, Nixon used the idea of black capitalism as a way to justify his opposition to antipoverty programs. It seems as though James Brown fell for this line because Nixon took the trouble to ask for his support. As Brown describes it, an assistant to the president who was calling on black businesses, visited him at his Baltimore radio station. As a result of this relationship, Brown got invited to the White House to meet with the assistant. "Sometimes I said hello to the president or talked with him for a few minutes. His working office was right across the hall."[57] Brown says that he endorsed Nixon in part because he knew he was going to win, and he thought the best strategy was to "try to get inside and have some influence."[58] But getting inside was always Brown's way of dealing with those in power, with whom he increasingly imagined himself a peer. His autobiographies are full of name-dropping, and there was apparently no U.S. president since Eisenhower whom Brown did not like. This personal desire to be a part of the world of the powerful and famous explains the contradictions in Brown's politics better than any ideology. The effect in the early 1970s, however, was to make James Brown look like a follower and not a leader, as photos of him with Nixon made him appear increasingly out of touch with his audience and, as the Watergate scandal deepened, the nation.

In 1972, Brown acquired his last well-known moniker, "the Godfather of Soul." It resulted from Brown's work on the music for a Black Mafia film, *Black Caesar,* but one must assume that the name caught on because of the popularity of Mario Puzo's and Francis Ford Coppola's *The Godfather.* The name captures the aura of power Brown had long sought—often with great success—to project. But to be a godfather is not the same as being a brother. The new title placed Brown in a position of power over soul music, rather than emphasizing his solidarity with black people. Moreover, a godfather may be an authority or a power, but he is not a leader. Brown himself acknowledged what was at least a change in self-perception when he said, "I'm no leader of no black community. I'm a role model, but I don't lead."[59] The Godfather of Soul was Brown's most enduring moniker, not only because it fits his domineering personality, but also because godfathers are typically not young men. Brown was thirty-nine when he became Godfather, which was already old for a practitioner of rock or soul.

Brown's songs beginning around 1970 also contribute to the sense that the star's self-centered character had become self-obsession. Who or what is being exhorted to "get on up" in "Get Up (I Feel Like Being a) Sex Machine"? If it's not the singer himself, as the title suggests, it must be a part of his anatomy, a reading that would seem to take the idea of cock rock into Viagra territory. It has been argued that " 'Superbad,' contains no hint of narrative; there is really no hero with whom the narrator can identify except for Brown himself. . . . 'Superbad' 's textual voices emphasize their identity with 'James Brown.' "[60] It's worth noting that several new monikers that Brown tried out failed to catch on. He never became widely known as "Mr. Sex Machine" or "Mr. Superbad." The failure of "Minister of the New New Super Heavy Funk" is particularly revealing, since it shows that Brown had lost the dominant funk identity to George Clinton.

Through the mid-1970s, Brown continued to have a significant black following, but even that was largely gone by the later years of the decade. The popularity of disco was one reason for this decline. Brown's music was a significant influence on disco, but the polyrhythms of the former made most of it unsuitable for the latter. Brown's attempt to bill himself as the "Original Disco Man" went nowhere. Trouble with the IRS brought down Brown's business empire, and he lost not only his radio stations but his home and most of his personal savings as well. But if 1979 was a low point for Brown, 1980 saw the beginning of a new climb. He appeared as the Reverend Cleophus James in *The Blues Brothers* (directed by John Landis), a part that, while nonmusical, drew on Brown's dancing and other bits of his onstage performances. The success of the film led to new concert opportunities and eventually to another film, *Rocky IV* (directed by Sylvester Stallone, 1985). There he appeared as himself, "the Godfather of Soul," and he performed "Living in America," which became his first top 10 single since the 1960s. The song is in many respects a remake of "America Is My Home," but its sentiment was more in keeping with the mood of the Reagan era.

Suddenly in demand again, Brown found himself performing frequently, and "Living in America" was followed by several more hits. But in 1988, Brown was arrested after a high-speed chase through parts of South Carolina and Georgia. He was being sought because his estranged wife Adrianne had accused him of shooting up her car and threatening her with a tire iron. Then, as he describes it, "after the fight with my wife, blind with fury and high as a kite, I took my shotgun with me into a meeting I had called in my office complex . . . and, I guess, scared the daylights out of everybody."[61] He was sentenced to six years in a Georgia prison, and the enforced layoff from performing and recording meant another period of decline. By the time he was released in 1990, after serving two years, rap had become the dominant form for black audiences, limiting Brown's ability to sell new records but also demonstrating the continued relevance of his music. By the 1990s, Brown was recognized as the musician most sampled by hip-hop artists.[62] At the time of his death at the end of 2006, Brown was touring again and had dates scheduled into August of 2007.[63]

Brown's two autobiographies can be seen as continuations of Brown's history of self-remaking. Each book tells of his rise from poverty but then confronts his later ups and downs. The plot is rise, fall, and rise again, the second book including one more repetition of the pattern than the first. Thus these narratives fall into the more recently popular genre of memoir, the trauma and recovery story. Brown presents himself in these autobiographies both as a success and as a survivor. While it's clear that Brown always thought of himself as the latter, the autobiographies make this an aspect of his public persona.

Despite all of his explicit self-fashioning, Brown's most important legacy may have been a role he might not have recognized himself playing: creator of the opening for African American musicians to act as public intellectuals. Brown himself did this at a minimal level compared to, say, Public Enemy in the 1990s, but he was taken seriously by his black audience and by white politicians alike. If Brown didn't offer much in the way of analysis, he offered compelling encouragement and direction. As Vincent observes, "Brown represented the political black man . . . the relentless black warrior that was 'Black and Proud,' and as the song says, 'ready to die on our feet, rather than be livin' on our knees.' "[64] He was the first major black performer willing to articulate black demands rather than merely black hopes.

CHAPTER FOUR

BOB DYLAN
The Artist

I first started waking up to the possibilities of rock lyrics being serious with *Blonde on Blonde*. . . . It said it was okay to be as serious as you wanted in rock.

Robert Hunter

Bob Dylan may not have Clark Gable's ears, but you can bet he's going to have as powerful an impact upon his generation as Gable did upon his.

Don Heckman

Bob Dylan emerged in 1965 as a rock star.[1] The story is by now well known. It has been told in numerous biographies and several documentary films, most recently Martin Scorsese's *No Direction Home*. "Dylan's electric set at the 1965 Newport Folk Festival may well be the most written-about performance in the history of rock & roll."[2] Though the previous March Dylan had released *Bringing It All Back Home* with one entire side of electrified songs, and his new rock & roll single, "Like a Rolling Stone," had already entered the pop charts, the folkies at Newport didn't expect this new Dylan to show up. And he did not show up with a rock band. Rather, Dylan had put together a pickup band of musicians at Newport and, as Robert Shelton describes it "rehearsed this instant group until dawn. They kept their plan secret until they walked on stage, Dylan, in a matador-outlaw orange shirt and black leather, carrying an electric guitar. From the moment they swung into a rocking electric version of 'Maggie's Farm,' the Newport audience registered hostility. . . . As Dylan led his band into 'Rolling Stone,' the audience grew shriller: 'Play folk music! . . . Sell out! . . . This is a folk festival! . . . Get rid of the band!' "[3]

Dylan's apostasy again met with now famous rejection at Forest Hills a month later and during his 1966 tour of England, where the electric portion of his concerts was routinely booed and where he was called "traitor" and "Judas." Yet the backlash in response to Dylan's changes was confined to a coterie of devoted folk music enthusiasts. For the rest of his ever-expanding audience, Dylan's earlier persona was understood to be an element of the new one. What to the Old Left and to folk purists was an incomprehensible abandonment of the authentic for the commercial was to the New Left and

Bob Dylan, still the committed folksinger, with Joan Baez at the 1963 Civil Rights March on Washington. (U.S. Information Agency/National Archives)

legions of young rock fans the embrace of their culture by one who had previously shared only their politics.[4]

What Dylan became during this period is "the artist." He was the first rock star to present himself as if he were in the same kind of business as Ezra Pound, Pablo Picasso, or Igor Stravinsky. His main medium was at first the song, but it quickly became the album, and, perhaps in the long run, it will have been his persona. After Dylan, it would be impossible to simply assume that a rock star must be culturally ephemeral. Dylan's artist persona enabled him to continue to comment on political and social issues without being classified as a "protest singer." Moreover, because since the mid-nineteenth century artists had styled themselves as opponents of the bourgeoisie, Dylan's new persona continued to register as a form of opposition or radicalism.[5]

As We See Him Now

It is hard even for those of us who lived through the period to recapture the Dylan who emerged in the mid-1960s. Those to whom Dylan still matters are probably much more aware of the details of his life than his fans were at the time. "In the faxless '60s, when TVs were still steam-driven and urgent correspondence was carried in the saddlebags of the Pony Express, news of Dylan's doings would often come limping along months after the event."[6] There was very little intelligent coverage of popular music back then, as the journalists captured in D. A. Pennebaker's cinema verité–style documentary of Dylan's 1965 tour of England, *Don't Look Back,* attest. Unlike Elvis, the Beatles, or the Rolling Stones, Dylan's star did not rise on television. He made his mark first through his songs and later through his records and coverage in mass-circulation magazines.

Of all rock stars, only the Beatles may have more print devoted to them than Dylan. The interest, unquenched by a stream of biographies, suggests just how much Dylan remains an enigma. He was enigmatic then too, but the questions surrounding him came from a different place—not his life but his lyrics. Then we knew him as a songwriter associated with folk music who became a rock star. We didn't know, for example, who Suze Rotolo or Albert Grossman were, and many of us believed that Joan Baez was Bob's girlfriend long after they had ceased to have anything to do with each other. We knew that Dylan had changed his name from Zimmerman, in homage to Dylan Thomas we believed, but we didn't know anything about his propensity to make up fictions about his past. The evidence wasn't readily available and the records were.

Now we know "the truth." Anyone who has read even a part of one of the biographies or seen Todd Haynes's film *I'm Not There* (2007) knows that Dylan has repeatedly refashioned himself.[7] It began before he became Dylan, when he called himself "Dillon," apparently after the marshal on the television series *Gunsmoke.* Then, according to one version, after reading *Bound for Glory,* Woody Guthrie's autobiography, Dylan "absolutely became Woody Guthrie."[8] To Robert Shelton, the critic whose *New York Times* review gave Dylan his first big break, Dylan "admitted that the change . . . grew out of a genuine need for a new identity: He simply wasn't pleased with his former bland, directionless self."[9] On arriving in Greenwich Village he told elaborate and conflicting lies made up to disguise his rather unexceptional middle-class background in Hibbing, Minnesota: "He was an orphan, born in Chicago or raised in a New Mexico orphanage or in various foster homes; his Semitic features were the mark of Sioux Indian Blood in the family; one of his uncles was a gambler, another a thief; he had lived in Oklahoma, Iowa, South Dakota, Kansas, and on the Mississippi River; he joined a carnival at age thir-

teen and traveled with it around the Southwest; he had played piano on Elvis Presley's early records."[10] As he told Shelton, "I shucked everybody when
I came to New York."[11] It wasn't until 1963 that *Newsweek* exposed the degree
of Dylan's self-fashioning, but that cover story, called a "hatchet job," probably didn't persuade anyone who was already a fan.[12]

Those who know only his music probably also recognize Dylan's history of
changes, but the records themselves don't advertise Dylan's conscious work
of self-invention. At first glance, probably no star seems as sincere as Bob Dylan.
This sense of sincerity, however, is a paradox, since Dylan's persona has
shifted more than any other star's. David Bowie and Madonna may have had
as many or even more guises, but they have always been presented as such.
Bowie played theatrical roles onstage, self-consciously bringing to life characters he had invented. Madonna, who explicitly urged us to "strike a pose,"
has presented herself less as a series of different characters than as a series of
different appearances. Her ability to change her looks makes her rock's cha-
meleon, but it masks a more or less consistent performer. Both Bowie and
Madonna play with literal disguise. Dylan's various roles never entailed such
radical changes in appearance. That may be part of the reason that his audience was largely willing to believe that each new persona represented a genuine instance of self-expression.

What is striking about Bob Dylan is that, though he has played a series of
roles, his fans have been asked to believe that all of them were authentic.
Dylan's first role, as one of the many imitators of Woody Guthrie, was hardly
original. Guthrie had long inspired such imitation by young men who, one
must presume, believed that they were in some way putting themselves in
touch with something genuine by playing at being Woody.[13] While Ramblin'
Jack Elliott (né Elliot Adnopoz) was the first performer to claim Woody's
mantle, Dylan wrested it from him in the early 1960s. When Robert Zimmerman became Bob Dylan, he took on a ready-made identity that carried authenticity with it. Dylan's topical songs of the time made him seem like the
genuine voice of the civil rights movement. Greil Marcus in *Invisible Republic*
reveals another element of Dylan's authenticity, tying him to roots deep in
the history of American music and thus making him the very emblem of
rock's musical authenticity.[14]

Time, in giving Dylan his first coverage in a national magazine, reported,
"An atmosphere of the ersatz surrounds him."[15] A few months later, *Newsweek*
revealed that Dylan had lied about his ordinary, middle-class background,

and questioned "why Dylan . . . should bother to deny his past is a mystery. Perhaps he feels it would spoil the image he works so hard to cultivate—with his dress, with his talk, with the deliberately atrocious grammar and pronunciation in his songs."[16] A few years later, when Dylan abandoned his role as political spokesperson, he didn't just say that he had changed his mind or that the earlier role was too confining. In interviews he utterly rejected that role, saying that he never wrote protest songs or took a political position. Ellen Willis, writing in 1967 in *Commentary,* was already able to remark, "Not since Rimbaud said, 'I is another,' has an artist been so obsessed with escaping identity."[17]

Dylan's shifting identity became more obvious beginning with the release of *Nashville Skyline* in 1969. There he took up the guise of the commercial country and western singer. His next record, *Self-Portrait,* was paradoxically an album of other people's songs performed, almost everyone agreed, wretchedly. Upon Dylan's return to touring in 1973, he appeared to reclaim his mid-1960s identity, but that moment was followed immediately by the role of confessional poet on *Blood on the Tracks.* It is harder to characterize the figure in whiteface of the Rolling Thunder Revue era, but by the end of the 1970s, Dylan appeared in another major incarnation, as an evangelical Christian. This switch strained the faith (in him) of his fans as no earlier one had. By the mid-1980s, after Dylan left behind the role of evangelist, people began to take his changing identities for granted.

There are, of course, different judgments of this pattern. The sympathetic biographer Clinton Heylin says, "Dylan's perennial reinventions of himself have led me to structure this book around each new guise he has taken upon himself," and *I'm Not There,* which uses six different actors to portray Dylan, makes these changes utterly fascinating and each persona seem genuine.[18] On the other side of the question, David Hajdu complains, "The irony of Robert Zimmerman's metamorphosis into Bob Dylan lies in the application of so much elusion and artifice in the name of truth and authenticity."[19] Hajdu suggests that the sense of authenticity Dylan conveys is itself a deliberate falsehood, thus compounding the sin of the original misrepresentation. While a minority have long agreed with Hajdu's judgment and written Dylan off as a mere poseur, his fans and many others have accorded authenticity to him in most, if not all, of his incarnations.

One way that some people have explained Jokerman Dylan is as an instance of the "trickster" figure. The trickster is by definition inauthentic at least some of the time, but the significance of the figure depends on authenticity as a norm or value. Without these, the trickster can be nothing special, since, in effect, everyone would be inauthentic and no one would ever be fooled. In this view, as Rob Wilson has put it, Dylan "embodies both belief and the innermost deconstruction of belief."[20] But that came only later, and in the 1960s Dylan's shifting identities were understood to be aspects of a more or less unified persona.

Art

In the early 1960s, popular musicians were often called "recording artists," but they were not regarded by the press or the public at large as having a claim to making Art. From the middle of the nineteenth century, the word *artist* was mostly reserved for painters, sculptors, writers, and composers, while the term *artiste* was sometimes used for actors and singers.[21] Although *artiste* evolved to mean something like "poser," we continue to distinguish between *art* meaning any skill or craft—for example, the art of wine making—and *art* (or *Art*) meaning works or the best works of visual artists, writers, or composers, and some filmmakers. If it remains true that the status of "popular music, dance, and film . . . as Art or art is still contested" today,[22] in the early 1960s the division between high Art and these popular forms was strongly entrenched. Clement Greenberg's 1939 essay "Avant-Garde and Kitsch," which condemned all mass culture, remained a touchstone of art criticism, and he and his colleague Dwight Macdonald continued through the 1950s to defend the highbrow and lament the existence of lesser taste cultures.[23] Indeed, the 1950s was a period in which cultural stratification was a major preoccupation of popular and intellectual periodicals alike.[24]

If one-half of Greenberg's title signaled continued cultural rigidity, the other, "Avant-Garde," pointed to changes in American tastes, at least among the highbrows. American critics and intellectuals had long been apologetic about what Europeans had called a lack of American Art. This deeply rooted sense of cultural inferiority began to give way to a growing sense of cultural pride and leadership. The government provided grants so that American literature and history could be taught and studied in Europe, where American Studies programs developed in many universities. At home, newly founded programs at Yale and the University of Pennsylvania were supported as part of the anticommunist crusade by major foundations. The capital of modern painting and culture shifted from Paris to New York with the rise of abstract expressionism, which was also promoted abroad with government subsidies. But if some parts of the avant-garde were given official blessing, others like the Beat writers and the Living Theatre remained beyond the pale. Such activities were defined by their alienation from the dominant culture.

Art was a contested domain in the early 1960s. The elite embrace of modern art did not immediately produce popular acceptance of it, but more Americans were becoming familiar with what had been the tastes of a very small percentage of the population. The rapid growth of higher education in the 1950s was one factor. Another was the growth of the media, which made more people aware of art and artists, both the accepted and the marginal. Everyone knew something about the Beats, for example, even though most people never read their work. The figure of the "beatnik" became a comic stock character, as the hillbilly had long been, and turned up in numerous contexts, perhaps most famously in Bob Denver's character, Maynard G. Krebs, on the *The Many Loves of Dobie Gillis*. The public remained suspicious that artists were, like beatniks, lazy, slovenly radicals who refused "normal" work and family life. But they were also fascinated by the freedom these very characteristics seemed to entail, and, increasingly, by the strange new work such artists produced.

If in 1960 the wall between mass and elite culture was beginning to crack, popular music, especially rock & roll, was still widely regarded as the antithesis of Art. Folk music was somewhat less disparaged, having been granted a special dispensation as authentically primitive—a quality much valued in high modern art. In condescending to folk music in this way, the culture denied its practitioners the status of artist. Nevertheless, there were connections between the folk scene and the art world, especially in New York. Bob Dylan experienced these connections, and they enabled him to acquire some of the liberal education he ignored while briefly enrolled at the University of Minnesota as well as an education that would have been hard to obtain anywhere else but New York. In his *Chronicles*, volume 1, Dylan reveals that he apparently took great advantage of New York's cultural resources.[25] Under the tutelage of his girlfriend, Suze Rotolo, he saw paintings by old masters Velázquez, Goya, Delacroix, Rubens, El Greco, and by modernists Picasso, Braque, Kandinsky, Rouault, and Bonnard.[26] In *No Direction Home*, Dylan tells us that he constantly read poetry at the apartments he crashed at during his early years in New York.[27] Rimbaud is the poet he has mentioned the most over the years, but *Chronicles* also mentions T. S. Eliot, Charles Baudelaire,

Walt Whitman, Dylan Thomas, and, especially Byron and Samuel Taylor Coleridge. The latter two, he claimed, helped him think beyond the three-minute song. In a somewhat contradictory passage, he credits hearing a performance of Bertolt Brecht–Kurt Weill songs, especially "Pirate Jenny," for giving him the inspiration to write complex songs like "A Hard Rain Is Gonna Fall," "It's Alright Ma (I'm Only Bleeding)," and "Mr. Tambourine Man": "If I hadn't gone to the Theatre de Lys and heard the ballad 'Pirate Jenny,' it might not have dawned on me to write them, that songs like these could be written."[28]

Dylan says he both recognized and kept at arm's length the Marxism expressed in Brecht's songs, and he depicts the performance that he attended as part of the Village scene. He participated in its avant-garde activities in other ways as well, attending plays by LeRoi Jones and the Living Theatre, and seeing films by Federico Fellini and other European directors. Among visual artists, he singles out Red Grooms as his favorite.[29] Grooms was part of the emerging pop art movement, which arose in opposition to abstract expressionism and embraced everything that Greenberg deemed kitsch. Pop broke down the divide between high and low by making bits of mass culture and everyday consumer products into paintings that hung in elite galleries and, soon, museums. Dylan would attack the divide from the other side, making rock & roll that had the seriousness and complexity of high modernism.

Becoming the Artist

One reason for the seriousness with which Dylan was taken is, as a recording artist, he was known for making albums rather than singles. The 33⅓ rpm long-playing record (or LP) was introduced in 1948 and by 1955 "accounted for half of all record revenues." But LPs were, as Elijah Wald has shown, "big records for adults," who constituted the vast majority of their market.[30] R&B and rock & roll were primarily sold in the form of 45 rpm singles well into the 1960s. Elvis's career was built exclusively on singles, and James Brown released only one significant album before 1970, *Live at the Apollo,* which he had to self-finance because his record company didn't believe there was a market. The early careers of the Beatles and the Rolling Stones were also dependent on singles, though the beginnings of the penetration of the album into the teen market was visible in their successful marketing of albums as well. It was not until after the Beatles' contact with Dylan that they produced their first album to be understood as a unified work, *Rubber Soul* (1965).

Before he became a rock star, Dylan was already identified with this more adult medium, and we can trace the development of his persona by examining the albums he released, including not just the music and lyrics but also the pictures, liner notes, and publicity as well.

In the 1960s, the appearance of popular musicians often seemed to be what was most important about them. The Beatles' hairstyles—and to a lesser extent their clothes—attracted far more commentary in the United States than their music. Adults were plainly threatened by this (relatively minor) violation of the gender code, which made the Four all the more Fab in the eyes of their young audience. After the Beatles breached the hair frontier, the Rolling Stones attacked accepted conventions of performance attire by looking as scruffy as possible. Dylan's earlier visual incarnations were carefully chosen, in keeping with the folk scene. On his first album, we see him in his cap and shearling jacket, looking the part of the folksinger. The clothes evoke work but from some other time and place—from where folk music supposedly came. The cover photo on *The Freewheelin' Bob Dylan* depicts him without the cap and with a woman on his arm walking down a snowy urban street. His hair is tousled, but otherwise Dylan looks remarkably ordinary here. On the next record, *The Times They Are a-Changin'*, he appears in a black-and-white photo frowning, wearing an open-collared work shirt and relatively short hair. Here Dylan adopts a more obvious identification with contemporary American workers and the political Left.

Dylan's third album, however, also pointed in a different direction. Instead of the traditional liner notes found on the first two, *The Times* featured Dylan's poetry. Called "11 Outlined Epitaphs," the poems in the main depict a world consistent with the lyrics and cover image, but they are apparently autobiographical and not explicitly political. They show the influence of modernist poetry, even if they don't constitute particularly successful instances of it. While Woody Guthrie figures prominently, some other names mentioned are not those one would have at first associated with Dylan's persona: François Villon, Bertolt Brecht, Brendan Behan, Edith Piaf, Modigliani, and William Blake, among others. The poems are in free verse—with only occasional rhyme—and, while individual passages are clear enough, the reader is required to make connections that are not obvious if the whole is to be understood as an argument or narrative. These poems probably mystified most people who bought the record at the time, and in turn began to make Dylan seem more like an artist.

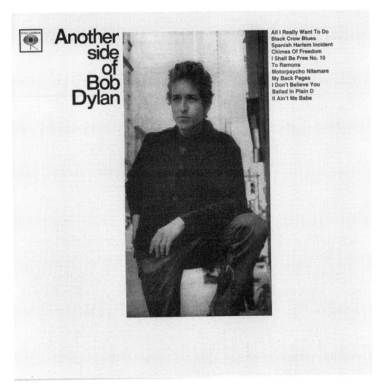

Dylan's fourth album, 1964, where he appears to be "the cynosure of hip." (album cover, Columbia Records)

The new direction is much more apparent on his next release, *Another Side of Bob Dylan*. The cover photo shows Dylan dressed entirely in black, his wavy hair longer and standing straight up. He's frowning here also, but the expression seems more thoughtful and less angry than in the photo on *Times*. Dylan apparently has morphed from a scruffy folksinger into someone dressed like a downtown artist. Someone who saw him a few months later at the Philharmonic Hall concert called him "the cynosure of hip, when hipness still wore pressed slacks and light brown suede boots."[31] Dylan here has moved from looking primitive or committed to looking stylish and "with it." The new look conveys an image of sensitivity, and in both respects it is consistent with Dylan's writing on *Another Side*. The liner notes are entitled "Some Other Kinds of Songs," and they consist of poetry similar in style to that found on the previous record, but they are not presented as autobiography and are considerably more opaque.

More important, the lyrics on *Another Side* are in a number of respects a departure from those on Dylan's earlier records. There are no topical songs on the album, and the majority, like "All I Really Want to Do" and "It Ain't Me Babe," are concerned with matters that seem more personal than political. There can be no doubt that Dylan saw *Another Side* as marking a shift in his career. As he told Nat Hentoff, who sat in on the recording session, "There aren't any finger pointing songs in here. . . . Me, I don't want to write *for* people anymore. You know, be a spokesman. Like, I once wrote about Emmett Till in the first person, pretending I was him. From now on, I want to write from inside of me."[32] The folk community recognized the change, and an open letter to Dylan in *Sing Out!* magazine complained that his "new songs seem to be all inner-directed, inner-probing, self-conscious" after several of them were performed at the Newport Folk Festival the month before the album's release.[33] One cut, "My Back Pages," was heard by many insiders as a "recantation," distressing Dylan's friends in the movement.[34]

One of the principles of modern aesthetics is the rejection of art's historic didactic function. Philip Sidney had held that poetry should "instruct and delight," and that view was widely assumed of all art up through the nineteenth century. But if the assumption of a didactic function began to be challenged by the Romantics, it wasn't until writers like Charles Baudelaire and Gustave Flaubert in France and Oscar Wilde in England began to assert the doctrine of art for art's sake that the incompatibility of art and instruction was promulgated. Dylan's songs offering explicit commentary on current events or taking explicit political positions—especially those that could be identified with a particular group or movement—were in conflict with the dominant conception of art.

Still, the changes reflected in *Another Side* probably loom larger in retrospect than they did at the time. It takes careful listening to the lyrics to apprehend the new direction. The musical style remains the same, and many of the songs have precursors on earlier albums. "Don't Think Twice, It's All Right," from *Freewheelin'*, is an earlier version of "It Ain't Me Babe" and an instance of Dylan's early interest in writing about relationships. But if relationship songs dominate on *Another Side*, "Chimes of Freedom," "I Shall Be Free No. 10," and "My Back Pages" continue to deal with more abstract issues and public matters. What they say about these issues is often new, but it is also not so forthrightly expressed, making it easy for the listener to assume continuity. "Chimes of Freedom" seems to be another treatment of a subject that is taken up in numerous songs from "Blowin' in the Wind" to "I Shall be Free." And, as critic Mike Marqusee observes, even in "My Back Pages," "there is continuity" with the earlier critique of American liberals and the assertion of youth's right to speak out and to define its own categories.[35] One of the new aspects of *Another Side* actually obscures the other changes. The surrealism of "Chimes of Freedom" makes it hard to be sure that a new position is taken, much less what that position might be. And "My Back Pages," which is on the whole pretty accessible, contains a chorus that tends to obscure the point of the song: "Ah, but I was so much older then./I'm younger than that now."

The characteristics of the evolving new persona allowed it to subsume rather than to reject the old. The culture had come to expect artists to express themselves on social and political issues and even to take radical positions in so doing. Dylan's list from "11 Outlined Epitaphs" includes several models, including Villon, Brecht, and Blake. By adopting the persona of the artist, Dylan hoped to shed the expectations that he spoke for any organized party or movement. But by this very act of freeing himself, Dylan continued to symbolize the desire for personal freedom that animated 1960s youth culture.

Dylan had actually always resisted pigeonholing. As he put it, "Folk music was strict and rigid establishment. If you sang Southern Mountain Blues, you didn't sing Southern Mountain Ballads and you didn't sing City Blues. If you sang Texas cowboy songs, you didn't play English ballads. . . . Everybody had their particular thing that they did. I didn't pay much attention to that. If I liked a song, I would just learn it and sing it the only way I could play it."[36] Dylan's quick move to writing his own songs also demonstrated his early distance from the preservationist impulse. Although folk musicians like Pete Seeger had written some of their own songs, their personas depended on those songs seeming to be part of a folk tradition. From the beginning, Dylan used such connections promiscuously for his own artistic projects.

Dylan's songwriting enabled a persona that differed from most other folksingers. Even before *Another Side*, Dylan was doing what society expected artists to do. Already on *Freewheelin'* he had established a distinctive personality. While he sang many songs in the voice of another or wrote them on behalf of oppressed others, he also recorded personal songs such as "Don't Think Twice, It's All Right" and "Bob Dylan's Dream." Moreover, the public conception of the artist's role included the idea of radicalism even as it also held that the artist was someone above politics. The tradition of the "lyrical left" goes back to the pre–World War I era, when radical politics and artistic experiment went hand in hand. And why was it that a mere singer and writer of songs could be so important to the Old Lefties as Dylan? Because this art was perhaps the only vibrant element of a movement that McCarthyism had recently decimated, but, in addition, that art was in itself understood as a politics, a rejection of the dominant capitalist culture.

Where the folksinger tried to keep old forms alive, the artist was charged with, as Ezra Pound put it, making it new. If Dylan had previously sung the news, he now sought to make news, that is, to paraphrase Pound again, to write songs that were news that stayed news. While *Another Side* had forecast this direction with "Chimes of Freedom" and "My Back Pages," Dylan's next album would fully embody it. *Bringing It All Back Home* was his first recording using electric instrumentation. One side of the album featured rock arrangements, while the other side consisted of solo acoustic performances. The rock elements of the album are usually seen as the major innovation, but the acoustic side was new as well. The first cut on that side, "Mr. Tambourine Man," is overtly about the power of art and the artist to take one away from the quotidian and self. The song suggests, however, that art will enable self-exploration, as several lines intimate, including: "Then take me disappearin' through the smoke rings of my mind, / Down the foggy ruins of time." The song's jumble of images also imply that self-exploration is likely to yield a mind more surreal than rational.

About the same time as *Back Home* was released, the Byrds' single of "Mr. Tambourine Man" became the first recording of a Dylan song to reach number 1 on the pop charts. The Byrds' version is defined by Roger McGuinn's chiming twelve-string guitar, and it is softer and sweeter sounding than Dylan's recording. Moreover, the Byrds' cover omits all but the second of Dylan's verses, putting the emphasis on the chorus, and making whatever meaning Dylan had intended still more obscure. Perhaps for this reason—but certainly also because of the lyrics Dylan did write—the song became widely understood to be about drugs. In early 1965 the words "take me on a trip," as the second verse begins, would not automatically denote LSD, but the song did convey a more general sense of mind alteration that might be associated with marijuana or heroin. If the song is about drugs, then Mr. Tambourine Man might be a drug dealer. But drug use had long been associated with avant-garde artists, and Dylan's possible connection to it served to further redefine him.

The next song on the acoustic side of *Back Home,* "It's Alright, Ma (I'm Only Bleeding)," reveals another face of Dylan the artist. As Marqusee observes, it is "as much of a protest song as anything else Dylan had written: a sweeping vision of a corrupt and dehumanized society and the fate of the sensitive, autonomous individual within it."[37] It is that last concern—or, more properly, the perspective of such an individual—that is new here. According to Nick Bromell, Dylan's earlier protest songs were "liberal" because they were sung on behalf of others, but with *Bringing It All Back Home* there is a radicalism rooted in "the perception of *oneself* as unfree, as oppressed."[38] The singer now understands himself to be denied the freedom he once portrayed as denied only to society's others. The song's social critique combines surrealism,

> Darkness at the break of noon
> Shadows even the silver spoon
> The handmade blade, the child's balloon
> Eclipses both the sun and moon

with more explicit charges:

> Advertising signs that con you
> Into thinking you're the one
> That can do what's never been done
> That can win what's never been won.

This is not topical songwriting like we get in "Who Killed Davey Moore" or "The Lonesome Death of Hattie Carroll." It is a much more sweeping indictment but one that implies that struggle is useless: "To understand you know too soon / There is no sense in trying." The film *Easy Rider* used "It's Alright Ma" to underscore just this point. Because activism is foreclosed, the artist is now free from its demands.

It makes sense, then, that the song also proclaims what might be called the artist's own creed, "That he not busy being born / Is busy dying." Dylan articulated this creed in the documentary *No Direction Home,* where he said, "An artist has to be careful never really to arrive at a place where he thinks he's somewhere. You always have to realize that you are constantly in a state of becoming." The song also proclaims the artist's freedom, "That it is not he or she or them or it/That you belong to." These last lines seem like a direct response to the claims that the Old Left and the folk purists had made on Dylan. As he recalled in *Chronicles,* "Ronnie Gilbert, one of the Weavers, had introduced me at one of the Newport Folk Festivals saying, 'And here he is . . . take him, you know him, he's yours.' I had failed to sense the ominous forebodings in that introduction. Elvis had never been introduced like that. 'Take him, he's yours!' What a crazy thing to say! Screw that. As far as I knew, I didn't belong to anybody then or now."[39]

"It's Alright Ma" and *Bringing It All Back Home* as a whole proclaim a new kind of authenticity rooted in the self rather than in tradition or solidarity. "Propaganda," the song tells us, "all is phony," articulating in four pithy words a commitment to the aesthetic and a rejection of the didactic. This rejection lies behind Dylan's repeated assertion during this period that he and his songs were not protest songs, that they had no messages, that he was not a spokesperson for anyone or anything. As he put it in *Chronicles,* "Being true to yourself, that was the thing."[40] The adoption of rock & roll on the other side of the album was a stylistic assertion of this point, which demonstrated Dylan's interest in formal experimentation. By continuing to use folk sources, here, especially, the blues transformed into rock & roll, Dylan invented a distinctive sound that was at that moment his alone. It augured "folk rock," a term he always rejected. The lyrics of the songs redefine the singer's struggle. "Subterranean Homesick Blues," Dylan's first single to reach the pop charts, is a song mainly about obstacles to individual freedom and to the aspirations of the young. "Maggie's Farm" turns a sharecropper's lament, "Down on Penny's Farm," into an angry proclamation of personal independence.

What might be most important, however, about *Bringing It All Back Home* is how strange it sounded. Having had Bob Dylan's recordings in our ears now for more than forty years, it is hard to imagine hearing them as audiences did in the 1960s. *Time* reported that "his voice sounds as if it were drifting over the walls of a tuberculosis sanitarium," while *Newsweek* said, "His singing voice scratches and shouts so jarringly that his success at first seems incredible."[41] While the folk audience, having heard precursors like Guthrie and Jack Elliott, had been able to place Dylan's voice and style within a known genre, the pop audience had never heard anything like him. Although this point had usually been cited as an explanation for why other artists made hit records of Dylan's songs before he did, the strangeness of Dylan's voice also accounts for his appeal to rock audiences looking for new sounds.

Dylan's early rock recordings did not disappoint those desires. The rock tracks on *Bringing It All Back Home* don't sound like the records that were popular in 1965. The records on the top of the charts in the spring of 1965 include Herman's Hermits' "Mrs. Brown You've Got a Lovely Daughter," Wayne Fontana and the Mindbenders' "Game of Love," and Freddie and the Dreamers' "I'm Telling You Now." While Motown artists Junior Walker and the All Stars had a hit with "Shotgun" and country singer Roger Miller a crossover success with "King of the Road," the pop charts were dominated by what might be called the prebubblegum of second-tier British invasion bands and their American imitators.[42] Needless to say, there was nothing sweet about Dylan's sound. The rock songs on *Bringing It* borrow from rock artists like Chuck Berry, but they owe more to the precursors of rock & roll, including Jimmy Rogers, Robert Johnson, and, of course, Guthrie. Perhaps to clue listeners in, the cover photo of what looks like a hip but bourgeois living room includes the album jacket of Johnson's *The King of the Delta Blues Singers* but also the jacket of *The Folk Blues of Eric Von Schmidt,* by Dylan's contemporary in the Greenwich Village folk scene. Dylan was doing here what rock & roll innovators have always done, recombining the elements of various musical practices to make new forms.

The Rock Star as Modernist

"Subterranean Homesick Blues" only charted at number 39, but Dylan's next single, "Like a Rolling Stone," was a genuine pop hit, making it to number 2. Greil Marcus, who has written an entire book about this record, finds virtually all of rock & roll summed up in its six-plus minutes, yet he also insists that it was immediately recognized as something utterly new. He quotes Bruce Springsteen, "The first time I heard Bob Dylan, I was in the car with my mother listening to WMCA, and on came that snare shot that sounded like somebody'd kicked open a door to your mind."[43] Like many others, Springsteen hadn't heard Dylan until "Like a Rolling Stone," and presumably these new listeners found his voice as surprising as their predecessors had. The record was new, startling, powerful, but it was also more recognizably rock & roll than anything Dylan had previously recorded. Mike Bloomfield's electric guitar and Al Kooper's Hammond B3 Organ compete with Dylan's folk guitar and harmonica and, of course, finally dominate the mix. The record sounded like it belonged on the radio.

Its success, as Marcus observes, put Dylan in the rarefied company of the Beatles and the Rolling Stones as a star who reached the largest audiences and did so with work that defied the assumption of popular music's triviality. What did audiences find so attractive about this record? One answer is that it is "permeated by a kind of ecstasy of schadenfreude. The ensemble rises and falls on waves of bitterness. The guitar gloats. The voice taunts: 'How does it feel?' "[44] The song takes to new heights the attitude Dylan first expressed in "Don't Think Twice, It's All Right," of vindictiveness toward women—who seem as a group to have disappointed Dylan. Where that song measures the attitude out, presenting it reflectively rather than emotionally, "Like a Rolling Stone" both reads and sounds like an angry screed. This put Dylan in the same terrain the Stones would mine over and over after "(I Can't Get No) Satisfaction," the number 1 record in the weeks preceding the release of Dylan's single. As I discuss in chapter 5, the appeal of this attitude to adolescent males derives from the power they feel women hold over them. More generally, adolescent males often experience the kind of disempowerment that the singer of "Like a Rolling Stone" once felt at the hands of the song's addressee. They were doubtless happy to glory in the comeuppance of one who held a higher social position. The song may also represent the wish fulfillment of most adolescents, male and female, since they suffer under the most rigid and oppressive social hierarchies.

Many have felt that the song's addressee is paradoxically Dylan himself. He's the one who should know how it feels "to be on your own, with no direction home, like a rolling stone." Muddy Waters and Hank Williams had both written about rolling stones, and Jack Kerouac and the Beats had styled themselves as such even if they hadn't used these words. The words fit Dylan so well that two works about him have been titled *No Direction Home*. I'm not sure how much this specific image of rootlessness attached itself to Dylan at the time, but all rock stars benefited from the presumption that they were not tied down to place or family or other mundane obligations. Perhaps the song's lyrics reflected their author most strongly in their style, which distinguished Dylan from other popular songwriters and from most modern poets as well. If some of the lyrics—the chorus in particular—are common in their diction and popular in their references, others are what might be called "poetic" or "rhetorical." The two levels of diction are well represented in the following lines:

> You used to ride on the chrome horse with your diplomat
> Who carried on his shoulder a Siamese cat
> Ain't it hard when you discover that
> He really wasn't where it's at
> After he took from you everything he could steal.

The contrast between the poetic imagery of the first two lines and the ordinary language of the last three is striking, and it works in part because of the way in which Dylan declaims the words, putting extreme emphasis on the final syllable of most lines, and fairly shouting key phrases, including the chorus. The use of repeated end rhyme fits with this presentation, and the last line rhymes with the first line of the chorus, "How does it feel." The chorus itself is structured as a rhetorical question.

The rhetorical quality of Dylan's songwriting was noticeable almost from the beginning, but the tendency had grown stronger starting with the surrealism of *Another Side*. One finds some of this quality in the Allen Ginsberg of *Howl and Other Poems*, but the closest poetry to Dylan in this sense is the early work of Robert Lowell. Though Ginsberg was someone Dylan read and, Lowell, insofar as I am aware, was not, the latter's turn away from the impersonality and understatement of modernist poetry in *Lord Weary's Castle* was characterized by apparent striving for stylistic effects. Ginsberg sometimes used such effects—for example, repetition—but only in the service of a larger argument. In Lowell's early poems, the ones before the confessionalism of *Life Studies,* the arguments take a backseat to sound and image. It is this kind of writing that characterizes such songs from the album on which "Like a Rolling Stone" appeared, *Highway 61 Revisited,* including the title track, "Desolation Row," "Tombstone Blues," "Queen Jane Approximately," and "Just Like Tom Thumb's Blues."

Unlike Lowell's early poems, however, or Ginsberg's for that matter, these songs shared a trait common to much modernist poetry, obscurity. "Desolation Row" in particular utterly resists paraphrase. It is in this song that Dylan makes reference to two American fathers of modernist poetry: "And Ezra Pound and T. S. Eliot/Fighting in the captain's tower." As these lines illustrate, the song, like Pound's and Eliot's poetry, is full of allusions. The range includes Shakespeare (Romeo, Ophelia), Hollywood (Bette Davis), and the Bible (Cain and Abel, the Good Samaritan). The song begins as if it is setting the scene for a narrative, but no coherent story is told. Rather, each verse describes a different scene, more or less coherent in itself, which may illustrate the idea of "Desolation Row," the words that conclude each. Such writing has given rise to an industry, unique to Dylan among rock stars, of interpretation. There are at least four books devoted solely to reading Dylan's lyrics, one of which, *Dylan's Visions of Sin,* by Eliot scholar and right-wing culture warrior Christopher Ricks, is 517 pages long.[45]

The ambition to high art can be found in many places in 1960s rock & roll, but Dylan is as much responsible for this ambition as anyone. Indeed, his lyrics may be the place where rock's sense of its own "seriousness," as Keir Keightley put it, was first apparent.[46] The Beatles seem to have acquired their own sense of seriousness by listening to Dylan, which they began to do before Dylan had released any rock recordings.[47] The Beatles are usually regarded as having made art. Their strategy was to borrow from and make reference to Western art music while at the same time introducing elements from other traditions, including classical Indian music and the English music hall. That trajectory reached its height in *Sergeant Pepper's Lonely Hearts Club Band* and came to an end by the time of the White Album. It is as if the Beatles proved that they could make popular music that was as complex and profound as classical and then returned to their roots, but with a difference. Rock & roll was now not merely what they played but what they played with—it had become material for their art.

Dylan's high-culture borrowings and allusions are literary rather than musical. His musical range shows the influence of virtually every sort of American popular music, and there is no equivalent in Dylan's corpus to the violins backing the Beatles on "Yesterday" or the orchestral sound of "A Day in the Life." Dylan's modernism yokes together innovative, often difficult lyrics with music that remains, whatever its genre, primitive. Like modernist poets and novelists, Dylan relied on primitive artistic forms as a source of authenticity.

Dylan's claim to the status of artist was based most strongly on his lyrics. Unlike most other rock stars, Dylan had established his reputation first as a songwriter. Since his music was usually borrowed from folk sources, it was as a lyricist that he made his mark. The poems he used as liner notes were an indication that he aspired to poetry, but these texts were not the ones people cited. And, there was the widely repeated explanation that he named himself after Dylan Thomas. Already in 1965, the *New York Times Magazine* ran a feature on Dylan headlined, "Public Writer No. 1?" with a subhead, "Who Needs Saul Bellow?' "[48] In 1966, after the release of *Blonde on Blonde,* a feature story in the *Saturday Evening Post* had the headline, "Bob Dylan, singer, songwriter, poet, who at 25 admits he's a millionaire but denies being a genius."[49] A year later, Ellen Willis could say, "It is a truism among Dylan admirers that he is a poet using rock-and-roll to spread his art: as Jack Newfield put it in the *Village Voice,* 'If Whitman were alive today, he too would be playing an electric guitar.' This misrepresentation has only served to make many intellectuals suspicious of Dylan and draw predictable sniping from conscientious B-student poets like Louis Simpson and John Ciardi."[50] Not all professional poets agreed. Kenneth Rexroth claimed that "probably the most important event in recent poetry is Bob Dylan." An informal survey of students at three Ivy League universities found that Dylan was their favorite "writer."[51] The *New York Times Magazine* revisited the idea of rock as poetry in 1969 and asserted, "Dylan must be called a poet because, like the Beatles, he speaks of, and transforms, experiences vital to the consciousness of his listeners."[52] By the early 1970s, the idea that rock lyrics are poetry was widely accepted by ordinary listeners and many young poets, even if it was sometimes derided in the academy.

The fact that the professors—back then, anyway—did not accept Dylan and his ilk as poets or intellectuals did not necessarily damage their standing among youth—and perhaps did exactly the opposite. The general negative reaction of the older generation to rock & roll was one of the grounds on which the younger one believed that they had achieved a special kind of enlightenment. In short, they *got it,* while everyone else did not. Dylan gave this sense of communal knowledge and generational alienation powerful expression in many of his songs, including "Subterranean Homesick Blues" and "Positively 4th Street," but "Ballad of a Thin Man" is his most explicit statement of it. The song's chorus, "Because something is happening here / And you don't know what it is / Do you, Mister Jones," describes the condition attributed to most adults. The verses describe a series of surreal encounters that could easily have been filmed by Luis Buñuel, each suggesting more strongly than the last just how estranged Mister Jones is from reality.

One former *Time* intern, Jeffrey Owen Jones, who interviewed Dylan on the eve of his 1965 Newport performance, claimed that Dylan had written

"Ballad of a Thin Man" about him, and indeed the song does begin, "You walk into the room / With your pencil in your hand." However, *Don't Look Back* suggests that Dylan may have had reporters in general in mind. While what is usually remarked upon there is Dylan's contemptuous treatment of the press, most of the journalists who interview Dylan don't seem to have a clue. Their questions reveal the abysmal state of popular music coverage in the 1960s. Journalists like Robert Shelton and Nat Hentoff, who wrote insightfully and sympathetically about Dylan, were mainly folk and jazz reporters. Dylan, along with the Beatles and a few others, would be one of the major reasons that rock journalism would become a reality around 1970. In the meantime, Dylan had to put up with reporters asking questions that were at best uninformed and at worst quite simply inane.

Dylan's artist persona was solidified by the release of *Blonde on Blonde* in the summer of 1966. The album also confirmed Dylan's status as a major rock star by including three songs that made it into the top 40 as singles. By this time, the expectation that Dylan should write topical or protest songs was no longer common in the United States, though the tour of the United Kingdom that preceded the album's release—recorded in *Don't Look Back*—showed that it remained strong there. The record represents a return to introspective and personal concerns of *Another Side* but presented now in the form of rock & roll. Where *Highway 61* had continued to present social critique—however fragmented or surreal—*Blonde on Blonde* excludes that larger picture entirely. But the private world of which this album gives us glimpses is very strange indeed. Consider "Visions of Johanna," maybe the most beautiful of Dylan's songs. Besides the obsession over an absent love, Johanna, all is murky. There is another woman, Louise, who is present, and, in one verse, "entwined with her lover." The verses only hint at the singer's emotions, and they describe instead fragments that might be the visions, except that Johanna does not appear in them. In the manner of expressionism, the song thus evokes a complex emotional state by means of images of the external world.

The music too was new. As Marqusee puts it, "On *Blonde on Blonde,* Dylan made the familiar deliriously strange. He took inherited idioms and boosted them into a modernist stratosphere."[53] The various tracks on the album do not have a single musical style, unlike *Highway 61,* where almost every cut is blues based. "Rainy Day Women #12 & 35" sounds like something you might hear a New Orleans funeral band play—at a party. "Visions of Johanna" is backed by the entire complement of studio musicians but sounding re-

Bob Dylan, aesthete, from *Don't Look Back,* 1967. (publicity photo)

strained and soft, allowing Dylan's voice uncontested dominance. "Leopard Skin Pillbox Hat" sounds like rock & roll pure and simple, save for Dylan's voice. "I Want You" borrows from traditional country music, while "Just Like a Woman" is a folk song with drums. At the time, the press lumped all of this variety together as "folk rock," but Dylan did not fit any genre, as his future stylistic shifts would confirm. It was the newness, the strangeness that resisted classification that distinguished Dylan from all the would-be Dylans the industry tried to market.

Moreover, Dylan's appearance also continued to evolve away from received categories of style. On the cover of *Highway 61* Dylan appears wearing a blue and pink print shirt open over a Triumph Motorcycle T-shirt. It's as if he was as intent on violating fashion codes here as he was in following them on his previous two album jackets. Beginning with this photo, his hair continued to get longer—or, as it appeared—bigger, so that in the *Blonde on Blonde* photos it curls up and out into a ragged orb. The look was captured in the pop art poster distributed with *Bob Dylan's Greatest Hits* (1967), in which his hair is abstracted to what appears to be a large aura surrounding a small head. Dylan's appearance, like that of the Beatles, had finally become itself iconic.

Around the time *Blonde on Blonde* was released, Dylan was seriously injured in a motorcycle accident. He suffered a concussion and broken vertebrae and was hospitalized for a week. The press portrayed "the accident as a near-death trauma," and at least one paper suggested that Dylan might never perform again.[54] Dylan cancelled his planned tour of the United States, due to begin in August and to last throughout the fall, and Dylan would not tour again until 1973. It would be a year and a half until another album of new material, *John Wesley Harding*, was released. As a result of this withdrawal from the public eye, Dylan's enigma deepened. As *Time* put it, "Dylan *in absentia* loomed larger than Dylan in the flesh; last year [1967] four of his LP albums broke the million-dollar sales mark, something none had done previously."[55] And, if *Time*'s coverage of the album seems little different from its earlier attempts, the press now seems to be taking Dylan much more seriously. *Life, Newsweek, Vogue,* and the *Saturday Review* all gave Dylan's new record respectful reviews or coverage. Most of the headlines hailed Dylan's "return," but the *Saturday Review* described *John Wesley Harding* as a "Self-Portrait of the Artist as an Older Man." This allusion to James Joyce was followed by the assertion that "like most good writers, [Dylan] has successfully disguised his own involvement. Songs such as 'Just Like a Woman,' 'It Ain't Me, Babe,' and 'Positively 4th Street' are very much Portraits of the Artist as a Young Neurotic, but skillfully hidden ones."[56] The new album, this reviewer thinks, is all about Dylan and the problems of identity that he speculates the motorcycle accident enabled him to address. The assumptions here are that Dylan's words are worth the trouble to interpret; he is being treated as one would treat an "artist" or a "good writer" but not previously a "pop hero."

In between *Blonde on Blonde* and *John Wesley Harding*, D. A. Pennebaker's documentary *Don't Look Back* appeared, first at a San Francisco premier in May of 1967 and then on college campuses and in art houses. The critics' reaction to the film was mixed at best, though even the negative reviews often confirmed Dylan's artistic status. Ralph Gleason said the film was about "the problem of the artist communicating with his audience," while *Newsweek* commented that "it shows a singing genius who does not know where his songs come from."[57] Those sympathetic to Dylan who disliked the film complained that it not only was out of date—Dylan performed solo and acoustic— but also that it failed to capture the inner man: "The film's audience, however, was made up, not of critics or unappreciative adults, but of *fans,* and to them the Bob Dylan who tore across the screen, singing and stinging victims, was exactly *on target.* Finally, Dylan fans could *see* as well as hear Bob."[58] What the fans perceived is revealed by Pennebaker as he recalled Dylan's reaction to the film: "We showed him the first rough cut. What he saw must have made him look like he was bare bones. And I think that was a big shock to him. But then he saw, I think, the second night, he saw that it was total theater. He was like an actor, and he suddenly had reinvented himself as the actor within this movie and then it was OK."[59] Dylan was undoubtedly performing for the camera, but in the very act of performing he was being the artist that his fans expected him to be.

Another element of Dylan's mystique was added in June of 1968, when *Rolling Stone* published a long feature on unreleased Dylan recordings, "The Missing Bob Dylan Album." Soon after, bootleg recordings of what became known as the Basement Tapes began to appear. These recordings, made with the Hawks, later to be known as the Band, at various nonstudio locations in and around Woodstock, New York, consisted of at least thirty new songs by Dylan.[60] The fact that these recordings were unauthorized, illegal, and relatively difficult to obtain made them all the more attractive. Interest in artists often is fueled by the rumor or knowledge of lost works, and Dylan's "near death" and seclusion doubtless intensified it, causing the Basement Tapes to become the holy grail of rock & roll. Their reputation continues to this day, with one critic calling the material Dylan's "greatest collection of songs" and another writing an entire book about them.[61]

In the 1960s Dylan evolved from a folksinger into the first rock musician identified as an artist. He presented himself as being in the same business as Ezra Pound, Pablo Picasso, and Igor Stravinsky. This persona enabled him to continue to comment on political and social issues without being classified as a protest singer. Because artists had since the mid-nineteenth century styled themselves as opponents of the bourgeoisie, Dylan's new persona continued to register as a form of radicalism. Yet it is also true that his songs became less political, and this fact was to some extent hidden by his identification as an artist. Dylan's claim to art made it possible for other popular performers to see themselves in this light and to be taken seriously as artists by the media and the public. Mick Jagger, speaking of the context for his writing "Satisfaction," explained, "When we started, people only wrote euphemistic songs about love. It wasn't until the Bob Dylan period that people started to write songs with real content in the lyrics."[62] The Grateful Dead's lyricist Robert Hunter said, "I first started waking up to the possibilities of rock lyrics being serious with *Blonde on Blonde*. . . . It said it was okay to be as serious as you wanted in rock." Many other rock stars, from James Brown, to Joni Mitchell, to Bruce Springsteen, to Public Enemy and Eminem, have benefited from Dylan's breakthrough.

Dylan and the New Left

Why did the New Left regard Dylan as a significant—if not the most significant—voice of the generation? The New Left, unlike the Old, never regarded rock & roll or mass culture in general as anathema. Todd Gitlin explains how mass culture in the late 1950s and early 1960s paved the way for the New Left: "Rock and roll and its dances were the opening wedge, hollowing out the cultural ground beneath the tranquilized center. Marlon Brando and James Dean embodied styles and gestures of disaffection. On the fringes, satirists of all kinds—*Mad*, Lenny Bruce, Tom Lehrer, Mort Sahl, Chicago's Compass and Second City cabarets—ridiculed a host of pieties. TV's Steve Allen and Sid Caesar and their offshoots and imitators carried some of the rambunctious spirit into the mainstream."[63]

Rock & roll became the most significant element of the culture of the late 1960s student Left. Nick Bromell describes the typical student of the late 1960s as "living to music," a phrase he borrows from a contemporary writer, John Cunnick: "I wake up in the morning and do a Master's voice thing in front of the speakers for a while; *then* I go outside. Music defines a total environment. . . . Go to a house and someone hands you a joint in front of a record player and it's assumed . . . that you are going to sit for a couple of hours, not talking, hardly moving, *living* to music."[64] Bromell glosses "living to music" as "the existential and visionary side of the 1960s; more mundanely, the inside of the experience of listening to rock, hearing it as a spontaneous epic poem produced miraculously by your peers for immediate use."[65] This experience reinforced the students' belief that they could change the nation, if not the world.

One of the functions rock & roll served was to produce generational solidarity, as I have argued Elvis Presley did. Bromell depicts the Beatles as having an even larger impact than Elvis, since the Beatles' reach extended to college students. He quotes Greil Marcus on the transformation that *Meet the Beatles* produced, turning folkies on to rock: "This was something that never happened before."[66] Simon Frith argues that "rock . . . is about difference and what distinguishes us from people with other tastes. It rests on an ideology of the *peer group* as both the ideal and reality of rock communion."[67] Elsewhere, Frith points to John Lennon embodying the connections between music and the movement: "It was Lennon who leapt more quickly (more desperately?) than the other Beatles at the unfolding possibilities of the 1960s rock and youth culture, and the importance of the Beatles in 1966–68 was not that they led any movement, but that they *joined in*. They became (John Lennon in particular), for all their established star status, comrades in the mid-sixties 'liberation' of leisure."[68]

In some respects, Lennon's trajectory was the opposite of Dylan's, into activism rather than retreating from the public. Nevertheless, Dylan was by far the most important rocker to the student Left. Unlike Lennon, Dylan had been enough ahead of the curve that he functioned as an opinion maker. His lyrics would provide the American New Left with more of its rhetoric and slogans than all Marxist writing put together. Some of the major histories of the New Left reflect this by their use of Dylan's titles and lines to name chapters or gloss events.[69] James Miller argues that by 1965 Dylan was a central influence on Students for a Democratic Society (SDS), the leading New Left organization, and he sees Dylan's development from the idealism of "Blowin' in the Wind" to the bitterness of "Like a Rolling Stone" as paralleling a similar development in SDS's outlook.[70] Even as Dylan's songs became less political, they were still used politically by the New Left. Thus, a line from "Subterranean Homesick Blues," "you don't need a weatherman to know which way the wind blows," supplied the Weatherman faction with a name and a "strategy."

Former SDS president Richard Flacks said, "To understand the *Port Huron Statement*," the organization's founding document, "you have to understand Bob Dylan."[71] That's plausible because the *Port Huron Statement* is unusual in its breadth of concern. Rather than stating a narrowly focused political program, the *Statement* deals with emotional and existential issues not typically associated with politics. It is this combination that one finds throughout Dylan's corpus but especially in the songs from the mid-1960s, when the Old Lefties saw him as abandoning them. The student movement didn't expect Dylan to hew to any party line, since it barely had one itself. He could continue to command respect and love because he was understood as an artist and not as a propagandist. If he was their voice, it was because they found in his songs truths about the world they recognized from their own experience. Moreover, in the world they hoped to make, everyone would be as free as Dylan claimed to be. In other words, Dylan's artistic individualism was consonant with the vision of the student Left, where individualism persisted despite the increasing influence of Marxism.

Dylan's history of shape-shifting did not render him less authentic for this audience. Indeed, one could go further and conjecture that it made him all the more authentic, since the students who made up the bulk of the movement had typically experienced recent radical changes themselves. They had moved from being Republicans or Democrats—buttoned-down and crew-cut, would-be homemakers or organization men, complacent and conforming, and assured of the basic goodness of American government and society—to a radicalism that rejected all of these identities and beliefs. Having recently undergone such a change, some at least would have been aware that other changes were possible, if not likely. The fixed, stable self they had previously taken for granted no longer seemed real. Like Dylan, they believed that "he not busy being born, is busy dying." It turned out that there was no more fitting icon of the New Left than the artist.

CHAPTER FIVE

THE ROLLING STONES
Rebellion, Transgression, and Excess

Rock stars, as one groupie once said, are groovy because they smoke more cigarettes, take more dope, drink more whiskey, stay up later, and fuck more frequently and in odder positions than most people. In other words, in post-everything bizarre America, they do the things everybody wants to do. . . .

And right at the top of the whole pyramid was Michael Philip Jagger, the number one rock star in the world.

Robert Greenfield

Rock & roll and the 1960s changed many things, but not everything. The Rolling Stones illustrate the intensification of consumer capitalism and the way in which rock stars continued the connection between consumption and celebrity. The Stones' 1969 and 1972 American tours thrust them to the top, not merely of rock & roll but of the whole entertainment world. They became entertainment royalty. While other stars at least pretended to worry about "selling out," the Stones had managed to evade the problem by incorporating excessive consumption as an element of their authenticity. Beginning their career as the Beatles' dark others, they embodied adolescent rebellion and became identified with sexual and social transgression. Because of the cultural transformations of the 1960s, the Stones became the height of fashion by retaining their personas as outsiders and rebels. By the 1970s, they represented the permanent dissatisfaction of a consumer culture, where you might be able to get what you need but you will always want more of it. In this they symbolize an economic order that rock & roll in general did not challenge, much less change. Thus the Stones are a cautionary example for those who would equate an oppositional stance with progressive politics.[1] Instead of representing communalism and other values of the 1960s New Left, the Stones stood for something like the individualism that would be the hallmark of Ronald Reagan's 1980s.

As I argued in chapter 1, movie stars were defined by the glamour of extravagant consumption. But if the movie stars were extravagant, they were

Mick Jagger with Mick Taylor and Charlie Watts on tour in 1969, from *Gimme Shelter*. (courtesy Photofest)

not excessive—their excesses being carefully covered up by the studios. The rock star, by contrast, is defined by excess, and it is the Rolling Stones who most thoroughly embody this definition. In rock journalist Robert Green-field's account, the definition of the good life that stars represented shifted from extravagance to excess by the early 1970s, when he was writing about the Stones' American tour. For the groupie he quotes, rock stars are groovy mainly because of their excesses. Unlike many rock stars, the Rolling Stones embraced stardom itself, embodying glamour and consumption, transformed by new tastes and styles, and commenting on them in their songs and by their behavior.

The Stones' rise to the top of the celebrity pantheon began in 1969, with their American tour ending in the free concert at Altamont. Earlier that year, the Beatles had broken up, making the Stones' new tour, their first in the United States since 1966, seem to fans almost miraculous. The Woodstock festival, held in August of that year, had put youth culture in general and rock & roll in particular front and center in the public mind. While the

Stones' music and performances certainly attracted attention, even the music writers seemed more interested in the Stones as celebrities. Beginning with the publication of Michael Lydon's story of the 1969 tour in *Ramparts* magazine, the most influential coverage of the Stones in the United States focused on the band's lifestyle. Also covering the 1969 tour were Stanley Booth, whose "biography" of the band uses the tour as its focus, and the Maysles brothers, whose documentary *Gimme Shelter* is probably the most familiar representation of the event.

Toward the end of the tour, on November 26th, before their Madison Square Garden concerts, the Stones held a press conference in the Rainbow Room at the top of the RCA Building in Rockefeller Center. In a moment included in *Gimme Shelter,* a reporter alluding to their first big hit "(I Can't Get No) Satisfaction," asked if the Stones were now satisfied. Jagger responded that they were "financially dissatisfied, sexually satisfied, and philosophically trying."[2] A few days later, the band would release *Let It Bleed,* which included "You Can't Always Get What You Want." This song might have suggested to some a more mature, accepting attitude, and perhaps even a responsible one that distinguished what you need from what you want. Musically, the contrast with "Satisfaction" was evident in the slow, almost hymnlike quality of "You Can't Always Get What You Want," emphasized on the album version by the use of the London Bach Choir to provide an introduction. Yet the song's obscure lyrics, which include references to drugs, do not appear to describe the achievement of satisfaction. Rather, the song could be a restatement of the theme of "Satisfaction," this time using irony. What the Stones signify is that, though you may be able to get what you need, you will always want more of it. They are prophets of the religion of consumerism, though it probably didn't seem that way in 1965, when "Satisfaction" was the number 1 single, and it may not be obvious even today.

One reason is the remarkable consistency of their persona over the course of their career. In contrast to Elvis, James Brown, Dylan, and even Bruce Springsteen, the Stones have always played the same role. Rather than mature, they have remained perpetual adolescents. But if the general character of this role is familiar, its nuances and complexities have continued to be elusive, because most of those who have discussed the matter have been engaged in the construction or perpetuation of that role. The key to understanding the meaning of the Rolling Stones in the late 1960s and 1970s lies in Jagger's admission that they remain "financially dissatisfied." It is worth recalling that the context for the Stones agreeing to do a free concert that would eventually be held at the racetrack in Altamont was criticism over the high prices they charged for tickets to the concerts on their 1969 American tour. The issue was significant enough that the first paragraph of Tom Dona-hue's review of the November 22nd show at the Oakland Coliseum included the following: "The 18,000 seat house was sold out for both shows at a top ticket price of $12.50, though the advertised top was $7.50 with the first twenty rows of $12.50 tickets being reserved for the 'In' crowd."[3] Ralph Glea-son, music critic for the *San Francisco Chronicle,* had complained about the cost of the tickets, holding that Jagger himself was morally responsible.[4] A reporter asked Jagger about Gleason's charge "that a lot of people who would like to see you can't really afford it." "Maybe we can fix something up for those people," Jagger replied.[5] The idea of doing a free concert apparently arose to offset the bad publicity the price controversy had generated. As other remarks Jagger makes at the press conference in *Gimme Shelter* suggest, the Stones also wanted to stage an event that would compete with and make up for their absence from Woodstock. Jagger denied that the Stones were "doing this tour for money," a statement contradicted by the later admission that he was "financially dissatisfied."[6]

If the ticket prices had produced some bad press, however, that was noth-ing new for the Stones. Bad press, in fact, had always been very good for them, and this latest instance was no different. That's because excess was al-ready part of the Stones' persona, and by demanding more money than any other rock band they did simply what their fans might expect of them. The Stones had always been perceived as rebellious and even dangerous, incar-nating the idea of male adolescence in the postwar West. They systemati-cally reversed many of the oppositions that structure dominant—or "adult"—values. In addition, the Stones embody a widely shared conception of male adolescent sexuality, defined by a lack of stable sexual preference or orienta-tion, by the omnipresence and frustration of sexual desire, and by feelings of impotence and insecurity projected onto women. This specifically adolescent condition explains the Stones' sexism and the misogyny of some of their songs. Excess is also associated with adolescence, but it is not restricted to it in our culture. Rather, it reflects consumer capitalism's most cherished value, the constant need for more of everything. While the early Stones seemed sexually excessive, by the late 1960s, they had become identified with a more general indulgence in all forms of pleasure and acquisition captured by the slogan "sex, drugs, and rock & roll." It is this oscillation between getting what you want and still wanting more that identifies the Stones with—rather than against—the culture that produced them.

Reverse Psychology

It should not be surprising to assert that to understand the Stones' persona, one has to begin with the Beatles, but the role of the two bands in defining rock stardom has been much less recognized. In the early 1960s the Beatles and the Rolling Stones made rock stardom a distinct cultural role. I have suggested that the contradictions in Elvis's persona are in part a result of his being a rock star before anyone knew what a rock star was supposed to be. The advantage that the Beatles' manager Brian Epstein and the Stones' manager Andrew Loog Oldham had over Tom Parker is that they had Elvis and other performers as models of careers that were defined by rock & roll and not by popular music and mass-market "entertainment." But the Beatles' and Stones' own sense of themselves are at least equally as important as their managers' strategies. From the start, the Beatles and Stones were more consistent in their personas than was Elvis.

Also from the start, the personas of the Beatles and the Stones were defined in opposition to each other. While the Beatles started the British invasion of America in 1964—and initiated what amounted to the invention of British rock & roll—the Stones followed quickly in their wake. The Beatles' cultural impact was no doubt much greater, and it has remained so. This is only partly explicable on the grounds of their temporal priority and larger initial media splash. What is especially curious is that rock critics, while recognizing the significance and pleasures of the Beatles, have tended to prefer the Stones. How, then, do we account for the relative lack of serious attention devoted to the Stones, especially when compared to the outpouring of the same for the Beatles? That the "good boys" should be so much more interesting than the "bad boys" defies most conventional wisdom.

In fact the Beatles were "bad" enough to attract attention, but they were also more easily recognized as "good" in aesthetic terms. A major reason for the disparity in attention is that the Beatles were formal innovators who made use of an enormous range of musical resources, while the Stones are formal traditionalists whose genuine innovations have generally not been perceived as such. To the musicologist, the Beatles offer formal change and a wide range of musical reference—and therefore something to write about. To the traditionally trained music critic, they offer a form of virtuosity—not that of either the classical or jazz soloist but of the pop orchestra—associated with polish, control, and discipline.[7] To those with literary inclinations, they provide wit, irony, and other verbal complexities. The Stones may be (or have been) the world's greatest rock & roll band, but their apparent lack of ambition to be anything more than this resulted in a narrower appeal than the Beatles offered.[8]

The Beatles and the Stones, in fact, represent two distinct aspects of the persona Elvis developed. The Beatles took up the gentle, innocent side, while the Stones embodied the cruel, sexually explicit one. Other differences add complexity to Elvis's contradictions. Elvis was white but sounded black, and he was a working-class kid who became rich enough to qualify as bourgeois but who never acquired bourgeois tastes. The Beatles were working-class kids who made good but did acquire such tastes, while the Stones were (at least some of them) middle class but presented themselves as working class. Where the Beatles "whitened" black music to a much greater extent than Elvis had, the early Stones devoted themselves to producing the most authentic-sounding reproductions of blues and R&B they could muster. To the mass audience— both the fans and their parents—these oppositions probably didn't register very clearly. The fans saw good boys and bad boys, with the proviso that there was something "bad" about the very act of playing rock & roll; the parents were more likely to lump both together as examples of that particular evil— they were threatening because of their challenge to gender roles and because of the power they seemed to hold over the "children." To most American listeners, the two bands' class and race were identical.

If the Beatles were "white" and the Stones "black," the opposition was not a matter of race but of their allegorical significance. The color associations are obvious enough. The jackets of the first seven albums released by the Stones in the United States follow the same formula, the band members' heads staring out at us against black backgrounds. The Beatles released the White Album, and their earlier covers show a much greater variety of colors. Moreover, the expressions on the faces of the Stones on these covers—and in most other early depictions—range from frowns to scowls. The Beatles were usually photographed smiling. The colors and facial expressions correspond to the moods of the bands' records. The Beatles' early songs (up through 1964) are almost relentlessly optimistic, usually depicting romantic relationships in a positive light. While, in 1965 and after, the view of relationships in Beatles songs becomes more negative and their range of subjects broaden, they seldom express anger or contempt. The Stones' songs are even more disproportionately negative in their dealing with relationships, and those that don't concern love typically offer a negative commentary on society. Many of the band's biggest hits express anger and frustration at individuals or society, while others convey contempt and disdain.

In cultivating this image, Andrew Oldham consciously set out to create the "anti-Beatles," though he did so only after he first tried to create the "next Beatles." According to Bill Wyman, writing of Oldham's first moves as the band's manager, "Our reputation and image as the Bad Boys came later, completely accidentally. Andrew never did engineer it. He simply exploited it exhaustively. In fact, his first move was to smarten us up by making us wear *uniforms.*"[9] Their first single, "Come On," was produced by Oldham to sound as much like the other British groups as possible and to downplay the band's blues affinities. The Stones' resistance to wearing their uniforms and their refusal to play "Come On" at their gigs led their manager to try a different tack. Instead of imitating the Beatles' formula, as many other British invasion groups did (the Dave Clark Five, Herman's Hermits, etc.), Oldham decided to make the Stones their opposite. According to Keith Richards, "The thing is not to try and regurgitate the Beatles. So we're going to have to be the anti-Beatles. . . . And Andrew started to play that to the hilt."[10] Instead of hiding it, Oldham could draw on the band's devotion to the blues and R&B to produce records with a sound appropriate to the band's iconography and lyrics. From very early on, the Stones' appearance distinguished them: "One look is sufficient to arouse curiosity. When they need a trim, they tackle it themselves. They mount the stage wearing exactly what they please, be it jeans, bell-bottom trousers or leather jerkins. Individuality is their password."[11]

Oldham's style of record production—heavily determined by the fact that he had no training or experience in music or as a producer—contrasts strongly with that of the Beatles' producer George Martin. The latter's creation of sweet and harmonious mixes helped make the Beatles' music infectious, while the jagged and raucous sound of the Stones' recordings was perhaps even more important than their appearance or lyrics in defining the Stones' image as angry young men. Although the Stones would borrow from the image repertory provided by the blues and R&B, their own image would be distinct. The bluesman might sometimes be angry or contemptuous, but his identity also typically involved the claim of sexual magnetism and an explicit intention to charm. He might be a braggart, but he was also a sweet-talker. Jagger was seductive by maintaining an angry stance; his edge was softened not by charm but by androgyny.

The Stones' sound, like Jagger's persona, was not a mere reproduction of its influences, but rather almost always *less* than them. In stark contrast to the pleasing harmonies and ringing tone of the Beatles, the Stones' music was rough, distorted, and dominated by rhythm. Where the Beatles made rock & roll sound more like pop, the Stones made it sound more like primitive blues. Consider the 1964 cover of Buddy Holly's "Not Fade Away." The Bo Diddley beat is there in the original, but that recording features the Crickets' voices prominently in the rhythm section, while Holly sings the lead with characteristic sweetness. In Holly's version, the song is an unambiguous affirmation of love. The Stones turn the same lyrics into a demand through Jagger's harsh, strident vocals and a rhythm track that uses even the guitars as percussion. If the lyrics to this song might lead one to classify it as a positive depiction of a relationship, the Stones' rendition does not distinguish the track significantly from their many other recordings carrying negative depictions of love. Indeed, the song seems of an emotional piece with such other early hits as "It's All Over Now" and "(I Can't Get No) Satisfaction."

The transformation of "Not Fade Away" is similar to the Stones' covers of Chuck Berry, Bobby Womack, Otis Redding, and the Temptations. The process makes rhythm dominant, forcing the melody beneath it. Instead of Berry's clean guitar lines, we get Jones's and Richards's distortions. In place of the horns or strings that often served as background for rock and soul records, the Stones give us nothing. Even comparing the Stones' sound to Robert Johnson's 1930s recordings—one of their most important influences—which mainly involve only his own vocals and guitar, the Stones still seem even more primitive. All of which is to suggest a rigorous minimalist aesthetic that was the original precursor of punk. By the time the punks took it up in the 1970s, it was already perceived by many as an aesthetic because Andy Warhol's Velvet Underground had embodied the connection. But the Stones' minimalism at first sounded precisely anti-aesthetic, and it was another manifestation of their strategy of reversal. Where music was often defined as the antithesis of noise, the Stones blurred that boundary. The Stones' minimalism in part explains the lack of critical attention to their music. The Stones' music did not seem worth extended commentary, yet that should not be taken to disparage the band's aesthetic success, which, it might be argued, was all the more powerful because of the rigor of their minimalism.

Embodying Adolescence

What the Stones did was to transform a musical expression of African American culture into an expression of white, male, adolescent experience. Since the term *adolescent* will play an important role in this chapter, it is important to define how it is being invoked. It is not my assumption that adolescence is a natural stage of human development, even though it does correspond to the predictable physical and psychological changes that occur with reproductive maturity. The idea of adolescence dates from the early twentieth century, when it was popularized by one of America's most influential psychologists, G. Stanley Hall.[12] While Hall believed that he had discovered a hitherto unrecognized stage of life, adolescence is better conceived as a cultural construction shared by Western, consumer capitalist societies in which schooling continues at least into the late teens and childbearing is postponed until the twenties. As a result, a period in between childhood dependency and adult responsibility becomes the norm. The prolongation of certain features of childhood frustrates desires for adult pleasures and independence, while the relative absence of responsibility allows for freedoms that will be less common later in life.

In the early 1960s as the Rolling Stones began their career, adolescence was a particular preoccupation of social scientists. According to Edgar Z. Friedenberg, an expert of the period, "What is most extraordinary about youth today is that adults everywhere should be so worried about it."[13] But Friedenberg himself elsewhere provides an explanation for this conundrum: "Must there be conflict between the adolescent and society? The point is that adolescence *is* conflict—protracted conflict—between the individual and society."[14] This conflict had intensified in recent years. The juvenile delinquency crisis of the 1950s had fostered increased attention to the teen years, and it made the studies that were produced quite prominent. Perhaps the period's most influential theorist of developmental psychology, psychoanalyst Erik Erikson, made adolescence the pivotal stage in his theory of psychological development in *Childhood and Society,* and he illustrated this with his account of Martin Luther's prolonged adolescence in *Young Man Luther.*[15] "For Erikson, adolescence constitutes the crucial staging ground of identity formation. It names the moment at which a person establishes, not so much the cognitive distinction between self and other (which clearly begins far earlier) but rather what might be considered a psychopolitical one."[16] This attention to adolescence by authorities and the parents and teachers whom they influenced meant that teens were increasingly likely to behave as the theories predicted. It could be argued that adolescent rebellion became more common as a result, as did sexual activity and other behaviors that would not have been tolerated—at least by middle-class parents—in earlier generations.

The Rolling Stones represent the distillation of white, male adolescence in the early 1960s. Their rebellious identification with various negatively marked people, practices, and signs is perhaps the most obvious example. The theory of adolescence says that people of this age group—but especially males—choose styles, behaviors, and identifications because they will incur disapproval from parents and other authorities. So blue jeans in the 1950s, long hair in the 1960s, and piercings and tattoos in the 1990s, by this theory, have the same meaning. Musical preferences are explained in the same way, with each new form of rock, from rockabilly to rap, taking the place of the last when it became familiar enough to no longer bother the elders. While it might be argued that all rockers—or, at least, all successful ones—must, therefore, position themselves as rebels, few have done it with the consistency of the Stones. Unlike Elvis, whose rebellion was confined to certain aspects of his appearance, performance style, and musical preferences, the Stones' rebellion is present in every aspect of their persona. Consider frequent Stones' sideman Bobby Keys's first impression of the group in 1963, when he was playing in Bobby Vee's band: "I was amazed. . . . They were the first band I'd ever seen who didn't wear uniforms on stage. Before the show, I remember Brian Jones saying, 'Look everyone else changes before they go on.' So they all switched their shirts around and they still weren't wearing the same thing. Then Jagger said, 'Excuse us, but the fucking amps keep going out.' I went, 'Huhhh? He said fuck. Did you hear that? He said fuck.'"[17]

When the band first performed on the *Ed Sullivan Show* in October 1964, it produced a reaction similar to the one Elvis's performance of "Hound Dog" on *Milton Berle* had in 1956. What bothered people was not the music or dancing this time but the band's appearance. Actually, the *band* wore jackets and ties, but Jagger was dressed in a sweatshirt and had disheveled and seemingly unwashed hair. According to one account, "The switchboard at CBS was overwhelmed with angry messages of parents objecting to the Stones.

Thousands of them."[18] Jazz critic Nat Hentoff complained that the band "looked very unkempt," while the *Toronto Globe and Mail* described the Stones as "a grubby lot."[19] Ed Sullivan asserted later, "I had not met the Stones until the day before they were to appear. . . . I was shocked when I saw them; *I promise you they'll never be back on the show*."[20] In May 1965, however, they were back on *Sullivan*, and they would appear several more times over the next few years.

Both the refusal to follow—and the active mocking of—show business conventions of dress and polite speech suggest a rigorous and perhaps even simple-minded strategy of reversal. Whatever standard might be applied to them, the Stones embraced the reverse or the negation of it. This strategy is crucial for understanding the permutations of the band's—and especially Mick Jagger's—persona over the course of their career. Bill Wyman describes the reaction produced by the first performance on *Sullivan*—the teenagers' approval and their parents' outrage—as an example of the "healthy polarization" that Oldham had successfully engineered in England. His chapter on their first U.S. tour is entitled "The Selling of Rebellion."[21]

This strategy—or, tendency, since it predates Oldham's strategizing—of reversal culminated in the Stones' flirtation with the occult and Satanism. Again, it was actually only the "real" Stones, Mick and Keith, plus Keith's girlfriend, Anita Pallenberg, who took an interest in these matters. There is some dispute about how seriously they did so. Kenneth Anger, who tried to recruit Mick and Keith to play Lucifer and his assistant in a film, regarded their involvement as dilettantish, and the Stones themselves always pooh-poohed the idea that they ever seriously believed in it. Nevertheless, popular music scholar Sheila Whiteley, among others, regards Jagger's association with the devil as an important element of his persona.[22] As I will discuss in more detail below, I think Whiteley overstates the case, since there is no evidence that the Stones' fans took the idea seriously. Rather, it makes more sense to understand the recordings that deal with Satan—*Their Satanic Majesties Request* and "Sympathy for the Devil"—as the logical extension of the bad boy role. To identify with the devil is, by one traditional set of values, the most radical reversal possible. Given that *Their Satanic Majesties Request* was regarded by almost everyone as the band's worst album, however, one might hazard the guess that such an extreme reversal must inevitably be a failure. In any case, attitudes toward Satan were not a source of serious cultural conflict in the 1960s.

Sex, however, was—both its practice and its representation. The Stones were in the forefront of this conflict from very early in their career. While the Stones' representation of sex and sexuality deserves the more serious consideration that it will get below, their progressively more explicit lyrics are of a piece with their more general testing of social taboos. So, an early cover of Willie Dixon's "Little Red Rooster" (1964) was not released as a single in the United States because of its suggestive lyrics. But by 1967, the more explicit "Let's Spend the Night Together" was released and managed to get significant (though not universal) airplay, even though it was billed as the B-side of "Ruby Tuesday." In 1969, they upped the ante again with "Live with Me" and offered such explicit lyrics as "If you need someone to cream on, you can cream on me" in "Let It Bleed."

We can observe the same phenomenon with album covers. The original design for the *Beggars Banquet* (1968) cover was a graffiti-covered lavatory wall. Decca Records rejected the design as well as the second proposal, a plain, brown wrapper with the warning "Unfit for Children." Two albums later, *Sticky Fingers* (1971) featured a cover by Andy Warhol: the crotch of a pair of jeans and a working zipper behind which was to be found a pop-up banana. Beginning with *Sticky Fingers'* "Brown Sugar," the Stones also began to push against the (then relatively new and insecure) proscription of racism. Characteristically, the racist suggestions of some of their songs were not taken any more seriously than their Satanism, no doubt in part because the band had historically championed black music and black performers.

Sex and Sexuality

The Stones' repeated testing of sexual taboos is consistent with their treatment of other social restrictions, including that which proscribes sympathy for the devil. When the Stones transgressed restrictions on sexuality, it was easy to see them as liberatory, given the continued influence of what Michel Foucault has called the repressive hypothesis, the idea that sex had been systematically silenced and stigmatized since the Victorian era. While Foucault's point was to raise doubts about the repressive hypothesis, the Stones must be seen as icons of changes in manners and morals—not merely because they dared to speak of sex but because they represented new and emerging sexual attitudes and practices.[23] At the time, this may have seemed to adults as just a continuation of the sexualization of culture that was observed in the 1950s. In retrospect, we can see in the Stones not only one rather regressive version of the "sexual revolution" but also intimations of more progressive changes in gender roles and of the emergence from the closet of homosexuality.

The Stones' sexuality was originally as much defined by adolescence as the rest of their persona was. One characteristic attributed to adolescent sexuality is that the individual's pattern of object choice is not yet established. In other words, a traditional psychoanalytic understanding of the adolescent is that he or she is not psychologically committed to a sexual preference. This was a major theme of 1950s culture in the United States, when adult homosexuality was often understood as a kind of arrested development. Literary critic Leslie Fiedler made much of this connection in his influential *Love and Death in the American Novel*.[24] The Rolling Stones managed to exploit the ambiguity of adolescent sexuality without producing a homophobic response. That this was an explicit strategy—at least on the part of Oldham—is clear from his own account of rock's appeal: "It was always the sex in rock and roll that attracted me. . . . The sex that most people didn't realize was there. Like the Everly Brothers. Two guys with the same kind of face, the same kind of hair. They were singing together to some girl, but really they were singing to each other."[25] Although it would be a few years before Oldham and the Stones would overtly thematize homosexuality, Mick Jagger's androgynous appearance and performance style covertly suggested homoeroticism from very early on.

To say that the Stones represent the sexuality of the adolescent male is not to say that this maleness is the same as the one often attributed to the band and to Jagger in particular. As Whiteley has argued, Jagger was no mere "cock rocker"; his "live performances disrupt any notion of 'normative' masculinity. Rather, they involve a self-presentation which is, at one and the same time, both masculine and feminine."[26] Jagger's sexuality was far more ambiguous from the beginning than that of Elvis or the Beatles. The now surprising androgyny of Jagger's early performances and appearances is attributable not just to his hairstyle but to his gestures, facial expressions, and perhaps most importantly to a kind of *softness* that all of these together produced. If Whiteley is correct to note that "there is little suggestion of the passive female in Jagger's performance," she is too quick to reassert binary oppositions when she likens him to a dominatrix.[27] It is a mark of the inventiveness with which he has recombined gender codes that one has trouble classifying Jagger's sexuality at all. This condition allowed individual fans to make whatever classification they imagined or desired.

Jagger's image is often understood as separable from the context of his performance with the band and its music, but the band as a whole seems to contain a butch/femme opposition, with Keith Richards, Bill Wyman, and Charlie Watts playing the former roles, and Brian Jones and Jagger playing the latter. Jones's stage presence does often appear to enact passive femininity, and he, not Jagger, was the first of the Stones to be subject to rumors of homosexuality. After Jones's death, Mick Taylor did not distinguish himself as butch or femme, but his replacement, Ron Wood, adopted the femme position—albeit more ambiguously. Wood became Jagger's chief playmate on stage, but his physique is anything but androgynous, and his face bears a good deal of similarity to Richards's. To confuse things further, in their stage antics, it is Jagger who is usually the top and Wood the bottom.

Thus Jagger's softness is just one aspect of his persona and of his role onstage. This feminine side of the lead singer contrasts with most other aspects of the band's image. Long hair certainly coded as female in the early 1960s; scruffiness and the impression of a lack of cleanliness did not. The Rolling Stones' rough and distorted sound and the content of most of their lyrics also had a distinctly masculine edge. "Satisfaction" is, of course, the Stones' most famous song, and it might be regarded as the international anthem of male adolescents. While only one of the song's three verses refers openly to sexual frustration, it is obvious that sex is the song's primary subject. It may no longer be the case that teenage boys are predictably sexually frustrated. The received wisdom is that more teenagers are having sex more often and at earlier ages. But when "Satisfaction" was released in 1965, most boys (at least those who were not rock stars) were not having much sex. Even masturbation was still suppressed in many households. Yet sex was increasingly present in the media. Hence, male adolescents in the 1960s often experienced the world as one big tease. "Satisfaction" gave expression to this frustration, not so much by naming its source—even the verse about sex is not explicit—as by evoking the feelings associated with it. This is done mainly through the use of repetition, not only in the song's chorus—"I try and I try and I try and I try"—but also by means of the guitar riff that is the song's most distinctive feature. The rhythm itself—relatively slow but pounding—suggests through syncopation that it is itself frustrated, as if it were pushing against some barrier. Adding the Fuzztone to the mix makes the music sound angry, and the song provides no release from the mood. "Satisfaction," according to critic Robert Christgau, is "the perfect Stones paradox—the lyrics denied what the music delivered."[28] But one could argue that it is satisfying because it is a statement of a problem and a musical discourse about the experience of it. The frustrated individual continues to demand long after demanding is productive, thereby increasing his frustration. The music of "Satisfaction" expresses this demanding rage while the lyrics explain it. Rather than mollifying the listener, "Satisfaction" is much more likely to incite his anger.

After "Satisfaction," the Stones' first single to reach number 1 on the charts, it is hard to find a Stones song that does not somehow express frustration. Their next two singles restated its themes and reproduced its mood, "Get Off of My Cloud" and "Nineteenth Nervous Breakdown" reaching numbers 1 and 2, respectively. The songs that don't express frustration are exceptions that prove the rule, because they are artistic failures. Their versions of the Temptations' hits, "My Girl" and "Ain't Too Proud to Beg" are examples. Jagger's "My Girl" is simply uninspired, and a song as close to the verge of banality as this one requires an emotionally convincing performance. By 1974, Jagger's persona was so well defined that no one could take seriously the idea that the singer wasn't too proud to beg. "Satisfaction," "Get Off of My Cloud," and "Nineteenth Nervous Breakdown" established the Stones' distinctive style and concerns, which are clearly gendered as masculine. One could argue that not until the 1990s, with P. J. Harvey, Alanis Morissette, and maybe Liz Phair, do we get female rockers who are as angry as the Rolling Stones. I'm not forgetting about punk here. There were angry punk women, but their anger tended to be generic rather than personal. While Jagger's lyrics might seem sometimes to offer social commentary, even these complaints are most often embodied in a female figure. So, "Nineteenth Nervous Breakdown" catalogs the faults of an otherwise unidentified woman. A degree of class resentment is clear enough, but the implication is that she has failed the singer personally. Here class is not in itself the issue but merely an explanation for the woman's neuroses.

The psychological function of rage is to release energy that is bound by the frustration of desire and that has not been dealt with in any other way. Thus rage satisfies the demands of frustration in a sense, and in this sense rage is orgasm. If one is emotionally satisfied by the Stones' angry music, it is because one identifies with the expression of rage and adopts this discourse as one's own. The Stones' music is, in the main, orgasmic in this way.

If it is true that the Stones did not record many love songs—as Christgau puts it, Jagger "wrote more hate songs"—relationships are still very often their subject, especially before *Beggars Banquet*.[29] This context needs to be kept in mind when discussing the Stones' misogyny. The songs expressing hatred of women are directed at onetime objects of affection. Played out in these songs are maneuvers in the battle of the sexes as fought out between individuals. The hostility arises not because women are assumed to be inherently inferior and docile but because they are feared as powerful and dangerous. This is a male adolescent's view of women, derived in part from the recent memory of the mother as a figure of both power and attraction but also from the typical confusion, insecurity, and rejection that boys feel when they begin to form romantic or erotic attachments. The Stones characteristically give expression to adolescent male fantasies of power in such relationships, either as dominance ("Under My Thumb") or freedom from emotional dependence ("It's All Over Now"). As Mark Edmundson puts it in his memoir, "The Stones knew that Eros was warfare by another name; that guys came pathetically underprepared for the struggle; that the other side had constant advantage. 'Under My Thumb,' where the guy actually is on top, running the show, is about a rare reversal."[30]

The most important sort of power to a male adolescent, however, is neither of these but, rather, the power of seduction. The boy wants girls to fall for him, to love him, and to desire him. The traditional stance of the bluesman is an almost perfect match for this fantasy, except that the bluesman is emphatically not a youth. If one adds the cultural differences that distinguish African American from European American experience (the average white teenager wouldn't have had a clue what a "mojo" was), then one can see why a somewhat modified persona was needed for the white adolescent's role model. Jagger re-created the role, less by what he sang than by the way he performed. Of course, the bad boy image made all of the Stones more seductive than their good boy counterparts. The Beatles were demigods; they didn't need to seduce. The Stones never had the same degree of following among young teen girls as the Beatles, but they acquired a reputation early on for getting into girls' pants with prodigious frequency. And if the Stones' music was the sonic equivalent of sex, then it ought to turn girls on. It is not surprising, then, that Michael Lydon, covering the 1969 U.S. tour, should record the following:

> In Phoenix three girls are sitting in the front row, obviously friends who came
> together: a pretty girlish blonde, a rather plain brunette with glasses and a cool

beauty-queen type who smokes her cigarettes in a holder. No dates. At first they are reserved and stiff, trying to look their best—do they have fantasies that maybe *He* will notice them? They smoke a lot. The blonde starts to smile during "Carol"; the brunette blushes when Mick puts the microphone between his thighs on "Sympathy." She recovers during the blues, but the beauty queen's jaw sags open the tiniest bit. Her tongue flickers out during "Under My Thumb" and she drops the holder. She doesn't pick it up. By this time the blonde's neatly coiled hair has somehow come undone on one side and, never taking her eyes off the stage, she vainly pecks at it with one hand. "Midnight Rambler" is too much for all of them. In its moment of eerie silence they watch as Mick slips off his belt and falls to his knees. He raises it above his head.

Well, now, you've heard about the Boston . . .

Bam! The belt comes down as the band hits a monster cord. The blonde almost falls back over her seat, the brunette covers her breasts and the beauty queen goes limp. Mick hisses,

Honey, he ain't one of those!

They're hooked. No more cigarettes. The brunette's glasses have disappeared, and as the lights go on they're on their feet. Tears start in the blonde's eyes. . . . I lose them in the crowd; my last glimpse is of the brunette, her hands above her head, palms up and fingers spread wide, her mouth open wide, singing, "No satisfaction, baby, no satisfaction," and she is beautiful now, transformed, her eyes bright as a bride's, her hair swinging loose around her shoulders.[31]

It is obvious that the critic describes a seduction of the three girls by Mick Jagger, but it is significant that the word appears nowhere in the account. The open mouths, darting tongues, and loose, swinging hair all suggest that this seduction has been achieved. It is not the actual ravishing of these women but rather their transformation from frigid virgins to sexually ready "brides." In other words, Jagger functions here as a kind of fluffer, who readies the women for sex without actually having them. They are had, as far as we know, only in the mind of the writer. In his identification with Jagger, the critic expresses his own fantasy and reveals one of the reasons for the singer's appeal to heterosexual men. Moreover, the observing critic makes the spectator the spectacle and reestablishes the conventional politics of looking. Where the shot / reverse shot editing of Elvis's TV performances established him as the object of the audience's gaze, here the performer onstage

Sexual excess was always part of the Stones' persona as illustrated by this still from *Performance* (1970), which also shows Mick Jagger's "softer" side. (film still)

becomes merely the occasion for the critic's description of the women in the audience.

It may seem as though there should be a contradiction between Jagger's androgyny and feminization, on the one hand, and his image as Don Juan on the other. But great seducers have rarely been macho men. In Hollywood, Rudolph Valentino, Fred Astaire, Cary Grant, and even Woody Allen were known for portraying lovers, while John Wayne and Arnold Schwarzenegger had no such reputations. The vulnerability that romantic love entails is at odds with the image of invulnerability that was an aspect of their personas. This suggests that, rather than understand the John Wayne type as "normative" masculinity, we should recognize that the culture gives us a number of competing ideals. Individual men are most often influenced by more than one of these. They imagine themselves sometimes as Wayne and sometimes as Valentino, sometimes as Keith and sometimes as Mick. Of course, there are masculine ideals that the Rolling Stones do not encompass, including those of the faithful husband and father. What the Stones represent is sex—and even love—without compromising autonomy or freedom. To be a Stone is to have unlimited numbers of adoring women to whom no responsibility is owed. According to Robert Greenfield: "Mick was always looking for action. Sexual fidelity, even to a woman he had only just married, was never his thing. On the road, Mick still liked to have it off with some young and fairly innocent looking girl he knew he would never see again. There were also on-going affairs with women willing to be with him on any basis he preferred. Such were the perks that came with being the world's leading rock star."[32]

Excess: Wretched and Sublime

If the Rolling Stones meant sex in the 1960s, by the end of the decade, without giving up that association, they began to be known as much for their excesses in general. Oldham, of course, had nurtured this aspect of the image from early on, and the press in England especially published a more or less continuous stream of gossip: "Having fashioned their 'bad boy' into the perfect press artifact for the head-line hungry hacks of Fleet Street, the Stones' story, an irresistible mélange of 'Sex, Drugs, and Defiance,' rolled on under its own steam. Abetted by Andrew Oldham prepackaged 'plants,' all this publicity played no small part in their infamous career."[33] According to Wyman, "Before the Beatles and the Stones blew the pop scene wide open, there hadn't been a great interest in the private lives of stars in the 'hit parade.' . . . I don't remember anyone caring much whether Petula Clark or Russ Conway was married, or what they were wearing. But now . . . the public eye was focused on everything we did."[34] While things may have been a bit different in the United States—where Elvis had certainly attracted his share of gossip—the Stones pushed it to a new level. Greenfield observes, "By his mere presence, Jagger changes any event that he is involved in. Any party that he gets dragged to becomes the party Mick was at."[35]

This excess of visibility is the condition for the association of the Stones with excess in general. Other bands behaved excessively: the Who destroyed their instruments and hotel rooms; Jimi Hendrix, Jim Morrison, and Janis Joplin died taking excessive amounts of drugs; Alice Cooper performed mock suicide at each one of his concerts. But none of these achieved the Stones' level of exposure or came near to equaling Jagger in social capital. "With his wedding to Bianca in 1971—an event which managed to fulfill the media's wildest fantasies—Mick became permanent property of the international wire services. . . . Together Mick and Bianca were double trouble, a split screen scandal. Socialites, movie stars, gilded sweethearts of the chic and glossy, jaded darlings of the Concorde crowd, top of the Best-Dressed lists, paparazzied dining at Maxim's, leaving Studio 54 with Andy Warhol—as mirror images of each other the Jaggers were celebrity clones."[36]

Even the music writers, whom one would think might write about the band's music, became more and more interested in the Stones as celebrities. The buzz surrounding the 1972 tour made the 1969 tour seem as though it had been ignored. Greenfield filed regular diarylike reports with *Rolling Stone*, which also hired Truman Capote to cover part of the tour. Terry Southern, the novelist and screenwriter showed up, as did novelist Richard Ellman, who was on assignment for *Esquire*. When Capote appeared in Kansas City, it was with Jackie Kennedy Onassis's sister, Princess Lee Radziwill. Capote never wrote a word of his *Rolling Stone* article, but his mere presence on the tour "gave the Stones an uneasy sheen of celebrity beyond the world of rock music, which annoyed other bands like Led Zeppelin, who were touring at the time and found themselves ignored even though they were outselling the Stones in every city."[37] After Capote left the tour, he appeared on Johnny Carson's *Tonight Show*. As Greenfield describes it, "He discusses drug intake on the chartered plane . . . and generally does the kind of advance publicity for the Stones money can't buy. . . . He makes the whole shebang sound like a great adventure."[38] By the end of the 1970s, a member of the entourage, Tony Sanchez—described by Wyman as "the guy who scored for Keith"—had published *Up and Down with the Rolling Stones*, which covers a longer period than the tour diaries, but is, if anything, more focused on lifestyle.[39] These representations—many of them reaching a wide audience—tell us that rock stars are different from you and me, not only because they have more money but also because they practice consumption unrestrained by morality, law, or even common sense. This excess is both wonderful and awful, a condition to be envied and a warning to those who might try to imitate it.

If the Stones' identification with sex in the 1960s included the idea that they were sexually excessive, it was not then rooted there, except perhaps to the extent that the adolescent's preoccupation with sex is thought to be always excessive. "Satisfaction," after all, is about not getting any. The Stones' music and lyrics continued to deal more with desire and its frustration than with satiation, but as their celebrity grew and public beliefs about the lives of rock stars increasingly entailed an assumption of something like continuous orgy, the Stones became the poster children for this lifestyle. By 1970, most people had heard about groupies and the free sex they offered to rock stars.

Greenfield quotes Marshall Chess: "When thirty-five chicks come to fuck the Stones, and there are only five Stones, that leaves thirty chicks, so anyone close to the tour gets one."[40] Of that same tour, Capote was reported to have described public sex between groupies and members of the entourage on the chartered jet. The incident was photographed by Robert Frank and would become the most notorious scene in *Cocksucker Blues*. It is no mere coincidence that the Stones stayed at Hugh Hefner's Playboy Mansion when the tour stopped in Chicago. The excesses associated with Hefner match those of the band, even if their styles and tastes differ. Yet according to Greenfield, the Stones' visit was excessive even by Hefner's standards:

> What Hef never realized when he began publishing *Playboy* is that all his fantasies would become real and that he would begin living a life filled with some of the most physically beautiful ladies on two legs. And that there would be A LOT OF SEX. . . . But even for the worldly-wise Hef, the Stones are taking it apart and putting it back together a new way. It's a little more intense and out in the open than it's ever been before. Although there have been groovy scenes before, and groovy scenes are a practice out at the L.A. Playboy Mansion where the gang is, well, uh, just groovier . . . it's never been quite like this; there have never before been so many knockdown-loaded people openly getting it on and inviting their friends to come along for a ride.[41]

The Stones' excesses were not merely sexual, of course. They also indulged in drugs. In this regard they outdid even the Grateful Dead, who gave the impression (false in the case of Jerry Garcia, at least) that they were in control of their drug use. The Stones' repeated busts contributed to the opposite impression. Keith Richards alone might have served as a poster boy for a campaign against drug abuse. Between 1967 and 1980, various Stones, their girlfriends, and retainers were busted on at least fourteen separate occasions, Keith accounting for seven of them. Charlie Watts, Bill Wyman, and Mick Taylor were never arrested on drug charges, and Wyman says he avoided drugs entirely. Here, as with much else, Brian, Mick, Keith, and, later, Ron Wood, were much more fully Stones than the others in the band. As a result of the publicity from all of these arrests and court appearances, the Stones became the first band to unite in the public mind "sex, drugs, and rock & roll."

Of course, in the 1960s merely taking drugs was not necessarily regarded as excessive behavior, and getting busted for them could be shrugged off as bad luck. By the 1970s, however, it became apparent that Keith's drug use far exceeded the usual definition of "recreational." While rumors of his heroin use had been around for much of the decade (police found heroin at his house in the south of France in 1972), Keith's arrest in Toronto in 1977 for heroin trafficking made it public knowledge. Even before that, gossip had Keith and Anita making periodic trips to Switzerland to have their blood changed as a cure for heroin addiction. Sanchez describes how he arranged one of these excursions in 1973. The extravagance and expense of the procedure and the travel necessary to arrange it almost trump the excessiveness of the addiction itself. Sanchez's comment is perhaps only a little bit more extreme than one might imagine the average fan's feelings to be: "I couldn't help wondering where all this blood was coming from or resenting the decadence of debauched millionaires regaining their heath, vampirelike, from the fresh, clean blood of innocents."[42]

Keith's continued survival in the face of the abuse of his body has become the stuff of legend. Writing in 1997, Greenfield remarked, "Had anyone told me twenty-five years ago that Ian Stewart, the Stones' original piano player, whose drugs of choice (in order of preference) were red meat, single malt whiskey, and golf would be long dead while Keith Richards, he of the lifestyle that challengeth human endurance, would not only be alive and well but living like Uncle Wiggily in Connecticut, I would have laughed myself sick and then gone out looking for yet another party after the show in some multitiered Hyatt along the road."[43]

As early as 1972, Keith looked like an old man, his face displaying the ravages of hard living. And he apparently did his best to live up to his reputation. By 1974, Sanchez reports, Keith "reveled now in the image the fans had of him as a debauched drug addict, and he carefully fostered it. 'I only ever get ill when I give up drugs,' he said to one interviewer."[44]

The accounts of the Stones' American tours depict the band as debauched royalty, with a train of loyal (or not so loyal) retainers and hangers-on. Indeed, the idea of the rock entourage may stem from these tours. Moreover, like the royals of the Middle Ages, the Stones didn't seem to live anywhere. Rather than having a home, they camped in various houses and hotels, some of which they happened to own. The accounts of tour life explain in part why the Stones could continue to be perceived as adolescents even after they were no longer young men. Their reliance on others for virtually all necessities meant that they never had to face the responsibilities associated with adulthood. So, even the dreadful events at Altamont Speedway don't seem to be something for which the Stones might be responsible. The Grateful Dead—who merely suggested that the Hell's Angels provide security—are sometimes blamed, while the Stones are depicted as not knowing any better. Stanley Booth's description of the band's feeble attempts to control the Angels reinforces this view, since it makes the band look like innocent bystanders.[45]

That's not to say that Altamont wasn't also perceived as another example of the Stones' excess, somehow consistent with their character even if not their fault. The Stones' lyrics are often cited as a connection. "Sympathy for the Devil" may have sounded either hip or silly before Altamont, but afterward evil became too palpable to maintain either position. Even the Stones themselves seemed to agree, since they didn't perform the song again until many years later. Several songs on *Let It Bleed* that the Stones performed at Altamont are, if anything, more disturbing, since they deal with actual instances of evil rather than with a figure symbolic of it. "Gimme Shelter," for example, demands shelter from a litany of threats. The lyrics "Rape—murder—it's just a shot away" seem to predict the situation at the speedway, and this song gave its title to the Maysles' documentary. But "Midnight Rambler," a song about a serial killer, might be the scariest of the Stones' Altamont set list. Where "Gimme Shelter" warns of violence, "Midnight Rambler" celebrates it. If it is less popularly associated with the Stones' aura of evil than "Sympathy for the Devil," it may only be because the lyrics of "Midnight Rambler" are harder to understand. And, while on "Sympathy," Jagger sings in the voice of Lucifer, on "Midnight Rambler" he moves between first and third person. Lyrics like "Well you've heard about the Boston Strangler/Honey, he ain't one of those," create a certain distance for the audience. Others, such as the song's concluding line, "I'll stick my knife right down your throat, honey, and it hurts," bring us up close and personal.

Those whom the Angels assaulted and killed were the most visible casualties of these American tours, but they were not the only ones. There were the kids who were beaten in most of the cities the Stones visited by whatever security forces had been hired, usually for the sin of wanting to get closer to the band. There were Margo and Mary, the participants in the airplane orgy Robert Frank staged for his movie, who end up in New York working in the sex trade. There was the Stones' manager, Marshall Chess, who ended up with a heroin habit. Even the journalists didn't come out unscathed. Stanley Booth reports that both he and Michael Lydon became caught up in the tour's sex and drugs, and he implies that Lydon's marriage was breaking up because of his womanizing. Booth's disapproval of Lydon's behavior doesn't prevent him from indulging in his own extracurricular activities before the tour is over. He ends his book with a coda: "Following the tour that ended with Altamont, I went to live in England and stayed until, after a certain weekend at Redlands, I decided that if Keith and I kept dipping into the same bag, there would be no book and we would both be dead."[46] In Booth's rendering, however, it is Brian Jones, who died before the 1969 tour (just after he had been kicked out of the band), who was the most tragic victim of the Stones' excesses—in particular, his own.

One might have understood the Rolling Stones differently if Brian Jones's example were representative. After all, we have understood debauched bohemian artists since Paul Verlaine and Arthur Rimbaud to be defined by their opposition to bourgeois proprieties, and we expect such opposition to be costly. Such persons should die young and poor. Certainly they should not be embraced by their society as the height of fashion. The Rolling Stones, however, are rich beyond their wildest expectations and, although they may no longer be at fashion's pinnacle, in 2005 and 2006 they mounted one of the most successful tours in popular music history, grossing in North America $138.5 million, with an average ticket price of $136.63 (about which few if any complaints were published), and setting a record $437 million worldwide.[47] In 2008 they were the subject of a concert documentary, *Shine a Light,* by Martin Scorsese.

Whatever the threat posed by the Stones' rebelliousness in the early 1960s, it was well contained by 1969. It might be argued that adolescent rebellion was contained in advance. Because this rebellion is defined as a feature of a natural stage of life, it is apolitical and cannot become revolutionary. Moreover, Leerom Medovoi has shown how such rebellion became integrated into American culture in the 1950s as a symbol of American democracy in the face of the Cold War.[48] Some of this would come back to haunt the body politic, when in the 1960s teenage rebellion turned into political activism. But the Stones had no politics, as "Street Fighting Man" makes clear. Their "opposition" was merely a stance, an immensely successful mode of presenting themselves to the world. That's not to say it was a pose, that the band was "inauthentic," since they didn't claim to be anything more than musicians and performers. It is, rather, a warning not to assume that cultural rebellion is politically significant.

CHAPTER SIX

THE GRATEFUL DEAD

Alchemy, or Rock & Roll Utopia

When we get on stage, what we really want to happen is, we want to be transformed from ordinary players into extraordinary ones, like forces of a larger consciousness. And the audience wants to be transformed from whatever ordinary reality they may be in to something that enlarges them. So maybe it's that notion of transformation, a seat-of-the-pants shamanism, that has something to do with why the Grateful Dead keep pulling them in.

Jerry Garcia

Almost everyone recognizes the Grateful Dead as a cultural icon of the 1960s.[1] What they and the sixties mean, however, is much in dispute. The decade has been cited by the Right ever since as the point where America went wrong, and sixties music is often blamed, or at least made to represent the decade's bad influence. In the wake of Jerry Garcia's death in the summer of 1995, conservative columnist George Will, writing in *Newsweek,* used a Reaganesque anecdote about a couple who abandoned their child to indict the Dead and the 1960s. No real connection is asserted between the couple and the band or the decade, but somehow they are responsible. Will claims, "The band has been a touring time capsule, keeping alive the myth that there is something inherently noble about adopting an adversary stance toward 'bourgeois' or 'middle class' values."[2] Will insists that "society's success depends" on these values—as if child-nurture were a value peculiar to the middle class. The idea that the Dead were in the 1990s a "touring time capsule" was not restricted to the far Right, and those on the Left don't usually see the Dead standing for the sixties they would like to remember, the nonviolent protests and civil disobedience that ended segregation and, eventually, the Vietnam War. The Dead aren't usually connected to either of these. Rather, they are mainly associated with drugs, out-of-date fashions, and a naïve belief that the world could be remade by living differently. In light of current attitudes, which assume almost any change is impossible, we need to reevaluate the San Francisco counterculture, a historically specific formation influenced by the Beats and instanced by, in addition to hippies and rock groups, the San Francisco Mime Troupe, the Diggers, and Ken Kesey's Acid Tests, among others.

If the Dead clearly qualify as icons, however, it is less obvious that they are rock stars. For some people, the Dead can't be *rock* stars because they don't play rock & roll music. This point has been made by numerous critics who hold that improvisation and other characteristics of their music put the Dead in a different genre. Members of the Dead family seem to agree that the band existed at some remove from rock & roll. Dennis McNally asserts, "The Grateful Dead isn't really a rock band and is only tangentially part of the American music industry."[3] While rock & roll was historically identified with youth, according to Bob Weir, the Dead's "music was not hormonal and *immediate* the way rock and roll was before the Beatles took the genre from teenage to adulthood. . . . The Dead started out with an appreciation of history, drawing from a century's worth of popular music forms as well as older classical influences. . . . Grateful Dead music is for people who have lived some; it's music that you live *with*."[4] In the end, however, the Dead are more like rock stars than they are like jazz musicians or bluegrass performers or any other familiar category that might be used instead.

The argument that the Dead didn't play rock depends upon an essentialist definition of the genre. If we understand that genres are based on family resemblances, rather than on essential traits, it is hard to argue that the Dead's music doesn't fit. Rock & roll has always been a hodgepodge of different styles, and the Dead may illustrate this quality better than any other act. In any event, the Dead's music is more recognizable as rock & roll than jazz, country, R&B, or any other large generic category, even though it draws on all of these. Moreover, the band's audience demographic and its behavior, the venues where the band performed—from the Avalon and Fillmore, to basketball arenas and football stadiums—and the instrumentation and amplification it used at these concerts are all consistent only with rock & roll as a cultural practice. Although some deeply invested fans and critics might insist otherwise, in the minds of the vast majority, the Dead were a rock band.

For others, the Dead can't be rock *stars* because they are not glamorous or sexy enough. Certainly if one takes Mick Jagger as one's model of star behavior, none of the Grateful Dead qualify. Clearly, when one calls Bill Clinton a rock star, it is not Jerry Garcia one has in mind. Unlike the Stones, the Dead did not relish the limelight. According to biographer Blair Jackson, Jerry Garcia was "distraught" that he had become a celebrity: "I liked it when you could just be a musician," Garcia told *Good Times*.[5] If it is true that the Dead did not, in many respects, behave like stars, there are several criteria by which they clearly fit the designation. One is their iconic status itself, which they attained early in their history, even though they had sold relatively few records; they remain as recognizable as any rock act short of the Beatles and Elvis. Moreover, using "box office" as a measure, the Dead were megastars at the time of Jerry Garcia's death, drawing the largest income from concerts of any musicians. It may be true that their audience was smaller and more devoted, but it extended well beyond its most visible members, the tour-heads who followed the group from concert to concert. The Dead are best understood as bringing a new dimension to stardom, one that is antithetical to its glamour (for which the Dead substituted a different sort of magic) and conspicuous consumption.

If we can agree, however, that the Dead were rock star icons of the counterculture, this chapter will explore what that means. In keeping with their drug use and the charge of "permissiveness," one might think that the Grateful Dead are, like the Rolling Stones, representative of excess and debauchery. But unlike the Stones, who were rebels without a cause, the Dead consciously sought to embody the idea of counterculture, meaning an alternative to the dominant social order founded on different rules and values. A Grateful Dead concert was "more than entertainment," and "the basis of the San Francisco [rock] community . . . was not pop but art."[6] For the Dead, drugs were never merely recreational but part of a larger experiment in changing consciousness. The psychedelic experience provided by LSD is at the root of the Dead's central trope, which I name "alchemy." What the Dead are about is magical transformation, or metamorphosis. Their lyrics, music, concerts, cover art— even their name—all may be understood on the model of base metal changed into gold. The Dead didn't think of their project as political, but bassist Phil Lesh called it "our collective transformation program."[7] Instead of decadence, then, the Grateful Dead represent the hope that the self and the world are capable of radical transformation. This vision that made change seem possible may be the most important legacy of the 1960s.

The San Francisco Sound and the Counterculture

To the casual observer, or even many ardent fans, "the San Francisco sound" is doubtless understood to describe a musical style, an auditory phenomenon. While it may be that other scenes associated with particular rock

The Grateful Dead at center of San Francisco's counterculture, Ashbury and Haight, 1967. (Herbert Greene, used by permission)

cultures—for example, Liverpool in the early sixties—were defined by distinctive musical characteristics, San Francisco in the mid- to late 1960s was not. The best Ralph Gleason could do—in his 1969 book *The Jefferson Airplane and the San Francisco Sound*—is to assert that music produced in San Francisco, even if it originated in Chicago or Texas, seems "to have a slightly different sound."[8] In fact, what the San Francisco bands who emerged in the mid-1960s—the Airplane, the Grateful Dead, Quicksilver Messenger Service, Big Brother and the Holding Company, and Country Joe and the Fish—share is not a musical commonality but the counterculture that to some extent pre-existed the music and that developed in conjunction with it. The music was made possible by the counterculture even as the music was essential to it. If, in the end, the music was the counterculture's longest-lived product, that should not lead us to neglect the fact of an actually existing counterculture that gave rise to it.

In 1966, an article in *Crawdaddy!* asserted, "The Grateful Dead figure to be important movers in imparting San Francisco's message to the world."[9] One is surprised now to imagine that San Francisco was thought to have such a message, but this idea was widely shared for a few years in the 1960s. If by November of 1968, Michael Lydon could ask in the *New York Times,* "Has Frisco Gone Commercial?," it is further testament to the idea that people had previously thought it represented something other than the music business as usual.[10] This sense was still apparent in 1984 to Simon Frith, who claimed, "The American rock arguments came most clearly from San Francisco, a self-consciously anti-pop, anticommercial community."[11] Frith's point was that some of the politics of that moment remained pertinent, even though by 1984—and a fortiori now—the tendency was to dismiss the politics and the music. Frith's piece, on the whole, is a part of that dismissal, despite the fact that it first appeared in a special issue of *Social Text* called *The 60s without Apology.* Frith proclaimed that "the rock revolution was far too easy. It proclaimed a Utopia without struggle." He preferred the pessimism of the Velvet Underground, the Sex Pistols, and the punk movement—itself by then already a matter mainly of memory.[12]

Frith's view is consistent with the way the San Francisco scene has been remembered, as he himself acknowledges: "In Britain as well as the USA, the 60s have a bad reputation."[13] He observes that, paradoxically, Left and Right meet in their dismissal of the decade for its permissiveness. When the sixties are fondly remembered by the Left, it is for political activism, and the San Francisco counterculture isn't usually understood as having fostered that. Rather, it is connected mainly to the "hippies," a word that calls up images of the wandering teenagers who ended up in Haight-Ashbury after the media began to cover it extensively. As feminist Alice Echols recently noted, "Bluntly put, the hippies aren't hip. In contrast to the Beats, who only acquire more cool and more relevance, hippies . . . seem sillier and more anachronistic with each passing year."[14] But the hippies were not always so easily dismissed. At the time, the radical political significance of the San Francisco scene was recognized by Warren Hinckle, the editor of *Ramparts* magazine, who observed, "The utopian sentiments of these hippies was not to be put down lightly. Hippies have a clear vision of the ideal community. . . . [I]t is a vision that, despite the Alice in Wonderland phraseology usually breathlessly employed to describe it, necessarily embodies a radical political philosophy: communal life, drastic restriction of private property, rejection of violence, creativity before consumption, freedom before authority, de-emphasis of government and traditional forms of leadership."[15]

The term *counterculture* is sometimes used as a synonym for 1960s youth culture in general. I'm using the term in a more restricted way, to refer to the less explicitly political and more cultural groups, practices, and events of the era. In these terms, the New Left and Students for a Democratic Society would not be part of the counterculture, while the Merry Pranksters and the Yippies would. The values espoused by the New Left and the counterculture were to a large extent similar. Both opposed the Vietnam War, social hierarchies, and restrictions on personal freedom such as drug laws. Moreover, there were instances, such as the fight over "People's Park" in Berkeley, where the two groups are indistinguishable.

But in the main they were characterized by different styles, different strategies, and different activities. The New Left, especially until 1968, was full of people who dressed and wore their hair conservatively and who did not regard drugs, if they used them at all, as anything other than recreation. The New Left wanted to change society as a whole via political means. This might be the ballot box or "participatory democracy," or, especially later in the decade, the taking up of arms. Revolution became the goal, though many continued to envision nonviolent revolution.

The counterculture, on the contrary, largely opposed "politics" as an aspect of the system and sought to change society by example, establishing new practices and institutions within but counter to the dominant culture. As Jerry Garcia put it, "I think everyone should take one step backwards and two steps sideways, and let the whole thing collapse. Nobody vote, nobody work—let it collapse."[16] The counterculture flouted straight society's conventions of dress and decorum and proclaimed the mind-expanding benefits of drugs. The opposition between the New Left and the counterculture is a sort of reprise of the nineteenth-century alternatives of scientific and utopian socialism. While most New Lefties did not embrace the old Marxist claims to science, they did believe in confrontation as an essential strategy. They practiced what might be called "traditional" protest politics. The counterculture tended to avoid confrontation and was suspicious of anything that might be called politics. But that doesn't mean that the counterculture really was without political significance; its politics by example were still intended to bring about change. Moreover, the utopian vision of the counterculture offered something the New Left seldom did, a vision of what a new society would look like. That vision was reflected in the alternative institutions that made up the counterculture, and it was disseminated most widely by musical means.

San Francisco's message—and its icon, the hippie—became widely known because of the massive media coverage of the Trips Festival of January 1966, a multiday extravaganza of music, dancing, light shows, and acid. That, according to Grateful Dead manager Dennis McNally, "was the first pebble of what would be a landslide of national media coverage of San Francisco rock/psychedelic culture."[17] There was a continuing stream of coverage of the San Francisco scene culminating in the summer of 1967, the "Summer of Love," which, Joel Slevin argues, "never really happened" but was "invented by the fevered imaginations of writers for weekly news magazines."[18] That summer began with the Monterey Pop Festival, which showcased the Airplane and other San Francisco bands alongside established acts such as Otis Redding, Buffalo Springfield, Simon and Garfunkel, and the Mamas and the Papas. The event launched Janis Joplin and Big Brother and the Holding Company as well as Jimi Hendrix, and D. A. Pennebaker's documentary film about it helped to disseminate a new image of rock & roll—defined not by teenage hysteria but by radical artistic and cultural experimentation.[19]

If most of the San Francisco groups had quickly followed the Airplane to the top of the singles charts, perhaps the distinctiveness of the scene would have been less clear. But Grace Slick, Marty Balin, and their band mates represented the exception rather than the rule. There were no other hit singles to come out of San Francisco, and only Joplin and Big Brother had a number 1 album, with 1968's *Cheap Thrills*. The San Francisco sound was understood to be a rejection of the industry's status quo. It developed outside of the usual channels, and by the time the record companies' A&R (artist & repertoire) men got around to signing most of the acts, they had already defined themselves well enough to be able to reject the standard packaging of their music. They did not have to follow the usual path to stardom of small club dates leading to local fame, "discovery" by an A&R man, and a record contract that permitted the company to repackage the act to optimize sales. The Dead took full advantage of the San Francisco scene and its counterculture. Most artists established themselves in the public mind by producing hit records. The Dead were courted so intensely by Warner Brothers that they had unlimited studio time built into their contract, and, as Garcia put it, when they went into the studio to record their second album, *Anthem of the Sun,* they were free to teach themselves how to make a record.[20] Although Warner Brothers Records wanted them to record songs that might be played on the radio, the band produced something closer to a single, seamless piece. As sound engineer Dan Healy explained, "It was our intention to create a complete trip."[21] The Dead did not set out with the same ambitions as most of the young men who formed rock groups in the wake of the Beatles. They were not focused on fame, money, or topping the pop charts. The Dead's utter rejection of commercial standards meant that they would not have a hit single or a platinum album until 1987, and the four albums they released in the 1960s failed to chart any higher than number 64.

The San Francisco sound was the product of more than resistance to the industry but of a whole array of alternative institutions, largely in place before the heavy influx of outsiders in 1967, including Ken Kesey's Acid Tests, Bill Graham's "dances," and the various Digger charities that enabled interdependent musical and cultural innovation. The musicians of San Francisco could embody the counterculture because a counterculture actually existed. The Beats played a significant role in creating the culture out of which these alternatives could develop, and their own institutions, such as City Lights bookstore, must be understood as instrumental in the birth of the next generation's counterculture. Jeff Kisseloff recalls the 1955 reading by Allen Ginsberg of his then unpublished poem "Howl" as the Beats' "coming-out party," and observes, "Ginsberg, along with Gary Snyder, another poet who read that night, provided a direct line from the beats to the hippies when they appeared onstage at the Hippies' coming out party, the Human Be-In, in Golden Gate Park in 1967."[22]

He notes that Ken Kesey, Neal Cassady, and the Merry Pranksters also connect the two movements, but he argues that even the way-out activities of the Beats pale before the Diggers, who combined street theater and anarchistic politics with daring, humor, and mischief. Peter Berg, one of the founders of the Diggers, had already been to college and served in the army before relocating from New York to San Francisco in 1963, where he became involved with what would also be an important countercultural institution, the San Francisco Mime Troupe. It was there that Berg came up with the idea of "guerrilla theater as a weapon in . . . an underground war against repression."[23] The Diggers, according to Berg, represent an extension of guerrilla theater. The name came from the radical Protestant sect in seventeenth-century England known for digging up town greens to plant crops for people without land. The San Francisco group began by giving out free food in Golden Gate Park, and then established a "free store," where people could come and take what they needed. Tie-dyed clothes, perhaps the most famous sartorial representation of the San Francisco counterculture, were invented in the Free Store as a way to make straight clothes "usable to the psychedelic generation."[24]

The Diggers' anarchism is reflected in the intentionally short life span of their projects. They weren't meant to be permanent institutions but to be temporary illustrations of their ideas of freedom and community. Still, during the two years the Diggers were active, their projects did, in fact, serve as countercultural institutions. The same can be said for Ken Kesey's Acid Tests, the Trips Festival, and the Human Be-In. The Dead were unknown outside of Palo Alto, where "they had been eking out a living by playing for the beer drinkers, at jazz joints and the like," until they became the house band for the Acid Tests, the large public parties featuring vats of Kool-Aid spiked with then (1965) legal LSD.[25] But Acid Tests were unlike any gig any band had ever played. According to Jerry Garcia: "The acid test was one of the truly democratic art forms to appear in this century. The audience didn't come to see us. They came to experience something altogether different. So we could play or not. So we had the luxury of being able to experiment freely in a situation which didn't require anything of us. It didn't require that we be good. It didn't require that we repeat a song. It didn't require that we be intelligible on any level. I mean, for a musician that's like carte blanche, you know, that was great fun."[26]

The San Francisco scene, however, depended on somewhat more traditional institutions as well. Frith complains that "the most significant people in the Bay Area turned out to be not musicians, but entrepreneurs," including Bill Graham and *Rolling Stone* publisher Jann Wenner.[27] While this reflects both Frith's dislike of San Francisco music and his Marxist opposition to free enterprise, he is not entirely wrong, especially with regard to Graham. Another legacy of the Mime Troupe, which he served as manager, Graham's first events at the Fillmore Auditorium were benefits for that group. The "dances" that Graham then began to promote there were instrumental in producing the particular character of the San Francisco sound, and they helped to change the practice of rock & roll in the United States. Graham's events were distinctive, not only because of the artwork used to advertise them and the psychedelic ambiance produced by light shows, but also because of their form. The pattern was to combine acts performing in disparate styles. A typical lineup might include a traditional bluesman like Muddy Waters, or a jazz combo, along with two of the local groups. Moreover, the dance setting made the audience much more participants than mere, passive spectators, and some of the traditional distance between performer and audience was dissolved. Whatever the economics of Graham's productions, his dances provided both an effective platform for the San Francisco bands and a center around which the community that supported them could gather more or less routinely.

As Arthur Marwick shows, a new entrepreneurialism in reaction to the conformity and restrictions imposed by corporations was an aspect of the cultural revolution of the 1960s.[28] If in the long run this tendency reinforced the status quo, in the short run, people like Bill Graham paradoxically helped to nurture a utopian vision of radical transformation. But right from start, the political edge of that vision was lost on many who wrote about the scene. For example, according to Tom Wolfe in *The Electric Kool-Aid Acid Test*, perhaps the single most influential account of the moment:

> The Acid Tests were the *epoch* of psychedelic style and practically everything that has gone into it. I don't mean merely that the Pranksters did it first, but, rather, that it all came straight out of the Acid Tests in a direct line leading to the Trips Festival of January 1966. That brought the whole thing full out into the open. "Mixed media" entertainment— . . . light and movie projections, strobes, tapes, rock 'n' roll, black light. "Acid rock"—the sound of the Beatles' *Sergeant Pepper* album and high-vibrato electronic sounds of the Jefferson Airplane, the Mothers of Invention and many other groups—the mothers of it all were the Grateful Dead at the Acid Tests.[29]

Wolfe's account of the Dead's influence is correct, and that particular claim has not been well remembered. But by emphasizing "style" and not mentioning any larger social vision, Wolfe's narrative contributed to the long-term misunderstanding of the band and the counterculture. Their role as perhaps the most familiar faces of the San Francisco scene gave the Dead much more notoriety than did their records. As a result, the Grateful Dead were mentioned in a hit song, "Hair" (recorded by the Cowsills in 1969), long before they had one of their own.

The Dead were always the band most associated with the hippies and the counterculture. According to Mickey Hart, the association is accurate: "The whole social thing was exploding, and we were just the soundtrack to it."[30] As

Simon Frith asserted in 1972 from a more traditional leftist perspective, "The Dead weren't just the source of good trips. They symbolized the original hippie ideals, the naïve attempts to combine total individual freedom with a loving community. Their music achieved the dream. It allowed each musician an individual freedom based on a complete instrumental trust."[31]

The political import of rock & roll is misunderstood if we focus mainly on protest songs, which were relatively few in number. Todd Gitlin makes the case that Barry McGuire's 1965 hit "Eve of Destruction" marked an important moment in the growth of the New Left, but it is hard to name another rock protest song that had a major impact.[32] As we saw in chapter 4, Dylan retained his political significance long after he stopped singing explicitly political songs. Most rock music did not deal explicitly with political issues, and references to drugs were by far the most controversial aspect of 1960s rock at the time. Among the San Francisco bands that emerged with the Dead, only Country Joe and the Fish were known mainly for their politics. Their song "Feelin' Like I'm Fixin' to Die" became the anthem of the antiwar movement, though it was never a hit record. The Jefferson Airplane never wrote anything quite so topical as this, but their music did have a political edge as early as *Surrealistic Pillow* (1967), where "Somebody to Love" (the band's first hit single) begins, "When the truth is found to be lies / And all the joy within you dies." The Airplane's recording of Jesse Colin Young's "Let's Get Together" gave voice to the sixties utopian vision and only slightly less explicitly to the idea of youth solidarity. They engaged openly in the identity politics of the youth culture with their album *Crown of Creation* (1968). The title track is an attack on the older generation, who thought of themselves as the "crown of creation." The song includes the chorus, "In loyalty to their kind / They cannot tolerate our minds / In loyalty to our kind / We cannot tolerate their obstruction."

"Crown of Creation" doesn't go much further than Dylan had earlier in the decade, when he had warned the older generation not to get in the way of change. The events of 1968—in Paris and Prague, at Columbia University and the Democratic National Convention in Chicago, and in the streets of many American cities after Martin Luther King was assassinated—made violent confrontation commonplace but also offered the hope that radical change was possible. The Airplane's next album, *Volunteers* (1969), is a response to this new political situation from the perspective of youth politics, and as such it lacks much in the way of a justification for revolution. The first track,

"We Can Be Together," begins as if it were a rewriting of Young's song, changing the inclusive "people" to an indefinite "we" who oppose the system, but it's no longer love that is being offered as the answer: "We are all outlaws in the eyes of America / In order to survive we steal cheat lie forge fuck hide and deal." The lyrics later identify private property as "our" target and assert "we are forces of chaos and anarchy," while the chorus of the song includes the line "Up against the wall."

This outlaw stance did fit the Dead; the confrontational version adopted by the Airplane did not. As lyricist Robert Hunter explained, "When Jefferson Airplane came up with that idea, 'up against the wall,' I was against them. It may have been true, but look at the results: blood in the streets. . . . There's a better way. There has to be education, and the education has to come from the poets and musicians, because it has to touch the heart rather than the intellect, it has to get there deeply. . . . That was a conscious decision."[33] Garcia expressed a similar sentiment in 1970: "On the West Coast it's already so crazy you can't believe it, with courtroom bombings and all that going on, . . . But . . . that isn't it—fighting and hassling and bloodletting and killings and all that shit; that ain't it. Whatever life's about, that's not it."[34]

The Airplane, of course, didn't really support violence, either. They were a much more commercial group than the Dead, having top 40 hits beginning with "Somebody to Love" in 1967. Though the title track of *Volunteers* may sound like a call to arms, it imagines revolution as dancing in the streets. Jerry Garcia sat in on *Volunteers,* and he was joined by the Dead's drummers Bill Kreutzmann and Mickey Hart on Paul Kantner and Grace Slick's Jefferson Starship album *Blows against the Empire* (1970), another project influenced by the New Left. The Dead were smuggled onto the Columbia University campus and played during the student strike in May 1968. According to McNally, the Dead "probably did more benefits than any band ever, and frequently for explicitly political groups, but they would sign nothing. They put their time where their beliefs were, but not their mouths."[35] In his autobiography, *Searching for the Sound,* Phil Lesh makes it clear that he felt their "collective transformation program" to be connected to the antiwar and other movements.

The difference between opposition and imagined transformation is subtle but necessary if we are to make sense of the Dead's place among the many political positions that emerged in the 1960s. If the Airplane imagined revolution—albeit, as a street dance—as the necessary means for social change, the Dead offer the hope of re-creating the social order by living differently. The band exemplified this in their organization, in their economics, and in their relations with their fans. More importantly, as artists the Dead offered a vision of transformation that they sometimes called "alchemy." Before the dawn of modern science, alchemy referred to the attempt to turn base metals such as lead into gold, and it is to the point that an "acid test" is "the metallurgical test for gold."[36] The Dead's alchemy is not the literal belief in magic but a trope. Artistically, the trope provides a way to comprehend what otherwise might seem to be the chaos of the band's work. Socially, it offers hope for transformation in the face of the failure of political confrontation to actually produce a revolution.

It is hard to discuss alchemy without the association to Owsley Stanley's chemistry. Owsley, who also built the band's first sound system and was its financial patron, supplied the band and the Bay Area with LSD. According to McNally, "Owsley's subtle approach to LSD making was unique, and critical to the history of psychedelia, because what he made was an immense quantity of extraordinarily pure LSD. Without him, there simply wouldn't have been enough acid for the psychedelic scene of the Bay Area to have ignited." Owsley was literally a student of alchemy, "having read the Rosicrucians and theosophy, the psychedelic experience made perfect sense to him."[37] At the heart of the psychedelic experience is radically transformed perception; objects seem to metamorphose before one's eyes. The claim made on behalf of this experience was that after having it, one's perception of the world was permanently transformed—not, of course, so radically as when under the influence of LSD but significantly nonetheless. Psychedelia thus could be said to have provided the Dead with an instance of actual transformation, different from, though rooted in, the hallucinatory effects of acid.

Visual Transformations

Although the term "acid rock" became well known, its referent is actually quite hard to pin down. Much of what the bands from the psychedelic scene in the Bay Area produced is generically not very different from the blues, R&B, and rock & roll that preceded it. But if the sound of acid is indistinct, the visual art associated with it is unmistakable. The Dead's early album covers epitomize this style, as did the now famous posters used to advertise concerts at the Fillmore Auditorium and Avalon Ballroom. While all psychedelic

The cover of the Dead's third album, *Aoxomoxoa*, 1969, by noted psychedelic poster artist Rick Griffin. (album cover, Warner Brothers)

visual art attempts to depict the world transformed under the influence of drugs, a more general theme of metamorphosis is sometimes apparent. The cover of the Dead's *Aoxomoxoa* (1969, art by Rick Griffin) is an image that connects death and rebirth. A bright sun shines on what seems to be a land-scape seen from underground through a fish-eye lens in intense, strongly con-trasting colors. On closer inspection the sun turns out to be an egg surrounded by sperm. In the center below the sun, a skull and crossbones are at the same time a penis and testicles, the source of the sun's circle of sperm. Trees and flowers to either side of the skull embody female genitalia or contain fetuses. The cover of *Aoxomoxoa* combines the idea of natural transformation in re-production with Ovid-like metamorphosis.

On later covers, concert posters, and T-shirts the Dead established their own iconography, the most familiar figure of which was a skull. This consistent iconography cannot be found in cover art until the 1972 live album, *Grateful Dead,* where the motif of the skull and roses first appears. Garcia claimed to have been creeped out by the death imagery, which perhaps explains its slow introduction. Yet it was Garcia who inspired the use of such images in the animated sequence that opens the film, *The Grateful Dead* (directed by Jerry Garcia and Leon Gast, 1977). This sequence, created by former *Sesame Street* artist Gary Gutierrez, at one level obviously represents a trip, in this case literalized in the form of a motorcycle journey. The images transform themselves instantaneously, making metamorphosis a central trope of what is not quite a story. At Garcia's request, a major motif is chance, represented most clearly by what might be called a cosmic pinball game. In this segment, a small humanoid figure sits in a spacecraft that shoots pinballs off into space, where they bang around against various bumpers and counters. The balls disappear into black holes before any score can be tallied on the board, where we find the image of Uncle Sam holding a poker hand. The last ball is shot directly at the board and smashes right through it, causing Uncle Sam to morph into a skeleton, who finds himself on the motorcycle in the next segment. As a whole, the animation sequence resembles many Grateful Dead songs, in that it is a fragment of narrative—in this case, parts of the middle, with the beginning and end omitted. "'Jack Straw' (*Europe '72*), by Bob Weir and Robert Hunter, is a good example of the Dead style. There's a story being played out, but it's never quite clear what the plot is. The characters are a couple of desperadoes, but the dialog never says what makes them so desperate."[38]

The Uncle Sam skeleton was Gutierrez's invention, but he took it from an image familiar to Dead fans, of Garcia in an Uncle Sam hat. Moreover, the image resonated with the U.S. bicentennial celebrated in 1976 and fit perfectly with the song that accompanies the largest part of the animation, "U.S. Blues." The song is a rare piece of political commentary that also illustrates perfectly the Dead's characteristic use of American culture. The lyrics begin, "Red and white / Blue suede shoes / I'm Uncle Sam / How do you do?" The yoking together of the flag and Carl Perkins's song tells something about each: that the song is as American as the flag and that the flag is one sign among many that the Dead can reinterpret in their art. The animation shows us an image of blue suede sneakers and, later, what might best be called a psychedelic interpretation of the flag is used as both foreground and background. The second verse suggests an identification between the Dead and

America—as Uncle Sam is said to have "Been hidin' out/In a rock-and-roll band"—and then connects him to P. T. Barnum and Charlie Chan. The real America, the song suggests, is not the one Richard Nixon represented in 1974, when this song was written, but the one represented by the Dead and their countercultural brethren.

Both Americas, however, partake of the same history, represented here by Barnum and Chan. Barnum, of course, was a great showman who, like the Dead and America, assembled a collection of wonders and "freaks" (the counterculture's preferred term for its own members) under the roof of his American Museum. Charlie Chan was, by the 1970s, an obscure character out of 1930s films, to most listeners a name without a clear referent. Those who knew the character might well have been familiar only with a cartoon version on TV from 1972 to 1974 and a poor film revival in 1973. Blue suede shoes, Barnum, and Chan all could be called part of the cultural detritus of America, of which the animation sequence also makes use. For example, there is a TV set that often flashes images of vaguely familiar faces. The motorcycle travels through a sort of "adult entertainment district." Even one of the Dead's own songs is treated as an allusion: we hear only brief bits of "Truckin'" as a radio tuned to some other station. Since "Truckin'" was the closest thing the Dead had had to a hit single at that time, the film seems to consign the band to the same fate as Charlie Chan. Yet, in recycling cultural fragments, the Dead transform and reanimate them by giving them an entirely new context. This is consistent with the way Garcia described his collaboration with lyricist Robert Hunter, as an attempt to rewrite American folk music. Songs like "Casey Jones" or "Cumberland Blues" are alchemical transformations of their well-known predecessors.

The cultural references of the animation sequence are not all matters of trivia. We see a mushroom cloud on the TV screen, reminding us of the great fear under which the Dead's generation grew up and of America's awful gift to human civilization. Eventually, the journey seemingly over, the Uncle Sam skeleton is basking on a raft in a swimming pool. But within seconds, he finds himself in a jail cell populated by many other Uncle Sam skeletons. The cell is guarded by a porcine policeman, and it has a view of an inverted Statue of Liberty from its window. The guard is shocked to find the inmates escaping when the Statue of Liberty smashes into the jail. At that moment Uncle Sam morphs for the last time into a face on the mirror ball above the concert in which the Dead are performing "U.S. Blues."

A word more needs to be said about this song. Its chorus comments on recent changes in the United States and its image. Uncle Sam might once have been basking in the pool under the summer sun, but those days are over, since "Summertime done come and gone." This remark, which is surely a reference to such events as Watergate, defeat in Vietnam, and the recent oil crisis, suggests a band more aware of social and political life than they are usually reputed to have been.

Transformed Space

The Grateful Dead, even disregarding the animation sequence, is an unusual concert film. It is as much about the audience as it is about the band, and it is clearly intended to convey the total experience of a Dead concert, rather than merely what happened onstage. Both this intention—which was articulated by Garcia—and the very fact, as it is generally acknowledged, that a Dead concert is much more than just the band's performance, are indicative of the special character of their concerts. Here, the Grateful Dead's alchemy can, in the experience of its fans, transform a basketball arena into a temple, the site of a quasi-religious ritual of rebirth. As a fan puts it, "Magic happens while the band plays."[39] This radically transformed space is built on the model of the psychedelic trip, but it also corresponds to the more traditional transformation of space of a church or temple during a religious ceremony. Most rock shows are structured by no more than a list of songs. There is characteristically some attempt to vary tempo and intensity, with the usual design being to build to a fever pitch just before a pseudo-ending and the encores.

Dead concerts, on the contrary, are almost liturgical in their structure. There are two sets, each having a distinct character. The first set is more like the typical rock concert. It consists mainly of distinct songs, which cover the range of styles and tempos typical of the band. There usually are several songs that may be bridged, as in "Not Fade Away" / "Goin' Down the Road," or "China Cat Sunflower" / "I Know You Rider." The second set is often structured cyclically, beginning and ending with the same song. In between, the band moves without significant breaks through a long series of different sorts of improvisations. "Dark Star," "The Other One," and "Drums" are the names the band's recordings give to some of these explorations, which differ each time they are performed. Included in the mix will be some distinct songs, and the set will usually conclude with an up-tempo rocker that will serve as

The Dead in Concert, 1974, not putting on a show: Jerry Garcia, Bob Weir, and Phil Lesh. (courtesy Photofest)

a coda to the cycle. Encores provide further grace notes, and this feature of the concert is perhaps the one most typical of the rock concert.

The Dead's style of performance—both musically and otherwise—is unusual. Most rock concerts are theatrical events, where the musicians attempt to present themselves in a visually interesting way. Almost all bands engage in some kind of dancing or in movement that may be more anarchic than that term would allow. Often rock shows involve elaborate stage props, such as the Rolling Stones' giant inflatable phalluses and blow-up dolls. The Grateful Dead perform on a largely unadorned stage, and they hardly move at all. Where most stars engage in at least some stage patter, the Dead seldom say anything more than "thank you" and "good night." The film *The Grateful Dead* demonstrates the degree to which the band's performance is not theatrical, by not presenting shots of the band from the audience's perspective, and by seldom giving a view of the full stage from any angle. Given this minimalism, one can conclude that audiences for the Dead find the music more important than do typical rock concert audiences, which is why the movie so often gives us close-ups of instruments being played.

Most rock bands strive in concert to reproduce the sound of their records, and audiences often praise the ones who are most successful at this. The best concert performers—and I would include the Rolling Stones, James Brown, and Bruce Springsteen among them—clearly see the concert setting as a place to modify or embellish the songs they record. The Dead do both of those things, but they do much more. The reason there is an entire subculture of "tapers," who record, collect, and trade recordings of Grateful Dead concerts is that no two shows are the same, and not only because the band has never played the same set list twice. No song is ever performed exactly the same way. The band is not just improvising but experimenting and inventing on stage. This makes Dead concerts compelling in a way that few other rock shows are. It also, however, means that the concerts are almost invariably uneven. By trying to make it new each night, the Dead risk doing some of it badly. The most devoted fans didn't seem to mind the lapses, but others, especially professional critics, found botched performances disappointing. Still, there were usually enough successful numbers to redeem most concerts.

It is not just the band's performance that makes a Dead show unique. It is also the audience. Bill Graham said that he became a Dead fan when he noticed that audiences at their shows seemed so happy, distinguishing them from the many other groups whose concerts he had promoted. The film *The Grateful Dead* devotes a great deal of footage to the audience. The choice expressed Garcia's interest in the audience and gives the movie a decidedly different feel from most concert films. Its fidelity to the actual experience of being at a live show, noted by many critics and fans, is largely a result of featuring the audience. While the Dead's music is not usually considered "dance music," during the 1960s, the band most often performed in venues where dancing was common. By the early 1970s, the arenas and stadiums that they played were generally too packed to allow most audience members to dance, but that didn't mean that dancing disappeared entirely. As the film documents, audience members found room to dance on the edges of the crowd. The film often captures them performing elaborate moves reminiscent of modern dance and apparently meant as a kind of interpretation of the music. As one fan describes it, "Everybody was dancing . . . but nobody was dancing with each other," suggesting that everyone was dancing with everyone.[40]

This gives the lie to the idea, propounded by some rock critics, that the Dead concert is a scene in which everyone is too stoned to move.

For many fans, the concert is a kind of family or tribal reunion. The idea of the tribe was important to the Bay Area counterculture, out of which the band emerged in the 1960s. One of the attractions of any rock concert is being together with other fans, but this attraction seems much stronger for Deadheads. They appear to enjoy each other as much as they enjoy the band. One tour-head, a girl whose family had "broken up," followed the band for "the family environment that it provides for me."[41] The Dead were about being together. Individuality was presumed, not proclaimed. This is demonstrated by the fact that there was little of the hierarchy that structured the Stones in the Grateful Dead. Ultimately, Dead concerts were as much about the audience as the band. As Mikal Gilmore has put it, "In every Dead show I saw, there always was a moment when it became plain that the audience's participation in these gatherings—and its sanction of the band—was as much the purpose of the shows as the musical performance. As often as not, I found that moment in the band's reading of Buddy Holly's 'Not Fade Away.' "[42] For Gilmore, the song's chorus "You know our love will not fade away," sung by the band and back to the band by the audience is a statement of their bonds to each other. The Dead's version of this song plays off both Holly's original love song and the Stones' angry cover, but it is transformed, by the band's arrangement and also by the different context of performance.

For the tour-heads, who are the subject of the documentary *Tie-Died*, the entire tour is a magically transformed space. As one such fan interviewed there reports, "My dream is to gather all my friends . . . and celebrate life together. I try to turn all of the places I hang out, like these places, into my church. It's a church in the aspect where all these folks have kind of a common not so much goal but a kind of a destiny following where we want to keep each other happy and find all of the good things in life."[43] The band also understood that their concerts had a spiritual dimension. According to Lesh, "We used to say that every place we played was our church. It was a pretty far-out church, but that was how we felt."[44] As early as 1971, Garcia could say, "The Grateful Dead play at the religious services of the new age."[45]

Musical Alchemy

The Dead's musical alchemy is not exhausted by their improvisation. Some of their performances illustrate alchemy by transforming one song, one melody, into another. The most compelling example is "China Cat Sunflower"/"I Know You Rider." This combination was first performed on July 5, 1969, at the Electric Theater in Chicago, and it was first released on *Europe '72*. It is significant that this combination was never recorded on a studio album. "China Cat Sunflower" was first released on *Aoxomoxoa*, and its lyrics were among those sent by Hunter to the band in 1967 as a kind of "application" that led to his becoming the band's leading lyricist. *Aoxomoxoa* is one of two distinctly psychedelic albums the Dead made in the 1960s (the other is *Anthem of the Sun*), and the music and the lyrics are accurately described as "trippy." "I Know You Rider," unlike, say, "Casey Jones," is an actual folk song that the Dead merely arranged rather than rewrote. The combination of these two songs reflects the two sides of the band's musical and cultural persona, psychedelia and experimentation on the one hand, and country/folk/blues roots on the other. This split was present in the band from the beginning. The band's first incarnation was as Mother McCree's Uptown Jug Champions, a group whose "folk purism" embodied the roots side. The Grateful Dead's eponymous first album (1967) draws heavily on this tradition for its material while adding electric instruments and rock & roll arrangements. As we have seen, *Anthem of the Sun* (1968), took the psychedelic experimentation of their live performances into the studio. *Aoxomoxoa* and *Live Dead* (1969) mark a movement back from the experimental edge by having distinct songs, but they remain strongly psychedelic. Those records were followed by *Working Man's Dead* (1970) and *American Beauty* (1971), which represent a return to country/folk roots performed more traditionally and featuring a new (for the Dead) vocal style, close harmony. One can place "China Cat Sunflower"/"I Know You Rider" as a bridge between these two moments.

"China Cat Sunflower" begins with a distinctive octave figure—octave intervals have a long association with whimsy and disorientation—on the lead guitar followed by a full instrumental intro in what could best be described as a stately tempo. Garcia's vocals duel with his guitar, and the lead line he plays is unmistakably Garcia. While his "noodlings" here do not drift randomly as they seem to, say, on "Dark Star," they are light and ethereal. They avoid, except at strategic moments, familiar blues, R&B, and rock riffs. The lyrics to the song make sense only if one is familiar with the conventions of the acid trip, popularized perhaps most widely in the Beatles' "Lucy in the Sky with Diamonds." Apparently these conventions are quite strong. Hunter reports, "Nobody ever asked him the meaning of this song."[46] Here is the second verse of "China Cat Sunflower":

Krazy Cat peeking through a lace bandanna
like a one-eyed Cheshire
like diamond-eye Jack
A leaf of all colors plays
a golden string fiddle
to a double-*e* waterfall over my back.

"I Know You Rider" belongs to all three of the Dead's roots musics, being best classified as country folk blues. Its lack of copyright or identification with any particular artist marks it as a folk piece. Its lyrics and much of the manner of performance and arrangement seem to derive from country, perhaps especially bluegrass. Its AAB form and chord pattern are blues based, and Garcia's guitar solos are in the style of blues guitarists. The song's first verse, which also serves as a refrain, is the antithesis of Hunter's psychedelic lyrics: A, "I know you rider, gonna miss me when I'm gone"; B, "Gonna miss your baby, from rollin' in your arms." Two of the other verses are equally homey, but the final verse is strange enough to recall "China Cat Sunflower": A, "I wish I were a headlamp on a north bound train"; B, "I'd shine my light through the cool Colorado rain." Still this lyric doesn't stand out especially well, and it doesn't change the general character of the song.

What is most powerful about "China Cat Sunflower" / "I Know You Rider," however, is the fact that the two faces of the Grateful Dead do not appear as anything but organically connected. The yoking of these two songs is the opposite of the modernist's favorite trope, the metaphysical conceit. The alchemy of these performances consists precisely in the difficulty of telling where "China Cat Sunflower" ends and "I Know You Rider" begins. Since the songs are so different, this obviously is in part a result of certain consistent features to the Dead's treatment of both of them. The most consistent of those features is the relation of the instrumental lead—usually Garcia's guitar, though at least at one point Keith Godchaux's piano—to the layered polyrhythms behind it and the vocals with which it interacts as call and response. In fact, the studio version of "China Cat Sunflower" includes a background vocal response to the lead vocalist in the form of the words "China Cat." The musical simplicity of this device together with a sort of bubblegum "toy organ" part give the studio version a stronger pop feel. The complexity of the live version pushes it toward jazz.

There are three verses to "China Cat Sunflower," with an instrumental break following each. The instrumentals last longer as the song progresses, the first break being longer than the intro, the second break longer than the first. This pattern establishes an expectation that there will be a fourth verse, but what we will get instead is "I Know You Rider." Moreover, the instrumental pattern of the breaks themselves prefigures the larger transformation. Each moves from Garcia's improvisation on the song's melody to a foregrounded chord change in the rhythm section. The final improvisation wanders far from the original melody, but not so far that we cannot imagine—and in fact, if we are unfamiliar with the track, probably expect—the song to return to that melody. This is the characteristic pattern of jazz improvisation, and it is a pattern that the Dead themselves frequently used. What is surprising and pleasing in the return of the original is that, having been led away, we hear the original anew, but we also experience a powerful sense of closure. We have come home.

"China Cat Sunflower," unlike most popular songs, is open both lyrically and musically. The lyrics don't tell a story, don't make an argument, don't go anywhere. The music, though it is rooted in a melodic line, changes in its presentation in each verse. There is little repetition here. What the final improvisation does is take us permanently away from, not only the melody of "China Cat Sunflower," but the entire musical package. And yet the mutation is so subtle that even familiar listeners may still be surprised when the band begins to sing "I Know You Rider." That song is, like most folk and blues numbers, based on repetition, not only in the lyrics and melody of the song itself, but in the very choice to perform what is legally a "traditional" rather than authored composition. It is no coincidence that the Dead's transformation moves from the experimentation of "China Cat Sunflower" to the familiar pattern of "I Know You Rider." The Dead's song brings us back to our roots; it takes us home—down home, we might say—just as surely as a typical jazz improvisation. The movement to "I Know You Rider" suggests that the psychedelia of the first song is but a brief "trip" that will safely end, not where it started, but where "we"—the band and its audience—regard as our home. Thus the performance of this pairing is musically reassuring, not revolutionary. The transformation of "China Cat Sunflower" into "I Know You Rider" is the Dead's project in miniature, an alchemy that makes one thing become its opposite before our very ears, a musical shamanism.

Business

The Dead's art embodied the idea of transformation, and their way of living also modeled it. While they became extraordinarily successful, they began without the ambitions that typically drove many young men who formed bands. The band itself was democratically organized. It didn't have a leader or a front man, as Mick Jagger was for the Rolling Stones. Even after the band's economic success, its members were never known for an extravagant lifestyle or for conspicuous consumption.

What distinguishes the Dead from the Stones is that for the former, accumulation was not an end in itself. One of the chief narrative threads of the Stones' history was their quest for financial success; the Dead, however, were financial failures throughout most of their career. According to Blair Jackson, Garcia cared so little about money that when he started to earn more of it from his multiple endeavors in the early 1970s, he stuffed checks in the glove compartment of his car and forgot about them.[47] One of the things that defined the Dead through their first decade was their desire to play for free. Lesh laments "that the institution of the spontaneous free concert has fallen prey to economic realities" and calls it "one of the most satisfying manifestations of our collective transformation program."[48] The Dead's free concerts were what impressed Eric Clapton most about the San Francisco scene: "Never heard of anyone doing that before. . . . There is this incredible thing that the musical people seem to have toward their audience. They want to give."[49] The same impulse is reflected in the band's unusual policy of allowing audience members to tape their concerts. Where most other rock stars treated their performances as intellectual property in need of protection, the Dead shared that property with their fans.

The Dead started out as a commune. They famously shared a house at 710 Ashbury Street, and even if they did so "without ideology," the image of the band and their friends on the steps of the place became one of the enduring images of 1960s communal living.[50] When the band could afford separate residences, they stopped living together, but communal practices continued. Although Jerry Garcia was publicly perceived to be the leader of the Grateful Dead, he always resisted playing that role—sometimes leaving the band directionless as a result. The band itself lacked a hierarchical organization, and

The Dead lived together in a commune at 710 Ashbury in 1967, not in country estates like the Stones. (Baron Wolman, used by permission)

from very early on it was described as a "family." The family included not only the performers but also the entire supporting cast and numerous significant others. In a striking contrast with the Stones, there was no sense that these others were part of an "entourage." They were the band's helpers and supporters, not a bunch of hangers-on. The Grateful Dead are the only rock band I can think of who could have been published in a "family album," as Jerilyn Lee Brandelius did in 1989.[51]

By the mid-1970s, however, the Grateful Dead founded their own record label and became a corporation. While the record venture was a financial failure, the band became among the most financially successful acts of the

1980s and '90s. In 1994, the last full year of their existence, they earned more than $50 million, 80 percent of which came from ticket sales. The Dead were the first major rock act to earn the bulk of their income from live performances rather than record sales. But they also made money by marketing and licensing Dead merchandise and by selling production services to other bands. Still the Dead were not your garden-variety capitalists. *Rolling Stone* reported soon after Garcia's death that the Dead's organization was downsizing, eliminating something like a third of its employees and putting the rest on half salary. This makes the Dead seem all the more like IBM or AT&T, but the reasons for the Dead's downsizing were different. " 'There was no money,' says an inside source who requested anonymity. 'That's the way the Grateful Dead work. They felt very strongly in sharing what they had. We all got bonuses at the end of a tour, and we have an incredible health plan and wonderful profit-sharing. You know Joe the schmo who works from paycheck to paycheck? They were counting on the [canceled fall] tour, that's what they were going to live off of. It's always been that way.' "[52]

What this suggests is that although the Dead sold their performances and merchandise as commodities, they did not treat the surplus value they realized from this practice as capital. We don't know how individual band members used their income, but the organization apparently returned much of the surplus to its employees. This looks like capitalism with a human face, since in this system workers are not exploited to the degree that they typically are, but it is not really capitalism at all. The Dead effectively exchanged the profits they realized for use values, for tangible goods and pleasures, and did not hold them to make even more profits. If the owners and management of most corporations behaved this way, we would have a different economic order.

The Dead also gave sizable chunks of their money to charity. In 1984, they created the Rex Foundation, whose grants between that year and 1995 totaled $7,180,261. Characteristically, the foundation had neither an endowment nor anything but the most minimal staff. Grants were decided based on the recommendations of an unpaid board. Though the foundation's giving had to be radically curtailed after Garcia's death, when the band's income dried up, it continues today. While some of the beneficiaries of the foundation reflect the Dead's left-leaning views, its giving strategy was not ideologically driven. Rather, the list of beneficiaries is quite eclectic; it includes many that can only be called pure charities, such as disaster relief funds of the Red

Cross and Salvation Army, and organizations that serve the poor, such as eye clinics in India and the Haight-Ashbury Free Clinic. The establishment of the foundation suggests a degree of social responsibility atypical among rock musicians.

This leads us back to George Will and his charges that the band promoted irresponsibility, permissiveness, and opposition to "bourgeois" values. It may be that Will didn't really know anything about the Dead, but I suspect that his real opposition to them is specifically to their failure to behave as proper capitalists or to sufficiently endorse consumerism. For finally capitalism doesn't demand repression; in recent years—at least until the current economic crisis—it demanded that the majority of the population spend their last dimes in order to keep capital accumulating. Rather, capitalism demands exploitation. If capitalists stop exploiting workers and accumulating wealth, the system will stop. Exploitation is the bourgeois value on which capitalist society depends. The Dead refused to exploit anyone, and thus they represent an alternative to the world the bourgeoisie made. But that alternative is not entirely at odds with the values of middle-class Americans. As David Gans puts it, "I think that the Grateful Dead embody the real American Dream. Not the materialistic American Dream of a house in the suburbs and a lawn of your own, and you know the sort of bogus consumer version of that. I think the Grateful Dead embody the real American Dream of self-determination. They created a culture, they created a music, they created a business entity among themselves, and they did so in a way that respected every individual in the band and the people around them."[53]

CHAPTER SEVEN

JONI MITCHELL

The Singer-Songwriter and the Confessional Persona

Why has Bob [Dylan] been so thoroughly canonized and Joni so condescended to over the years? Maybe, in part, because when Joni was uppity, she was considered a bitch, and the media retaliated. From day one, however, Bob could be as uppity as he wanted, and the great mammoth rock press lauded his behavior as rebellious, clever, renegade and punkishly cool. Maybe it's also because Bob's songs are inherently more masculine (go figure) and have therefore been viewed as more universal, while Joni's writing, which has a more feminine perspective, is put in a box labeled "girl stuff."

Ani DiFranco

The women's movement that represented American feminism's second wave found relatively little expression in rock & roll, Aretha Franklin's recording of "Respect" notwithstanding. Joni Mitchell's emergence as "rock's leading lady" in the early 1970s shows how the movement did impact popular music. As a singer-songwriter and as a women's artist, Mitchell represents two new dimensions of rock stardom. Mitchell certainly had a significant male audience, but she became known as a performer who expressed a distinctly female perspective. Mitchell has long rejected the label "feminist," but her stardom needs to be understood in the context of the women's movement's influence and the changes in consciousness and behavior that it helped to foster. Mitchell's songs illustrate the notion that the personal is the political by the way in which they deal with the power dynamics of intimate relationships.

Mitchell's success also demonstrated that a singer-songwriter could become a rock star, and her confessional lyrics gave an added dimension to the tension between persona and private self. While critics such as Lester Bangs influentially attacked the singer-songwriters as the antithesis of rock & roll, it can be argued that rock & roll was the practice in which the singer as songwriter first emerged with Chuck Berry and then the Beatles.[1] But as a distinct kind of performer, the singer-songwriter is a creature of the early 1970s, when performers such as James Taylor, Carole King, Carly Simon, Jackson Browne, and Mitchell herself began to perform their own songs.[2] Taylor and Mitchell in particular were described as "confessional" songwriters by association with the then influential school of poetry that included Robert Lowell, Sylvia Plath, and Anne Sexton. Although Mitchell has denied that she was influenced by the confessional poets, in many respects the term better describes her work than it does the poetry. Mitchell's success at creating a sense of direct address to the listener defined her persona. This represented another modification of stardom, where the intimacy that fans had imagined they might have with the person behind the persona is now offered as integral to the persona itself. Mitchell's confessional persona may have made it more difficult for her audience to accept her transformations as she moved away from the confessional mode beginning in the later 1970s.

The pop singer Jewel suggested in 2005 that Joni Mitchell was more an icon than a star, because "she is quite unknown to a lot of people."[3] I think Mitchell remains a star, but it is true that she has not had a commercial hit album or song since 1975 (when *The Hissing of Summer Lawns* reached number 4 on the *Billboard* chart). Whatever her current status, in the 1970s she was a major star, "Rock 'n' Roll's Leading Lady," as *Time* put it.[4] And if we can agree that she is an icon, what does she represent? When David Wild interviewed Mitchell in 1991, it was all too clear to both her and her interviewer that she was, as she said, "Spokesperson for a Generation" and "That Woodstock Girl."[5]

While those associations remain, they are no longer quite so obvious, and we are now able to see that Mitchell's cultural significance is much more interesting and complex. The title of Sheila Weller's 2008 triple biography, *Girls Like Us: Carole King, Joni Mitchell, Carly Simon—and the Journey of a Generation*, suggests one way in which the generational association has become more nuanced. In Weller's formulation, she represents the journey not of an entire generation but of the girls of that generation.[6] This view is supported by historian Judy Kutulas, who argues that the three women represented an alternative to traditional expectations of love and marriage that fused free love, the counterculture, and second-wave feminism. These performers created songs where "the woman was the subject, not the object, modeling her own sexuality: her feelings, her delight, her satisfaction."[7] It's not just that she is a woman—though there are precious few female rock icons—but that she stood for women, not in an overtly political sense, but rather in the world her songs depict. Mitchell clearly had male fans; she is, though, an icon more for women than men. Unlike Janis Joplin and many other female singers who seemed to present themselves mainly for men, Mitchell developed a multidimensional and conflicted persona that allowed her to build such a powerful identification among her female fans. Although her gendered appeal may be the reason that to this day Joni Mitchell has not received the recognition she deserves from a rock press still dominated by male writers, she nevertheless succeeded in providing rock & roll with a woman's voice and vision.

Mitchell has often rejected the idea that she is a feminist, saying in 1991, for example, "That's too divisional for me."[8] But that should not lead us to discount her pathbreaking role or her significance as a political figure. Her rejection of feminism is of a piece with Dylan's abjuration of "finger-pointing songs" and the Grateful Dead's opposition to "politics." As Ani DiFranco has explained, "She is such a notable feminist in terms of her own life."[9] DiFranco notes that Mitchell has retained control of the publishing rights to her songs and that she has had complete artistic control of her albums. In other words, Mitchell insisted on retaining power over her own life in a way that women (and many men) in the music industry often have not. She famously refused to marry Graham Nash, then the man she was describing as the love of her life, because she feared having to sacrifice her artistic goals to play the role of helpmeet and homemaker. She became the first woman in popular music to be recognized as an artist in the full sense of that term. She rose to popularity at a time when women were still primarily singers of other people's songs and who were marketed almost exclusively on their sex appeal. Though Mitchell undeniably had the latter, it was not what made people buy her records or love her songs. Whatever Mitchell's stated views of feminism, what she represents more than any other performer of her era is the new prominence of women's perspectives in cultural and political life.

The Emergence of the Singer-Songwriter

Joni Mitchell was able to become a rock star without conforming to any preconceived notions of what rock or stars should be. She adopted and adapted folk, pop, jazz, and rock styles, carrying all of them off convincingly. One could argue that Mitchell exemplifies the way rock absorbed other practices, the '60s folk scene out of which she emerged being almost completely absorbed by rock by 1970. But her career also reveals the degree of resistance that rock has often shown to musical innovation. Her work with jazz great Charles Mingus, for example, was rejected by rock critics and audiences. It is to take nothing away from her originality and her achievement to suggest that Mitchell's success owes something to the phenomenon of the singer-songwriter, the name that rock culture gave to performers like Mitchell, Leonard Cohen, James Taylor, and Jackson Browne. It was the emergence of this category that allowed Mitchell's distinctive persona to develop and her music to find a popular audience.[10]

Writing about singer-songwriters in general and Joni Mitchell in particular poses an interesting challenge in a book about rock stardom. For one thing, such performers exist at the most remote extreme from those such as David Bowie and Brian Ferry, who flaunt the artificiality of their personas, the singer-songwriters' appeal resting on their convincing us that we as listeners are being given access to their very souls. As a result, singer-songwriters may seem to lack star personas altogether or to manifest ones that are indistinguishable from their private selves. It is one of my tasks to show how this experience of direct address is produced; my assumption is that the Joni Mitchell the songs reveal is as much a performed role as is Mick Jagger's, Bob Dylan's, or even Brian Ferry's, and that would be true regardless of the singer's intentions. Secondly, there is the long-standing objection to treating singer-songwriters as rock & rollers; they often have been relegated to the margins of its history—as in *The Rolling Stone Illustrated History of Rock & Roll*, where no singer-songwriter gets his or her own chapter. Those critics who championed rock & roll purism see the singer-songwriters as representing something like the nadir of "rock," the bastardized form that they see as emerging in the 1960s.

Surely the strongest statement of this view is offered by Lester Bangs in "James Taylor Marked for Death."[11] There was more, I think, to Bangs's condemnation than aesthetics, however. Such critics identified rock & roll with a particular version of masculinity that Taylor's songs didn't fit. He was too sensitive, too vulnerable, and not angry. Joni Mitchell and other female singer-songwriters also suffered under this macho aesthetic, but they weren't as likely to be so viciously attacked. They were, after all, only women, and what more could one expect? After the moment of punk in the mid-1970s, the anti-singer-songwriter hysteria declined, but the critics of that moment had left their mark. Singer-songwriters are still often written out of rock history. The truth is that the singer-songwriters of the late 1960s and early 1970s reflect the development of forms and styles that were nurtured and practiced in rock & roll rather than in folk or pop. The singer-songwriters, in other words, are part of rock & roll as a cultural practice and represent one of its most important aesthetic outgrowths.

Of course, historians and critics of rock & roll have always made an exception for one singer-songwriter, Dylan. As Dave Marsh observes, "The *singer-songwriter* archetype was Bob Dylan, but Dylan was so changeable that the reference was confusing."[12] I would argue that Dylan only became a singer-songwriter after Taylor and Mitchell had created the role. I mean this in two senses. One is that Dylan couldn't be perceived as a singer-songwriter until the category was created. Before that Dylan existed in a class by himself, and there is a sense in which he still does. Secondly, Dylan's work prior to *Blood on the Tracks*—his great contribution to confessional songwriting—did not in the main depend on the sense of direct address that defines the singer-songwriter. Dylan's very early work is folk, and folk derives its authority from the claim to represent "the people" rather than the isolated self. Dylan's songs were heard as public music and not private revelation, even though as early as "It's All Over Now, Baby Blue," he was writing songs that were rooted in his private experience. There are detailed autobiographical references in several songs on *Another Side of Bob Dylan,* and Joni Mitchell has said that she was inspired by the directness of "Positively Fourth Street," Dylan's screed against the folk community.[13] Despite this, Dylan continued to be imagined as the "voice of a generation" and not as a tortured soul. This has a great deal to do with the style of his lyrics and music, which do not often suggest vulnerability. Moreover, beginning with songs like "Chimes of Freedom," Dylan gives us virtually the opposite of direct address. We get instead heavily coded lyrics that disguise much more than they reveal.

But if Dylan only belatedly took up the singer-songwriter mode, he was indispensable to its emergence. That may seem obvious, but so too are Elvis and the Beatles, Chuck Berry and Little Richard. Prior to Elvis, popular music of most genres—some kinds of jazz were exceptions—assumed that the performer was acting as a medium for the song, a product either of a professional songwriter or of tradition. The song was not understood as the personal expression of the singer; that expression was present only in the performance. The best a great interpreter of songs might do was to become identified with certain songs. Frank Sinatra did this more frequently than anyone else of the prerock era, but his songs were a glossy surface. They were defined by his vocal style, but they helped to define the larger style, perhaps even a lifestyle, that Sinatra embodied. "My Way" tells us of the singer's insistence on doing it his way, but it doesn't give us a clue what that way is. To mention another extreme, Woody Guthrie was a singer who wrote most of the songs he performed, but his lyrics imitate the public and traditional forms of folk, while his music depended heavily on folk tunes. A great deal more of Woody's personality is revealed in his prose and his drawings than in his songs.

Elvis, like Sinatra, was an interpreter of other people's music. The difference, however, is that Elvis did not record standards, songs that other people commonly interpreted. The songs for which Elvis came to be known were not merely identified with him. They came to seem as if he had written them, as if they were his personal expression. It doesn't matter that Big Mama Thornton had already released a recording of Leiber and Stoller's "Hound Dog." Elvis's recording and television performances of it made the song his just as surely as if he had written it. More importantly, Sinatra and the other singers of the swing era came off as self-conscious stylists, while Elvis appeared to be revealing his inner core by the intensity of his singing and dancing.

Prior to the Beatles, most rock & roll recording followed the pattern of pop, in that singers usually recorded the work of professional songwriters. By recording mainly their own compositions, the Beatles set a new pattern for the rock & roll of the 1960s. However, the Beatles were not rock & roll's first auteurs. Carl Perkins, Little Richard, Bo Diddley, Buddy Holly, and others recorded their own songs, but Chuck Berry is perhaps the most important 1950s precursor of the singer-songwriters. This is true in spite of the musical dissimilarities, for Berry's music, lyrics, and performances were all distinctively his own. Like the other rock & roll songs of his era, Berry's lyrics do not depend on the convention of direct address. In fact, what is probably his most personal song, "Brown-Eyed Handsome Man," is indirect in numerous ways. Though it is likely that this is a song about Berry himself, it is sung in the third person. And, while the protagonist is described as brown-eyed, this is clearly a reference to his race. The song thus celebrated black pride long before most popular music would begin to deal with such matters. The point here is not that Berry invented the conventions of the singer-songwriter style but that he represented a significant change in expectations of popular singers. Berry was not just a performer; he was an artist expressing himself in all of the various media in which he worked.

After the Beatles, performers who did not write their own songs were suspect, and, as we have seen, after Dylan, popular singers were regarded as genuine artists. But rock & roll's development also featured another trend that would enable the singer-songwriters. From the beginning, rock & roll consisted in a mixture of other styles, not just country & western and R&B, but gospel, Tin Pan Alley pop, and jazz, and this is not to mention that country and R&B were (and remain) very much mixed forms themselves. What happened during the 1960s, however, was an opening of rock & roll to influences previously remote from it, while at the same time its original roots were being brought to the surface. Folk, classical, and jazz elements all became significant at various times during the sixties, and all of these new elements set the stage for the singer-songwriters.

The Confessional Mode

The key record for the emergence of the confessional mode is James Taylor's *Sweet Baby James,* and especially the song "Fire and Rain." This is not to say that Taylor was the first of the singer-songwriters. Laura Nyro, Leonard Cohen, and Randy Newman had all released significant recordings earlier that were part of the emergence of the singer-songwriter. But it was *Sweet Baby James* that clearly marked a distinctive new mode. Neither Newman nor Nyro had recorded such personal material, and their music and lyrics remained connected to Tin Pan Alley. Cohen's lyrics were personal—he was an early influence on Mitchell—but they were also often obscure and his popularity in the United States was limited. Somewhat like Nyro's *Eli and the Thirteenth Confession, Sweet Baby James* is striking in its musical diversity, with explicit invocations of blues, jazz, folk, and rock & roll, and including a version of the generically ambiguous "Oh Susanna" by Stephen Foster. In another words, in spite of the frequent use of acoustic guitar, the relative softness of the sound, and the foregrounding of an individual singer's own words and music, this was clearly not a folk album. Nor was it folk rock à la the Byrds or Simon and Garfunkel, but another, different remixing of rock & roll's components. More important than its musical innovation, however, was the fact that *Sweet Baby James* was the first record to make confessional songwriting a popular success.

What is remarkable about "Fire and Rain" is the starkness of the pain and despair it reveals. Pop music had long featured laments about lost love, but being pop they seemed to be conventional rather than personal. We can, for example, speculate that Cole Porter's life as a gay man entailed experiences that made him able to give such powerful expression to unrequited love and longing. But that expression did not lead his listeners to conclude that he was writing autobiographically. His songs were understood as expressing universal rather than particular experiences. "Fire and Rain," however, advertises itself as autobiography. Contemporary stories about Taylor report listeners asking if his girlfriend had been killed in a plane crash ("sweet dreams and flying machines in pieces on the ground"), or if he had recently experienced a religious conversion ("won't you look down upon me Jesus"). Yet besides the reference, obscure to most listeners, to Taylor's early band, the Flying Machine, the song does not require the listener to guess the names of those it describes, like a roman à clef. Rather, the sense that we have that this song is autobiographical is conveyed by its manner of performance and lyrical style.

How is this autobiographical effect achieved? In the first place, the song names a specific time that suggests a particular event: "Just yesterday morning they let me know you were gone." The lyrics seem to be telling us about the singer's life, not just about the general experience of loss. Moreover, this song is about loss—not unrequited love—and the effects of loss on a particular psyche. It is not the named woman, Suzanne, who is the cause of the singer's pain. While the exact cause is not named, what is clear is that it is radically beyond the singer's control. This sense of helplessness is a hallmark of the confessional mode, and in this case the events are so overwhelming that they threaten the singer's very survival. Suicide is never named in the song, but its threat exists just over the lyrics' horizon. Extremity is also characteristic of the confessional. To have loved and lost is a conventional experience that doesn't require confession. Suffering of the magnitude described in "Fire and Rain" is not something that previously characterized popular song but rather typified one's private communication with a psychiatrist. The music that accompanies this lament seems plain, but it is plaintive. It punctuates the lyrics but never threatens to displace them in the foreground. The song is presented in slow tempo, the verses sung in an understated, almost reportorial manner, while the chorus is only somewhat more of a wail. This direct manner contributes to our conviction that the song is true. The song seems artless, but therein lies, precisely, its art.

Songs like "Fire and Rain" came to be called "confessional" because they resembled a distinctive body of poetry that emerged in the 1960s. Robert Lowell's *Life Studies,* a book that combines explicitly autobiographical poems with a brief bit of prose autobiography, is usually taken to be the founding document of the movement. Lowell's students Sylvia Plath and Anne Sexton brought the style to a wider audience, Plath's suicide giving added confessional force to her posthumously published *Ariel*. The power of this poetry derived in part from its sharp break with the aesthetics of high modernism, governed as it was by T. S. Eliot's dictum that poetry is an escape from personality. While the modernists were read as tackling the largest philosophical, religious, or formal issues, the confessional poets reported on their private psychological struggles. If modernist aesthetics demanded the fiction of formal distance, another important confessional poet, John Berryman, expressed the confessional credo, when, in an interpretation of Lowell's "Skunk Hour," he asserted, "When Shakespeare said 'two loves have I,' reader, *he was not kidding*."[14] In other words, the confessional poets proclaimed the autographical character of their work.

And yet, it is also worth observing that the critic who first named the movement, M. L. Rosenthal, did not define it in terms of the accuracy of its correspondence to the facts of the author's life nor as a matter of guilt to be expiated. The key issue is the way that the self is presented in the poems, the poet appearing as him- or herself and not in the convention of an invented "speaker."[15] As another literary critic explained after Rosenthal's term had gained wide currency, "A confessional poem would seem to be one in which the writer speaks *to* the reader, telling him, without the mediating presence of imagined event or *persona,* something about his life. . . . The sense of direct speech addressed to an audience is central to confessional writing."[16] Rosenthal's emphasis is on the "self-therapeutic" motive for confession, which he found, in 1960, to be best represented in Robert Lowell's *Life Studies*.[17] Rosenthal praises Lowell's poems in terms very similar to those that will be applied to Joni Mitchell about ten years later: "he does not spare himself in these poems"; "uncompromising honesty"; "audacious intimacy."[18] The critic, however, does not value Lowell's poetry merely on these grounds. He reads them not as self-absorbed but as revealing "the whole maggoty character" of American culture, "which [the poet] feels he carries about in his own person" and thus looking "at the culture through the window of psychological breakdown."[19] Certainly many readers found a similar kind of critique in the poems of Sylvia Plath, which have long been understood as significant feminist statements. At the same time, Rosenthal believes "one implication of what writers like Robert Lowell are doing" is "that their individual lives have profound meaning and worth, and that the therapeutic confession will lead to the realization of these values."[20] This combination of social critique and the affirmation of the meaning of individual experience is also to be found in the work of the singer-songwriters.

Of course, "confessional" has many meanings, and it is doubtless true that, as the idea of confessional poetry became more widely known, the specifics of its use in literary criticism were often lost. As a result, the term has been widely misunderstood in popular usage and by some of the musicians to whom it has been applied. It is not clear whether confessional poetry directly influenced singer-songwriters like James Taylor or Joni Mitchell. The latter, as we will see, has specifically denied that it was an influence. But there were connections at the time that seemed significant even if they were in fact mere coincidence. For example, James Taylor was treated in the same private mental hospital, Mc-Clean, as Lowell and Sexton, and all three wrote about the experience, Taylor in "Knocking Around the Zoo." Indeed, the threat of madness that lurks everywhere in confessional poetry also lurks in the background of Taylor's first two albums (although it might be said to lurk a bit like a cartoon monster). This says nothing about Taylor's exposure to the poetry of Lowell or Plath, but it does suggest a context of reception and interpretation for his work.

One element of this context is what we might call a particular experience of adolescence, here characterized not by the rebellion that the Rolling Stones expressed but uncertainty, anxiety, and alienation. At the time, these emotions were widely believed to be typical among later adolescents, and the popularity of existentialist literature—which treated these three states of mind as inherent in the condition of modern humanity—among this group seems at least to confirm their interest in these feelings. Confessional poetry individualized these existentialist themes, and Sylvia Plath's poetry in particular was very popular among older adolescent girls. This same late-high-school and college-age group, but including more males, also made up the core of the singer-songwriters' audience. But even if only a minority of Taylor's listeners had heard of—much less read—confessional poetry, surely this poetry prepared cultural mediators to value and make sense of the songs he and other singer-songwriters wrote. Finally, both phenomena need to be associated with larger cultural ones, including the expanding reach of celebrity that made the private lives of the famous ever more public.

There are important differences between the confessional mode of songwriting and confessional poetry. For one thing, the poetry is rarely as open or direct in its presentation of the self.[21] It retains elements of the complexity

Eliot correctly predicted would define modern verse, so that the reader often has to work to figure out just what the poet is confessing. A related difference is that the extremity of the poetry is often much greater. We don't find any Holocaust imagery in Mitchell, but Plath makes use of it in *Ariel*, in poems like "Lady Lazarus," and suicide, more or less explicitly, is often discussed by her and other confessional poets. Paradoxically, this extremity made the poetry seem radical by comparison to the dominant poetic style that favored understatement, but it would have made a young popular songwriter sound all too immature and typical. We will find such extremity in rock, albeit in a much less serious form, a bit later in the 1970s with Alice Cooper and some heavy metal acts.

Mitchell observed these differences in a 1996 interview with *New York Times* music critic Stephen Holden:

> She heatedly rejects any comparisons of her work to that of women like Sylvia Plath and Anne Sexton. "The only poets who influenced me were Leonard Cohen and Bob Dylan," she insisted. "What always bugged me about poetry in school was the artifice of it. When Dylan wrote, 'You've got a lot of nerve to say you are my friend,' as an opening line, the language was direct and undeniable. As for Plath and Sexton, I'm sorry, but I smell a rat. There was a lot of guile in the work, a lot of posturing. It didn't really get down to the nitty-gritty of the human condition. And there was the suicide-chic aspect."[22]

This analysis would find support from some literary critics, for example, Irving Howe, who criticized Plath for the way she represented a suicide attempt in "Lady Lazarus." He accuses her of "enlarging the magnitude of her act through illegitimate comparisons with the Holocaust" and of "a willed hysteric tone, the forcing of language to make up for an inability to develop the matter."[23] In describing Plath and Sexton as "posturing," Mitchell is claiming greater honesty, and apparently, a more authentic confession. But Mitchell had other objections: "To this day she bridles at the application of the term 'confessional' to her 1970s' songs because to her, confession implies information extracted under duress. The term she prefers is 'penitence of spirit.' "[24] This connotation of "duress" was not one associated with the term in its application to the poetry, where almost the opposite situation was assumed, that the poet was desirous of unburdening him- or herself. In any case, Mitchell has not always been unwilling to use the term. In a 1979 interview she said she "became a confessional poet" because her fans' adoration was "too much to live up to. I thought, 'You don't even know who I am. You want to worship me?' . . . I thought, 'You better know who you're applauding up here.' It was a compulsion to be honest with my audience."[25] The word "compulsion" might be read as an admission that at one time she did believe she was under a kind of self-imposed duress, about which she has since changed her mind.

If we take a confessional poem or song to be defined by "direct speech addressed to an audience" without the mediating presence of "persona," then many of Mitchell's songs seem to fit better than most of the poems that have been called confessional. Indeed, her own statements about her work suggest that such direct expression was her goal. As she said of *Blue,* the most confessional of her albums, "I have, on occasion, sacrificed myself and my own emotional makeup, . . . singing 'I'm selfish and I'm sad' [on 'River'], for instance. We all suffer for our loneliness, but at the time of *Blue,* our pop stars never admitted these things."[26] Indeed, Mitchell does differ from other stars, whether in music or elsewhere, in her willingness to assert that her songs are about herself. Because she asserts their honesty, however, some of her listeners may assume that the meaning of her songs is to be discovered by finding out information that they do not explicitly reveal. This may have encouraged the tendency already prevalent in the public at large to assume that works of art like films or songs must have a one-to-one relationship with specific people. "Thirty years after it was released, her fans still have heated debates . . . equally adamant that the song 'Blue,' for instance, can only have been written about one man: James Taylor/David Blue/Graham Nash/Leonard Cohen, pick a name, any name."[27] But these assumptions reflect a misunderstanding of art in general and the confessional mode in particular. What such artists reveal is not an external cause of the work but emotional states the artist has experienced. In making these emotions available to an audience, the circumstances that gave rise to them are necessarily transformed. *Blue* or any other work is or is not confessional by virtue of the conventions it uses. We experience something as a confession when it takes the form of a confession. Even though the emotions are real and details are taken from life, the songs are necessarily works of art or artifice, that is, fictions.

To call something a fiction is not to say that it is a lie; rather, it is to point out that its meaning exists not in its reference to particular people or events but in its generality of reference. The details of a poem or novel allow us to experience the world of that work as if it were real, but its fictional character allows us to use it as a model, a hypothetical world that we can make our own. Joni Mitchell's songs have mattered to so many people not because of the individuals they may or may not refer to but because they help them make sense of their own lives, to understand their own emotions, or to experience deeply someone else's emotional world. The conviction that songs like "Blue" or "Fire and Rain" do represent particular people and events is part of what defines their authenticity. What's important to understand is that that conviction is produced by the fiction, and not the other way around. We hear honesty because of the style of the language and the music.

One of the most powerful characteristics of Mitchell's persona, then, is honesty. There is, of course, a paradox produced when Mitchell—or, I would argue, any artist—successfully conveys honesty and makes her audience believe that they are being directly addressed. The implication of this belief is that that persona and self are identical, that in other words there is no persona. But even though we may accept that in "River" it is Mitchell herself who is "selfish and sad," we as fans can only add that information to our understanding of the Joni Mitchell star persona, since we cannot know the private person. However, the conviction that the songs are true may encourage many to believe that they can know the real Joni, increasing the "tension between the possibility and impossibility of knowing the authentic individual" and making them look all the harder for the missing information that they hope will relieve it.[28] What such listeners fail to understand is that this tension is a necessary condition of the star system and of fiction.

Joni Mitchell Naked

From the beginning of her career, people have believed that Joni Mitchell was speaking for them. A review of her first album asserted, "This record is a profound expression of I, a woman—I have yet to meet a girl who doesn't feel that Joni speaks for her."[29] Of course, the popularity of many rock songs can be attributed to the idea that the audience felt that those songs expressed their experience. The Stones' "Satisfaction" may be the most compelling example of this. What's remarkable about Joni Mitchell's career is that her audience continued to feel that way after she began to speak directly *to* them.

Blue was the first album of Mitchell's that is definitely confessional and that leaves the more public "folk" mode behind once and for all. Her previous album, *Ladies of the Canyon,* was a mixture of the two modes. Some of the songs, like "The Circle Game," which had been composed earlier, remain in the folk style dominant on her first two albums, *Song to a Seagull* and *Clouds*. What distinguishes the earlier songs as folk is a degree of impersonality that allowed them to be recorded easily by others. "Both Sides Now" was a hit for Judy Collins, but numerous others, including Frank Sinatra and Bing Crosby, recorded it. After *Blue*, Mitchell's new material was much less frequently covered until the 1990s, when younger artists whom she influenced started to record her songs. "Both Sides Now" and "The Circle Game" could be considered philosophical. They describe how life in general is, and they do not detail private experience. The song "Woodstock," also on *Ladies*, is public in a somewhat different way, the celebration of a public event, also something folksingers had long done.[30]

Not surprisingly, Mitchell's folk persona differed from her rock persona, which emerged in the early 1970s. One gets some sense of change from the title of a 1974 magazine article, "From Folk Waif to Rock & Roll Lady," though neither "waif" nor "lady" gets the personas in question quite right.[31] Knowing that the article was a review of a live performance helps to explain the use of "waif," since Mitchell's discomfort in front of large crowds did sometimes make her look like a little girl stranded in a strange place. As one report described a 1970 performance in Boston, "Fragile, giggly and shy, she had the most obvious case of nerves I have ever seen in a professional singer. Her ringing soprano cracked with stage fright and her frightened eyes refused to make contact with the audience."[32] Moreover, "waif" conveys the idea of vulnerability, an aspect of her persona that actually became more pronounced after her confessional turn. In her folk mode, however, Mitchell seemed a bit too knowing and a bit too competent for this label to fit. Her image included contradictory elements, as *Rolling Stone* explained in 1969, prior to the release of *Clouds*: "Joni Mitchell is a fresh, incredibly beautiful innocent/experienced girl/woman."[33] Her beauty and her voice made her the object of male fantasies, but these ambiguities and the complexities of her songs suggested that she might be a difficult conquest. This seems to have been the premise of an ad campaign Warner Brothers Records cooked up for *Clouds*. The campaign consisted of a series of narratively related ads in *Rolling Stone*, each headlined with a double entendre such as "Joni Mitchell is 90% virgin," "Joni Mitchell takes forever," and "Joni Mitchell finally comes across."

This campaign was at odds with much of the star's already established persona, however. Mitchell's appearance—tall, thin, with long, straight blonde hair—made her a recognizable type in the popular music scene of the

1960s. Among the other performers it included were Judy Collins, Marianne Faithfull, Mary Travers, and Michelle Phillips. These women were attractive, but their sex appeal was subtly packaged. They weren't presented to the public like movie starlets, or even as artists such as Lesley Gore and Dusty Springfield had been, with elaborate coiffure, makeup, and dress—much less like the Lolitaesque sex kittens common since Madonna pioneered the look in the early 1980s. The associations that went with Mitchell's type include bohemianism, which in the late sixties had become identified with hippiedom. In a *Look* article from 1970, Mitchell is pictured in her southern California home with the caption "Graham and I are talking about marriage."[34] She appears highly domestic, seated at a grand piano in a room full of antiques, her hair pulled back behind her ear. Another photo shows her out in nature, playing the dulcimer "atop a Hollywood hill." The previous year, the *New York Times* ran a story about her relationship with Graham Nash, headlined, "In Her House, Love": "It's a lovely house, sunny and friendly and filled with the easygoing spirits of the Laurel Canyon music scene." The hippie theme is carried through in the description of Mitchell's appearance: "With her blond hair in braids, and wearing a peasant blouse and sailor pants, Joni looks younger and less mysterious than one might expect from hearing her songs. Her face, lacking the forcefulness and luminescent quality it takes on when she performs, looks like a forthright farm girl's, with freckled pale skin, watery blue eyes, and prominent teeth and cheekbones." Graham is quoted as saying, "She bakes better pies than Myrtle."[35]

Perhaps it was this image of Mitchell together with the more confessional character of *Ladies of the Canyon* that led Warner Brothers to direct its campaign for that album toward women. It is more of a woman's record, beginning with the title track, which describes three different ladies—Mitchell's neighbors, presumably—in their domestic spaces. Moreover, there is a shift in the perspective of Mitchell's songs from a more gender-neutral one, in older songs like "Both Sides Now" and "Circle Game," to one more distinctly a woman's in "Conversation," "Willy," and "Rainy Night House." When these songs were first heard, they were unusual simply because they are narrated in a woman's voice. Most of the popular songwriters before and after rock & roll had been men, and even when they wrote songs for women, those songs tended to reflect men's fantasies, hopes, and fears. Mitchell, on the contrary, tells us what particular events are like for her. "Willy is my child, he is my father" is not only obviously a line only a woman could utter of a partner in

Joni as "folk waif" at her Laurel Canyon home, 1968. (Baron Wolman, used by permission)

a heterosexual relationship, but it also gives us a sense of the complexity of that relationship, since neither "child" nor "father" denote the role we expect a lover to play. "Willy" anticipates the songs on *Blue,* in that it represents an inner dialogue, revealing the psychological life of a particular individual "I." Its analytic stance will characterize much of Mitchell's work through *Hejira.* It distinguishes her confessional writing both from poets like Lowell and Plath and from singer-songwriter contemporaries such as Taylor, Carole King, Carly Simon, and Jackson Browne. The poets usually revisit familial relationships, and poets and songwriters alike are more prone to complaint than analysis.

Blue is by now regarded as Mitchell's breakthrough record and her enduring masterpiece. It leaves folk music behind for a style that is closer to cabaret singing (*Stereo Review* called the songs "torch songs") or to "art songs," as *New*

York Times reviewer Dan Heckman would suggest.[36] The change was recognized at the time by Heckman, whose review was headed, "Joni at a Crossroads." Timothy Crouse in *Rolling Stone* gave a quite precise account of it:

> The curious mixture of realism and romance that characterized Joni Mitchell and *Clouds* (with their sort of "instant traditional" style, so reminiscent of Childe ballads) gradually gave way to the more contemporary pop music modern language of *Ladies of the Canyon*. Gone now was the occasionally excessive feyness of "rows and rows [*sic*] of angel hair / And ice cream castles in the air"; in their place was an album that contained six very unromanticized accounts of troubled encounters with men. . . . [*Blue*] is less picturesque and old fashioned sounding than Joni's first two albums. It is also the most focused album.[37]

Like Taylor's "Fire and Rain," the songs on *Blue* seem simple but aren't. "River," for example, begins with an instrumental evocation of "Jingle Bells," itself surely an instance of simplicity. Transposed into a minor key, this music evokes the joy of the season the singer does *not* experience and hence desires a river she "could skate away on." Mitchell's performance on *Blue* is also complex, but its style isn't easily categorized. There is little that one would call rock & roll, and the only obvious example of that style is what I assume is a sort of pseudo-sample on "This Flight Tonight," where we hear a few lines of a girl group record the singer is listening to on her headphones. There are folk elements, including the guitar accompaniment on about half the songs. But the vocalization itself is not the straightforward, sing-along style of Peter, Paul, and Mary or Mitchell's own "The Circle Game." Rather, she bends lyrics and melody for purposes of emotional expression. So, for example, "River" ends with the line "I could skate away on" sung dissonantly, to be echoed at the end of the instrumental coda by a dissonant final cord. The fact that this song, like four others on the album, is recorded with only piano accompaniment also moves it away from folk. The result is that these songs, though their performances are highly crafted, sound to us as if they have not been consciously crafted at all. Mitchell's performance communicates an emotional immediacy that makes us believe that we are experiencing truth rather than art.

If *Blue* were to appear today in the wake of Prozac and the widespread public discussion of depression, it would surely be read as a record of that malady—and Mitchell has in recent years said that she was depressed when she wrote these songs: "Depression can be the sand that makes the pearl.

Most of my best work came out of it."[38] When it appeared in 1971, however, the title connected with "the blues," a much less specific and frightening conception of unhappiness that, of course, has a long history of musical expression. There are no musical blues on *Blue,* but it is an account of different emotional blues. The mood of the record, however, does not, to my ears, sound "doleful," as Timothy White asserts.[39] The songs are never depressing, and they never exhibit unrelieved sadness. Compared to the early James Taylor, the singer of these songs seems positively healthy. It's not suicide that haunts this record, but rather loneliness. The songs don't present a sense of crisis, but of a continuing internal struggle. As a whole, then, the album evokes a complex mixture of emotions.

I don't mean primarily that different songs exhibit different moods but that each of the songs is emotionally complex in itself. None of the songs escapes sorrow and loneliness entirely. In several, however, it does not seem to be the dominant mood and even when it is dominant it is opposed at least by the hope of change. "Carey" and "My Old Man" are songs where sorrow and joy are balanced. "Carey" is a call to celebrate in the face of an impending separation that the singer, for conflicting reasons, desires and not an explicit lament about leaving. "My Old Man" first celebrates the man's presence before it laments his absence, which is temporary and occasional. The song concludes with "My old man / Keeping away my lonesome blues," a positive note that also admits to a condition the singer herself cannot overcome. "All I Want" is darker, but it still contrasts the pain the singer and her lover cause each other with love's ecstasy, "When I think of your kisses / my mind seesaws." Perhaps the most powerful contrast of moods occurs in "A Case of You," which begins "Just before our love got lost" but which proclaims in the chorus:

Oh, you are in my blood like holy wine
You taste so bitter and so sweet
Oh I could drink a case of you, darling
And I would still be on my feet.

One might argue, then, that *Blue* is more marked by ambivalence than by any particular emotion. The album's first song, "All I Want," illustrates the point. "Oh, I hate you some. I hate you some. / I love you some. / Oh I love you when I forget about me." Ambivalence is characteristic of neurotic states, but it is also a product of the work of analysis. Mitchell's work depends heavily on the discourse of, if not psychoanalysis proper, then the therapy of the talking cure in a general sense. Her songs are less like the plaintive wail of Plath than like Lowell's shrewd and often lacerating self-analysis. The Joni Mitchell that gets produced in her recordings often seems less patient than analyst, even if her analysand is most often herself. She thus, unlike Taylor, does not present herself as a victim but as complicit in her own misery. So "River" confesses, "I made my baby cry" and:

> I'm so hard to handle
> I'm selfish and I'm sad
> Now I've gone and lost the best baby
> That I ever had

These lyrics also illustrate another aspect of *Blue*'s construction of a confessional stance in their plainness. Reading the lyrics of some cuts, we would hardly recognize them as songs. Rhyme is often missing or sporadic. Lines are sometimes strung out far beyond what the typical rhythmic pattern would permit. Some of the lyrics are conversations. "A Case of You" begins

> Just before our love got lost you said,
> "I am as constant as a northern star"
> And I said, "Constantly in the darkness
> Where's that at?
> If you want me I'll be in the bar"

Mitchell is able to get away from the conventions of popular song lyrics because of the versatility of her voice, which turns her free verse into songs. Yet, the lyrics wouldn't stand up well as poetry. They are too plain for that. Plath and Sexton confessed their inner demons in a kind of declamatory rhetoric that turned private complaints into public discourse. Mitchell's songs don't make that leap. Although they are not in general so private as to be obscure, the language doesn't sound inflated. One seldom has the sense with Mitchell, as one often does with Dylan, that she is working hard for rhetorical effect. We believe in this voice because it seems natural, seems to be speaking the language in which one might think of one's self in private.

Even *Blue*'s packaging appears designed to convey openness, honesty, and authenticity. The cover art is presented entirely in blue tints. The front cover features a grainy photograph of the singer, more or less face forward, but with only the right side clearly visible. Her eyes are either closed or nearly so.

The cover of *Blue,* 1971: not a glamour photo. (album cover)

Though the image is indistinct, she may be singing into a microphone. While we assume that this is a performance pose, her mouth is closed into a frown. This is not a star image, but the antithesis of the usual glamour treatment given female performers. The cover promises an album that will present the truth about this striking but troubled individual.

Mitchell's future albums will never again reach the level of confessionalism embodied on *Blue.* But I think it can be argued that this album defined her persona more than any other. Future albums will pull back from the edge and they will explore various styles, but they serve only to deepen and complicate the role Mitchell has already carved out for herself. Contemporary accounts often use the word "vulnerable" to describe Mitchell. In a review of a 1972 London concert, *Melody Maker* added, "She's some kind of high priestess, virginal and vulnerable, not to be vilified. . . . It seems almost like heresy to criticize her."[40] This validates Mitchell's observation that she was being worshipped. If she thought the songs on *Blue* would make her fans less wor-shipful, however, she would be disappointed. Since stardom is based on an imaginary personal relationship, the intimacy of that album could only make fans feel more devoted. In fact, Mitchell's audience continued to grow as long as she stayed with the confessional mode.

The *Melody Maker* review also reveals a difficulty posed by Mitchell's per-sona. There is something of a contradiction between "priestess" and "vulner-able," the former conveying power and distance, the latter weakness and ac-cessibility. Moreover, confessing one's failures is not necessarily a sign of weakness, and another reading of *Blue* would be that these songs are about a woman tough enough to survive these trials. Several reviews did find the theme of survival, and *Rolling Stone* would say, "Her appeal is in the subtle texture of her toughness, and her readiness to tell secrets and make obscure and difficult feelings lucid and vocal."[41] The description of Mitchell as "vir-ginal" raises further problems. *Blue*'s lyrics make clear that this is inaccurate; in fact, one attraction of the album is that it tells us about a woman who has lived and loved; she is a somewhat world-weary adult, not an ingénue. The difficulty here may be that the virgin-whore binary to which women have been typically subjected limited the alternatives. As Sheila Whiteley has ar-gued, on *Blue* Mitchell was grappling with "the problems associated with the feminine mystique" and trying to deal with the conflict between the desires for freedom and commitment now that life outside of marriage was imagin-able.[42] The difficulty the culture had in imagining a new role for women might explain the degree to which domesticity seems to figure in stories about Mitchell. *Time* would even have a story about being invited to Joni's house for dinner.[43]

Blue obviously continues the distinctly female perspective we saw in some songs from her previous album. Just as clearly, this meant that Mitch-ell would attract a significant female following—presumably the worshipful ones observed by *Melody Maker*. But these songs don't exclude male listeners, and they are less gender specific than "Willy" or "Conversation." The dilem-mas of romantic love are ones that men share, and the conflict between free-dom and commitment had, until Mitchell's own era, been one experienced mainly by men, because men were the ones whom society permitted to have options other than marriage. Certainly if one judged by male music critics of this era, one would have to say that men not only liked her music but, by and large, seemed to get it. This debate about Mitchell's audience was alive at the time. Loraine Alterman in the *New York Times* articulated the issue precisely in early 1974: "There's no doubt that men as well as women can relate to Mitchell's songs; but because she is a woman her work does have a special meaning to all women who are caught in the basic dilemma of knowing they must realize their own potential at the same they still want to find that one love."[44] *Time* described her as "the reticent feminist who by trial and error has charted the male as well as the female ego."[45] As Mitchell herself put it later, "For a while it was assumed that I was writing women's songs. Then men began to notice that they saw themselves in the songs, too."[46] Indeed, one of the things that Mitchell's work teaches us is that love feels pretty similar on both sides of the gender line.

Still, there is another kind of appeal that Mitchell may have had for male listeners. As the repeated mention of her vulnerability suggests, Mitchell's expressions of pain and loneliness could invite a rescue response. This is most strongly evoked by the album that follows *Blue, For the Roses*. At first this album seems lighter in mood, not least because of its more robust production. *For the Roses* yielded Mitchell her first hit single, "You Turn Me On I'm a Radio," a bouncy country-rock record that is atypical of the album except that it describes a difficult relationship. Its style and the humorous, sexy metaphor of the title make it harder to hear the serious subtext. The singer is issuing an invitation to a man who apparently can take her or leave her. She is waiting for him even if he comes with a dark cloud, and she will come when he whistles. It's not an expression of unconditional love, but it does express a kind of self-abasement not found on *Blue*. And there's plenty more of this, expressed in much less upbeat form. On "Woman of Heart and Mind," she criticizes a faithless lover but nevertheless says she will be there for him. "See You Sometime" is a lament written to a former lover, whom she'd still like to see sometimes. "Blonde in the Bleachers" complains, "You can't hold the hand / Of a Rock 'n' Roll man / Very long." Where the songs on *Blue* depict a singer responsible for her own fate even when it turned out badly, these songs present her as a more passive victim of men or circumstance.

This more familiar feminine role is supported by the album's photography. The cover of *For the Roses* is a color photo of Mitchell seated in front of a woodland lake dressed in what looks like a sort of pioneer garb, suggesting self-sufficiency but also isolation. Inside, there is a long shot of the back of her nude body facing a bay, implying vulnerability and inviting men to rescue her from her loneliness. Mitchell is said to have wondered if the many men who complimented her on the nude photo had listened to the record.[47] Still, the image seems appropriate to the confessional character of Mitchell's songs.

From Triumph to the Prison of Authenticity

It is one thing for a poet to write autobiographically, and another for a rock star. Living under the glare of the media spotlight meant that Mitchell's honesty would not always be praised. In the early 1970s, *Rolling Stone* called her "The Old Lady of the Year" and published a diagram of Mitchell's known and supposed relationships with other musicians.[48] Mitchell was a celebrity almost before she became a star, but, like Jerry Garcia, she has never been comfortable in that role. The desire to escape from the fishbowl had sent her to Europe before she recorded *Blue,* and it would send her to the wilderness of northwest Canada prior to recording *For the Roses.* There she lived alone without electricity for nearly a year, trying to get her head together and get back to the garden. About this time, she claims to have read every work of psychology in the library in an attempt to figure out her own unhappiness. Although she says that she found the books unhelpful, their influence is perhaps to be found on *Court and Spark.*

There the more passive, more vulnerable Mitchell of *For the Roses* was quickly supplanted. *Court and Spark* would be Mitchell's biggest commercial success, and it would yield hit singles, "Help Me" and "Raised on Robbery." Its mood is much more upbeat than *Blue,* but the mood is conveyed far more by the music than by the lyrics, which represent Mitchell at her most analytic. These are, as Loraine Alterman said in reviewing the album, not love songs but "songs about love."[49] The lyrics convey a sense of complex self-reflection, as in this example from "People's Parties":

> I feel like I'm sleeping
> Can you wake me
> You seem to have a broader sensibility
> I'm just living on nerves and feelings
> With a weak and lazy mind
> And coming to people's parties
> Fumbling deaf dumb and blind

The distinctiveness of *Court and Spark* was widely hailed by reviewers who almost to a person understood that these songs were, as Ezra Pound said of poetry, "news that stays news." Their insight into relationships and to human emotions more generally was frequently noted. Because its canvas was bigger than *Blue's*, this album seemed to reflect not just Joni Mitchell's troubles but those of the entire culture, achieving exactly the impact Rosenthal had praised in Lowell's *Life Studies*.

It was not the only great album of self-analysis to be released in the mid-1970s. Bob Dylan's *Blood on the Tracks*, a record of the dissolution of his marriage to Sara Lownds, also came out early the following year. Appearing after the "sexual revolution" of the 1960s, the emergence of second-wave feminism, and other upheavals that called into question traditional patterns, these records were relatively early markers of a new way of thinking about love and courtship that would find its way into self-help books, novels, and films. The new discourse of intimacy would compete with the older discourse of romance, even as it took romantic love as one aspect of the intimate relationships it analyzed.[50] Mitchell's need, as she described it, to "confront" relationships made her someone who did this kind of analysis before it was widely urged upon us.[51]

Not only did *Court and Spark* cement Joni Mitchell's role as popular music's leading analyst of modern love, but it also demonstrated once and for all that she was no longer a folksinger. For the first time, she was recording with a band. The bigger sound itself did not make the singer seem vulnerable, but as Malka Morom observed, "When she went with a band, there was something muscular about it. There was a certain power and confidence that was conveyed through the bass and the drums. And no one had ever heard her sing like this before."[52] Mitchell herself said that she didn't "want to be vulnerable anymore."[53] Corresponding to the new sound and her new role as a front woman, was a new look. Her hair was not so long and not so straight, and she traded her hippie clothes for chic new styles. There were also new vocal styles, ranging from rock ("Raised on Robbery") to jazz (most obvious on her cover of "Twisted"). This new Joni, even though her band had its roots as much in jazz as rock, seemed to put the question of the genre of her music to rest. They mounted a well-received fifty-city national tour, and the show was recorded for a live album, *Miles of Aisles*. She was now being called "Rock and Roll's Leading Lady" and a "Superstar."[54]

Mitchell's next studio album, *The Hissing of Summer Lawns* (1975) represented a new departure, both musically and lyrically. The record explored African music and moved further into jazz, while the lyrics focused on social

JONI MITCHELL HEJIRA

On the cover of *Hejira,* 1976, Joni as artist. (album cover)

commentary. The record reached number 4 on *Billboard,* but the reviews were mixed at best. *Rolling Stone* decided it was the worst album *title* of the year. The reception of *Hissing* suggests the degree to which Mitchell's persona had been fixed by critics and fans alike, who wanted from her more of the same. Critics did recognize that her next album, *Hejira* (1976), was a return to the themes of her previous work. By this point, however, not all of them were happy with that move, either. With punk becoming the critical bandwagon of the moment, Mitchell's musical and lyrical complexity had gone out of favor. English professor Perry Meisel, writing in the *Village Voice,* complained that despite her "reputation as a lyricist, the poetic element in her work has been a growing source of embarrassment to many listeners" and lamented what he called *Hejira*'s "dearth of melody."[55] John Rockwell of the *New York Times* liked the record but still complained of Mitchell's "narcissism" and "self-absorbed introspection."[56] The moment of the rock artist that Dylan had initiated was coming to an end, as the critical establishment embraced primitivism. Even *Blood on the Tracks* had been criticized by Jon Landau for not including a great pop single.[57] If few shared the Lester Bangs aesthetic in 1970, by 1976 a version of it dominated rock writing.

Mitchell has said that the compliment she most appreciated was that she made raceless, genderless music. Unfortunately, American culture in the 1960s and 1970s made it impossible for a star persona to be raceless or genderless, and critics, as she has complained, often ghettoized Mitchell. She noted that she was usually compared only to other female performers, especially singer-songwriters such as Carole King and Carly Simon, who were also selling lots of records in the early 1970s. To be called rock's "Leading Lady" is a somewhat debatable honor, since in 1974 the competition was slim. Mitchell should have been recognized for what she was, the best songwriter of her generation and one of the most important rock stars. Rock & roll, however, was a male-dominated practice, which meant not only that women were treated as second-class performers but also that an aesthetic that privileged supposed masculine qualities would determine the preferences of critics and fans alike. Rock & roll was rough and primitive, not polished and sophisticated, as Mitchell's work increasingly seemed. One advantage Dylan had over Mitchell was that regardless of how complex his lyrics were, his music and singing always had numerous rough edges.

In addition to such stylistic judgments, there were also judgments about the stance the singer took toward the work. Mitchell sings about complicated emotions and a self that is sensitive and ambivalent. Anger is just one emotion among others, and it is more often discussed than expressed. While *Blood on the Tracks* is undoubtedly a confessional album—as Ellen Willis pointed out in a contemporary review, it is the portrait of a man struggling with emotional complexity—its dominant emotion is anger.[58] Moreover, as befits Dylan's masked character, the songs are not direct and open expressions of the singer's feelings or experiences but complex narratives in which we have to work to uncover what they tell us about him. *Blood on the Tracks* is a great album, but Joni Mitchell made at least three that are its equal, and only gender bias can account for the general failure to recognize this.

The decline in Mitchell's popularity after the triumph of *Court and Spark* cannot entirely be ascribed to changes in critical fashion or gender bias. *Hejira* was Mitchell's last confessional album. It was also the first of three records that were recorded with hard-core jazz musicians, including Jaco

Pastorius (whose melodic bass on *Hejira* so befuddled Perry Meisel) and Charles Mingus. On the cover of *Hejira*, Mitchell appears in a black-and-white photo wearing a beret. It is a photo of an artist that also proclaims itself art rather than advertising. Perhaps more than any popular musician of her generation, Mitchell understood herself as an artist, but that understanding and her public persona were at odds. Artists are private and inscrutable; it is the nature of genius not to be understood or available to the public. Popular notions of the artist, which fit Dylan to a tee, did not fit Mitchell's openness and honesty. Her fans believed that they knew her intimately because she had shared intimate secrets with them. We expect the trickster to change shapes; we are disconcerted when our best friend does. The authenticity on which her early 1970s work traded could not support the experimentation of the later years of the decade, which was heard as artifice and pretension. Had her fans who knew her not so believed, they might have been more willing to trust her aesthetic impulses.

Even if Mitchell's popularity declined after the mid-1970s, she has remained an icon, representing, among other things, a woman's ability to remain true to herself and her art. As Ani DiFranco suggests, she continues to be a feminist icon, regardless of her own statements about feminism. Her later work, however, did become less distinctly feminine, as she has discussed in several interviews. She told *Rolling Stone* in 1992, "I came into the business quite feminine. But nobody has had so many battles to wage as me. I had to stand up for my own artistic rights. And it's probably good for my art, ultimately. . . . So over the years I think I've gotten more androgynous—and maybe become an honorary male."[59] This suggests that, although women may not identify as easily with Mitchell as they once did, she still represents for them someone who shattered the glass (or maybe it was more like concrete) ceiling, a star on her own terms.

CHAPTER EIGHT

BRUCE SPRINGSTEEN

Trapped in the Promised Land

By the time he finished the 155 shows of the *Born in the U.S.A.* tour, Bruce Springsteen had become an inescapable icon in American culture.

Eric Alterman

Eric Alterman, a political journalist whose books include, *Why We Are Liberals* and *Kabuki Democracy: The System vs. Barack Obama,* is just one of many commentators—a high percentage of whom normally work on beats other than popular music—who have treated Bruce Springsteen not merely as a cultural icon but as someone who has made a significant contribution to American political discourse: Robert Coles, Jefferson Cowie, David Masciotra, and Louis Masur, among others. These interpreters' books are strong evidence that the Boss is widely understood as standing for more than most rock & rollers. Yet these writers, in the main, are not much interested in his public persona but in reading his lyrics and interpreting his music and performance. I see their work more as contributing to the public persona than interpreting it. My focus here is on what is essential to that persona, and thereby I hope to explain why so many have found so much in Bruce Springsteen.

Rock & roll had always been understood to exist on the margins of the cultural mainstream. It was the music of rebellious youth and disaffected subcultures. Bruce Springsteen's work has carried on this tradition, but paradoxically he is also the best representative of the music's movement from the periphery to the center. The trajectory of his career can be seen as something like the reverse of Bob Dylan's. Springsteen was first called "the new Dylan," largely because of their shared literariness, and especially the predilection for doggerel that characterizes Springsteen's earliest songs. Now the contrasts between the two figures are striking. Dylan began as an explicitly political folksinger who became known for his protest songs. He rather quickly moved into other forms and other personas while retaining much of his former identity. Springsteen began more as a rock & roll aesthete, like the Dylan of *Highway 61 Revisited.* But Springsteen's career became increasingly political, with such projects as the Guthriesque album *The Ghost of Tom Joad* and later

The Rising and *We Shall Overcome: The Seeger Sessions.* While Dylan's embrace of rock & roll widened his audience and lent the music a new seriousness, Springsteen was proclaimed by critics to be rock's future at a time when it seemed to be in decline. Where Dylan's career is marked by radical shifts in persona, Springsteen's consists in relatively subtle reinventions, most of which involve the remaking of his physical appearance, including his very body. And unlike Dylan, Springsteen's career was altered by the advent of MTV and the way in which his music videos helped to vastly increase his popularity at the expense of his heretofore taken-for-granted authenticity.

In the long run, Springsteen replaced Dylan as the most important musical commentator on American society. Indeed, Springsteen surpassed Dylan by writing songs that addressed political issues in the complexity they deserve. And, where Dylan had posed the binary of speaking for someone else or for himself, Springsteen was willing to assert his own identification with the working class and with America. That combination gave him an authority rare in recent American history. This chapter focuses on how the artist's persona has come to embody many of the contradictions that trouble contemporary American culture: being a patriotic American critical of America; being an extraordinarily successful individual who identifies with the working class, the homeless, the dispossessed; being a performer so popular that, despite his efforts to position himself as an outsider, he is perceived to be mainstream. But it's not just Springsteen himself who became mainstream. The acceptance of *The Rising* as a successful commemoration of the tragedy of 9/11 shows that rock & roll itself became central to American culture.

Print Persona

Even before he became a star, Bruce Springsteen was proclaimed to be rock & roll's future. Given his rise to stardom, one cannot assert that that prediction was entirely false, but it was not true in any simple sense, either. Rock in general did not follow Springsteen's lead. Springsteen emerged after rock stars had become both entertainment royalty and genuine artists but also at a point between major movements in rock. The 1960s were over, but punk, new wave, and other innovative aesthetics were yet to come, and even disco was not yet widely heard. One could argue that Jon Landau was speaking for many when he said that he needed the rejuvenation that Springsteen brought to rock & roll.[1] That renewal came, as it would with punk and grunge, from going back to rock's beginnings, not to repeat old formulas, but to remake them with the seriousness of self-conscious art.

Bruce Springsteen's persona has, to an unusual degree, been constructed in print media by critics. While print has played some role in the construction of most rock stars' personas, other media have typically been more important. Elvis Presley's persona developed on television, but Springsteen didn't perform on the tube until 1992, long after his persona was well formed. The persona of the Grateful Dead was constructed mainly in live performance and through news coverage of the San Francisco counterculture. Live performance has also been extremely important in Springsteen's career, but in the beginning the performances were not seen by very many people. They reached the public secondhand through the press. It might be argued that Springsteen was the first rock star whose reputation was made by critics.[2] Although his first two records received respectable reviews in places like *Rolling Stone* and *Crawdaddy!*, it was his live shows that made the critics rave.[3] Moreover, his signing by the legendary John Hammond—discoverer of Billie Holiday, Benny Goodman, and Dylan himself—gave him a pedigree and an imprimatur.

Most important, of course, was Jon Landau's famous proclamation in Boston's *Real Paper* that "I saw rock and roll future and its name is Bruce Springsteen," which set in motion a flurry of press coverage that would include cover stories in both *Time* and *Newsweek*.[4] But while Landau's vision of rock & roll's future—he apparently saw his own future, as well—is familiar to many, the article is even more laudatory than this phrase reveals.[5] The piece begins with autobiography, the story of Landau's well-nigh religious involvement with rock & roll: "Through college, I consumed sound as if it were the staff of life. Others enjoyed drugs, school, travel, adventure. I just liked music: listening to it, playing it, talking about it. If some followed the inspiration of acid, or Zen, or dropping out, I followed the spirit of rock 'n' roll." The faith, however, had started to fade for Landau—until Bruce, that is: "And on a night when I needed to feel young, he made me feel like I was hearing music for the very first time. When his two-hour set ended I could only think, can anyone really be this good; can anyone say this much to me, can rock 'n' roll still speak with this kind of power and glory?"[6] It is to the point that the intonation and rhetoric of the revival preacher have long been part of Springsteen's show and of his songs.

There were other important pre–*Born to Run* pieces by Dave Marsh in *Rolling Stone* and by John Rockwell both there and in the *New York Times*.[7] If we add to this Greil Marcus's review of *Born to Run* and earlier praise from Lester Bangs, we recognize something like unanimous agreement of the rock critic establishment: Springsteen is a star, fit to be ranked with Elvis, the Beatles, the Stones, and so on.[8] All of these stories appeared before the artist had achieved a successful recording career; that is, before he was in fact a star he was already being made into one. The *Time* and *Newsweek* cover stories are important, however, not merely for making the connoisseur's secret known to a mass audience, but also for initiating at this early moment the debate about Springsteen's authenticity.

The critics, of course, had at least by implication declared Bruce the real thing, rescuing him from the cloud that Mike Apple's early selling of the Boss as the "New Dylan" had produced over him. *Time*'s Jay Cocks agreed with them. What he liked about Springsteen was consistent with what Bangs, Marcus, Marsh, and Rockwell liked: "His music is primal, directly in touch with all the impulses of wild humor and glancing melancholy, street tragedy, and punk anarchy that have made rock and roll the distinctive voice of a generation. Springsteen's songs are full of echoes—of Sam Cooke and Elvis Presley, of Chuck Berry, Roy Orbison and Buddy Holly. You can also hear Bob Dylan, Van Morrison, and the Band weaving among Springsteen's elaborate fantasias."[9] The potentially contradictory claims that the artist is both "directly in touch" with what rock represents and that his music is full of references to rock's history are presented as entirely complementary here, and these qualities show why Springsteen can be rock's future: only someone aware of its past can reinvent rock and not merely repeat it. This article of faith among American rock critics distinguishes their judgments from those of British rock critics and the many in each new generation of musicians and fans who have insisted on a need to reject rock's past in the name of the latest style.

The first generation of American rock critics learned their business in the era of the New Criticism, and their tastes favor artists who can be read as complex in the ways that metaphysical poetry or modernist fiction can. The critics often called Springsteen a poet in these early days, and it is not surprising that they would favor an artist to whom words are so important. Nor is it surprising that the critics found and enjoyed the tension and irony in Springsteen's songs or the observation that even in as romantic a song as "Rosalita" Springsteen can include the line "Someday we'll look back on this and it will all seem funny." The real, here, is thus a complicated realm. Authenticity lies not merely in primal expression or being in touch with life in the streets but in having the skills to frame this content appropriately.

It's not unfair to say that all of this was lost on Maureen Orth, the lead writer on *Newsweek*'s cover story; she was not a rock critic but a reporter who had written "sporadically" about the music. Titled "Making of a Rock Star," her *Newsweek* piece focused on what she calls "The Hype" surrounding the artist: "Springsteen has been so heavily praised in the press and so tirelessly promoted by his record company, Columbia, that the publicity about his publicity is now a dominant issue in his career. And some people are asking whether Bruce Springsteen will be the biggest super-star or the biggest hype of the 70s."[10] Ignoring the rock critics' praise of Springsteen, Orth quotes one of the relatively rare negative reviews—by *New York Times* music (not rock) critic Henry Edwards, who called "his melodies either second-hand or undistinguished and his performance tedious" and who asserted that "given such flaws there has to be another important ingredient to [his] success: namely, vigorous promotion."[11] It is worth remembering that high-culture purists had long attributed rock's success to promotion, since it was beyond their ken to understand how the music could be genuinely appealing.

The *Newsweek* story concludes with Springsteen's then manager, Mike Appel "pacing around the Manhattan office once occupied by Dylan's manager, Albert Grossman." Appel is depicted as a kind of raving huckster, quoted as saying things like "'What you have got to do is get the universal factors, to get people to move in the same three or four chords. It's the real thing! Look up America! Look up America!'" Instead of giving the artist the last word, she gives it to his promoter. Her concluding comment locates the irony of Bruce Springsteen not in his work but in his persona: "Hypes are as American as Coca-Cola so perhaps—in one way or another—Bruce Springsteen *is* the Real Thing."[12]

Since then, Springsteen has been the subject of a consistent stream of periodical coverage as well as numerous books. In 1979, only four years after *Born to Run* and the twin cover stories, Dave Marsh published the first of his biographies of the Boss. It took nearly ten years for the first biography of Dylan to appear. Both of Marsh's biographies were best sellers, while more recent books by Eric Alterman and Robert Coles received widespread attention. In these representations, Springsteen could be constructed as a complex character with a nuanced political significance and an at least implicit aesthetic value higher than that of all but a very few popular musicians. But the limits of star construction in print are also suggested by Springsteen's career. In 1984 he became a superstar on the release of *Born in the U.S.A.*, but that increase in popularity had much more to do with music videos and the character of the record itself than it did with print coverage. Print, it seems, can create "cult" stars, but other media make superstars.

The debate over whether Springsteen is the real thing has continued throughout his career, but its terms have changed. I will detail several major shifts, but I begin with this one: in *Time* and *Newsweek* in 1975, there is no suggestion that Springsteen's truth or falsity lies in his representation of the working class—because he is not perceived as doing so. It's not until the release of the album *The River* (1980), and especially its title track, that his lyrics begin to assert a working-class identity. At least through *Born to Run*, Springsteen represented youth more than class. Yet, despite these changes in persona, the politics of his music remain relatively consistent. The problem to which his songs always return is the gap between the American Dream and American reality, and one could argue that no popular musician, including Dylan, has been taken more seriously as a political figure.

Growing Up

From the beginning rock & roll was the music of youth, but it was not primarily music about youth. As Lawrence Grossberg has put it, "If rock is 'about' growing up in the U.S. . . . it does not describe or represent that experience."[13] In fact, one of the attractions of rock & roll to youth was that it seemed to be about concerns that were "adult," especially sex. While Dion may have had a hit with "Teenager in Love" and Frankie Lymon sang with the Teenagers, the more typical stance of rock lyrics was expressed in lines like "she was just seventeen" from the early Beatles hit "I Saw Her Standing There." "(I Can't Get No) Satisfaction" expresses a problem characteristic of adolescent males, but it is sung in the voice of a man. Moreover, when rock songs do adopt an explicitly adolescent perspective, it is expressed directly in the voice of the teenager. In contrast, the songs on Bruce Springsteen's first album, *Greetings from Asbury Park, N.J.* (1973) are about growing up, the title of one of its songs. As that title suggests, it is a reflection on adolescence sung in the voice of one who has lived through it and who continues to identify with that younger self.

Springsteen's depiction of the teenager's world is more self-conscious than the one typical of his 1950s and 1960s rock & roll forebearers. Their music seemed to express the angst and the desire of their young listeners, while his seems to be sung in the voice of a teenager thinking about these issues. Springsteen thus makes explicit what had been the covert political content of rock & roll, generational conflict. The resistance that the music expressed has been directed toward the power of adults. In a 1984 interview, Springsteen states perhaps the basic psychological fact of rock & roll, that children lack power in the face of their parents and society: "When you're young you feel powerless. If you're a child, you're lookin' up at the world; the world is frightening."[14] He holds that this feeling never quite leaves you, but that it reaches a crisis around the age of fifteen or sixteen, when a lot of fantasies are power fantasies. It might be argued that adolescence is the time of life when this sense of powerlessness becomes a central developmental issue. Sexual and physical maturity are signs that the adolescent is entitled to the power that his social standing still denies him. Many of Springsteen's earliest songs— "Spirit in the Night," "Growin' Up," "It's Hard to be a Saint in the City," and "Blinded by the Light" (all from *Greetings from Asbury Park*)—are expressions of powerlessness, the frustration it breeds, and the fantasies of power and dominance it engenders.

The importance of these themes to Springsteen's persona is confirmed by two "autobiographical" narratives incorporated into his performance of "Growin' Up" during a broadcast concert from the Agora Club in Cleveland in 1978. Springsteen introduces the song with a story about getting sent home from Catholic school for "pissing in my desk." The nuns at the school—of whom it is reported only the parents were more afraid than the kids— recommend to the Springsteens that they take their son to see a shrink. On his visit to the doctor, the boy reveals his secret: "I was a teenage werewolf." That revelation leads into the first part of the song, which begins, "I stood stone-like at Midnight suspended in my masquerade / I combed my hair till it was just right and commanded the night brigade." Here the claimed "truth" of the boy's actual experience of powerlessness and rebellion is contrasted with the fantasy of power portrayed in the image of the werewolf and in the song's lyrics.

The second narrative from the Cleveland concert is more revealing, and it illustrates the flip side of the adolescent's mentality, the dream of success. Here a somewhat older Bruce tells about the time his parents, worried about his vocation, sent him to see the parish priest. The parents instruct their son to say that he wants to be a lawyer or an author, but "don't tell him nothin' about that goddamn guitar." The priest decides that the question of Bruce's calling is too difficult for him to handle, and, repeating the same instructions given by the parents, sends Bruce out to find God. E Street Band saxophonist Clarence Clemons knows where to go, but first they have to get Bruce's Rambler painted so that God won't refuse to see him. "There will be guys up there in Eldorados, Lincolns." They drive out to a dark hillside behind a cemetery, and Bruce climbs to the top, where he discovers that "the place is packed." He kneels down and explains to God that his mother wants him to be an author and his father wants him to be a lawyer, but "I got this guitar you see. . . ." Then amid thunder and lightning, a loud voice proclaims, "Let it rock."

This story of divine calling is also a fantasy of victory over parental authority, but here the fantasy is one that might plausibly be realized—which, of course, it already has been, albeit by different means. Success here is achieved despite the parents' advice, but one presumes—and as Springsteen explicitly acknowledges in another version of this story—it is what they wanted for him. Here Springsteen, like James Brown before him, presents himself as the embodiment of the American Dream. Springsteen has explained that he wanted to become a rock musician to meet girls, make tons of money, and change the world a little bit, but this last ambition doesn't become evident until later in his career.[15] The first two are embodied in a song from *The Wild, the Innocent, & the E Street Shuffle* (1973), "Rosalita (Come Out Tonight)," where success is depicted in much the same terms as F. Scott Fitzgerald used: it qualifies him as a suitor to a woman whose parents had previously rejected him. "Rosalita" might be Springsteen's most unambiguously hopeful song. Not only does it celebrate the record company's big advance, but it also presents an image of a place to which the lovers might escape, "a little cafe, where they play guitars all night and all day."

Springsteen's next release, *Born to Run* (1975), was his breakthrough recording. In addition to its critical success, the record was a smash, becoming the first to earn the industry's new platinum award for $1 million in sales. Here the analysis and doggerel of *Greetings* have given way to narrative and plain speech. The songs virtually all tell stories, some of them, such as "Meeting across the River," quite elaborate. Whether in the first or third person, they all invite the listener into a distinctive youth culture. The record asks us to share that culture, to experience its hopes, dreams, thrills, disappointments, and defeats. As Lester Bangs observed, "It could almost be a concept album."[16] But its unity is less conceptual than emotional, and most of the songs are distinctive enough that they tend to make you forget their connection to the others.

One thing that the songs all share is a place, industrial New Jersey towns like Freehold, where Bruce grew up. As rock musician and film scholar Robert Ray noted in 1978, "Springsteen is a regional writer who, when inspired, can transform an ordinary locale into a setting for the most exotic romance. What Faulkner did for the drab farming towns of the Mississippi Delta, Springsteen does for the grimy suburbs of New Jersey—he makes them fascinating."[17] This captures exactly the duality of *Born to Run*, where a very particular and real New Jersey is transformed into a world Springsteen's audience recognized as its own dreamscape. So, as in Faulkner, region is transcended and a new fictional space is created. Also as in Faulkner, the space evoked is not exactly one that most of his listeners had ever actually experienced. Even in 1975, it felt just a bit dated, describing something closer to the 1950s or early 1960s than the mid-1970s. Some of that temporal distance may in fact have been a matter of class, since the subculture described on *Born to Run* is working class. It doesn't describe war protests or drug use but cars and crime. Its denizens are not going to college, and their future is often imagined only in the desire to get away from wherever it is they are.

Springsteen began recording in the same year the film *American Graffiti* (1973) began the 1950s revival that would include the TV series *Happy Days* and *Laverne and Shirley*. While his songs deal with a teenage world similar in some respects to theirs, his use of it is not nostalgic but creative or aesthetic. This world has much in common with that of James Dean and Elvis Presley, but Springsteen's version is more romantic and his characters are more desperate. Actual 1950s teenagers lived at home and went to high school—as did Dean's character in *Rebel without a Cause*. Springsteen's characters are a bit older and are typically depicted on the streets, living in a world of their peers and their desires. They are the product of his reinvention of the previous generation's popular culture, and it was this reinvention that attracted both critics and fans.

Despite the success of *Born to Run*, Springsteen's persona through the period of his first three albums is hard to classify. The failure of the "new Dylan" moniker to take hold and the enormous but nonspecific claims of "rock & roll's future" left Bruce something of a mystery. The pictures on the covers of *The Wild, the Innocent, & the E Street Shuffle* and *Born to Run* make Bruce, with

A bohemian Bruce and Clarence Clemons on the cover of *Born to Run,* 1975. (album cover)

his facial hair, seem vaguely bohemian. He and his band mates don't look the part of the characters they are singing about. One element of this is Clarence Clemons's prominence on the cover of *Born to Run,* since we are unlikely to imagine that the world Springsteen has invented is nonwhite. Yet, at a time when there had been very few integrated bands, Bruce's choice to pair himself with Clarence, as Louis Masur observes, must be read as a "message of racial egalitarianism" and thus, I would argue, is an early indication of the political consciousness that would later emerge.[18] Still, at this point these disjunctions contribute to the sense that the artist is singing about a world to which he knows he does not belong. Beginning with his next album, however, the artist and his material will seem more organic.

A Working-Class Hero

The cover photo on *Darkness on the Edge of Town* announces the album's new direction: we see a clean-shaven Springsteen staring directly out at us against the backdrop of a window covered by closed venetian blinds and bordered by

Darkness on the Edge of Town: adult Bruce, 1978. (album cover)

some faded, flowered wallpaper. The artist is wearing a black jacket (or perhaps a robe) open to expose a white undershirt, his hair is tousled but somewhat shorter than in previous photos, and his expression is neutral, neither smile nor frown. On the reverse, there is a similar photo without the jacket. In each, the harsh lighting produces large shadows behind the subject, contributing to the downbeat mood of the pictures, which seem to be from the mise en scène of television soap opera. This person is no longer a teenager, clearly not having fun, and he could easily be working class.

The cover is appropriate to the mood and milieu of *Darkness,* where the scene of Springsteen's songs shifts from teenagers and their hopes and dreams to the disillusionment and struggles of young adults. Here success becomes more ambiguous, failure more real, and striving and labor have replaced play as the characters' typical activities. As Anthony DeCurtis has put it, "songs like 'Factory' and 'Racing in the Street' portray the lives of the working-class people he had grown up with in stark, existential terms. The choices available are a grim descent into numbness or exultant, if potentially destructive, sensation seeking."[19] For the first time, class begins to emerge from its association with youth to become a significant category on its own. "Factory" is the song most consistently devoted to what it calls "the working life," but many others make reference to working-class jobs. The songs on *Darkness* are not yet critical in the way that "The River" and many later ones will be, but they do describe the world from the point of view of those for whom the American Dream has failed or who are still struggling to realize it.[20]

And yet the dream of success is not lost; rather, it is made both harder to reach and raised to a new, metaphysical level of significance. Success is now identified with the "promised land," a name that carries both biblical and American historical associations. The seventeenth-century Puritans who settled Massachusetts saw their own migration into the wilderness as foretold by the Old Testament promise. Ever since, Americans have repeated versions of this trope—Ronald Reagan used it effectively in his 1980 presidential campaign—which is part of what is meant by the phrase "the American Dream."

While on *Born to Run*, "Thunder Road" could urge, "Oh-oh come take my hand/Riding out tonight to case the promised land," it sounded like the inflated rhetoric of seduction. On *Darkness*, the singer of "Badlands" and "The Promised Land" is philosophizing, not wooing a lover. The songs give us two sides of the same American coin. In the first, he asserts that his faith and hope will raise him above the backbreaking work in the fields of the badlands, where "Poor man wanna be rich,/rich man wanna be king,/And a king ain't satisfied,/till he rules everything." "The Promised Land" also names something that the singer must take on faith, and his manhood seems to depend on the belief in it. This song might be understood as a revolutionary anthem, if it weren't for the fact that sheer power of conviction—rather than political activism—is what it celebrates. The promised land appears at first to be victory in an auto race, but it becomes by the end of the song a vision of violent transformation: "There's a dark cloud rising from the desert floor/I packed my bags and I'm heading straight into the storm/Gonna be a twister to blow everything down/That ain't got the faith to stand its ground." While the anthemic quality of these songs renders the belief they describe heroic, it's not clear that Springsteen means us to identify their attitude with his own. It is clear that he never mistakes present-day America for the Promised Land, but the emotional power of this song tends to sweep this reality aside. Redemption is still possible in leisure or faith or, as "Racing in the Street" puts it, driving to the sea and washing the sins from our hands.

The mood on *Darkness* is considerably less hopeful than it had been on the earlier records, but hope itself seems in many songs to be grounds for belief in change or escape. By *The River* (1980), however, the images of freedom have become much more modest and ordinary: "When I'm out in the street/I talk the way I wanna talk." "Hungry Heart," Springsteen's first top 10 single, makes escape an illusory moment in what turns out to be a vicious circle. The title track offers no escape at all, however, as teenage love turns into a dead-end job and a forced marriage. If the sea once symbolized redemption, the river now represents only a memory that haunts the singer "like a curse." Where "Badlands" and "The Promised Land" proclaimed the power of believing in ones dreams, "The River" asks, "Is a dream a lie if it don't come true/Or is it something worse."

During *The River* tour, Springsteen began performing reggae star Jimmy Cliff's song "Trapped." In Cincinnati, he introduced the song by reporting that while on the European leg of the tour he had learned a lot about America from a book he had happened across, a book that made him rethink American history. While he did not announce the title of the book in Cincinnati, it has been identified as Henry Steele Commager and Allan Nevins's *The Pocket History of the United States*.[21] Written by two New Dealers, the book presents a liberal, pluralist conception of American history. By introducing the song in this way, Springsteen made it clear that he was singing Cliff's "Trapped" as more than a lament about a bad relationship but as a critique of oppression.

As an album, *The River* is a depiction, and at times a celebration, of working-class life, as the cover's photos of kitschy wedding decorations and the half-buried automobiles of Cadillac Ranch suggest. It is not primarily a political album, and its forays into social criticism are limited. Springsteen's next album, *Nebraska* (1982), represented a radical departure. Recorded on a four-track cassette recorder, the songs are performed solo with the artist accompanying himself, mostly on acoustic guitar. There are no anthems to be found. The lyrics and the vision are as spare as the production. The world they depict is much darker than anything Springsteen had previously presented, and focus is on criminal violence, which is treated with almost clinical detachment. This stance prevents the identification of the artist with the milieu and its denizens, and it makes this apparently personal album feel like the most impersonal of his career. The aesthetic here reminds one of Truman Capote's *In Cold Blood,* the paintings of Edward Hopper, and late-nineteenth century naturalist fiction. Like the latter, *Nebraska* is peopled with characters who seem to have no real choices, and the album offers nothing in the way of solutions. Indeed, the thrill killer in whose voice the title track is sung might be said to sum up the album's point when he offers the explanation for his crimes: "Well sir I guess there's just a meanness in this world."

Nebraska was certainly a significant event in Springsteen's development as an artist, but it did not have much impact on his persona. The opposite might be said of his next album, *Born in the U.S.A.* (1984). Relative to his pre-*Nebraska* recordings, *Born in the U.S.A.* exemplifies the artist's more or less consistent development as a songwriter and performer, but the album and other media representations connected with it demarcate what, for the public, became a new Springsteen. This was in part a response to the album's popularity, which put Springsteen into the entertainment industry stratosphere. But it was also a matter of a self-conscious remaking, in which the one-time bohemian/juvenile delinquent was now entirely transformed into a "working-class hero," as *Newsweek* put it in 1985.[22] The magazine observed the transformation in a series of photographs labeled "Five Faces of Springsteen." While the pictures do represent different looks, they break down into two groups, those from the 1970s, which suggest youth culture, and those from the 1980s, which convey a working-class identity.

The most striking change is in the star's body. One might call Springsteen skinny in the 1970s photographs; the 1980s version shows a man who has done some serious bodybuilding, and the sleeveless shirts he wears show it off. The effect is not to make him look like a bodybuilder, however, but like a laborer. This is consistent with the roles Springsteen played in two narrative videos for songs on *Born in the U.S.A.* Directed by John Sayles, the videos feature Springsteen as an auto mechanic ("I'm on Fire") and a heavy equipment operator ("Glory Days"). These videos stand out not only from most of Springsteen's, which have typically been performance videos, but also from the dominant style of music videos in the mid-1980s.

Although the music video as a genre was characterized by avant-garde strategies such as self-reflexivity and pastiche, these videos border on naturalism in their style. This is especially true of "I'm on Fire," where the auto mechanic desires a wealthy woman on whose car he works. A prolog sets up what seems to be mutual attraction—since we never see the woman's

Bruce as auto mechanic in John Sayles's video for "I'm on Fire," 1985. (frame enlargement)

face—we can only judge from the tone of her voice and the fact that she insists that he alone work on her car. After the music starts, we see the mechanic—apparently in the evening of the same day and now cleaned up and looking like he might be going on a date—get off his bed and drive the woman's vintage Thunderbird to her house "way out in the hills." These scenes are connected by long dissolves that make them seem dreamlike, and it is unclear whether they are meant to represent a literal dream. When he arrives at the woman's house, as if he has come back to reality, shots of it and him are again connected by straight cuts. He contemplates ringing the doorbell but decides against it and leaves the keys in the mailbox. This vignette not only associates Springsteen with a working-class occupation, but unlike much American culture, it insists on the gulf between the working class and the bourgeoisie. It works for all audiences because it illustrates the fundamental truth that desire is about wanting, not getting.

"Glory Days" is somewhat more complex, since it deals with three levels of reality. The video opens with a shot of Springsteen in the cab of a pile driver.

The scene fades into one where he is alone on a diamond pitching baseballs at a backstop. As the music begins, there is a cut to Springsteen and the E Street Band playing in a small bar. Most of the video is taken up with this performance, which is, however, intercut not only with scenes from elsewhere in the bar but also of Springsteen as the operator/pitcher watching a baseball game on television, apparently in his living room. While one could easily read the bar scene merely as a Bruce Springsteen concert, it could also be understood as an instance of working-class leisure, putting the entire video within the experience of that class. The video concludes with the pitcher throwing to a young batter, who asks him who he pitched against today. The pitcher replies, "San Diego. Nettles got me with two out in the ninth." The exchange reveals that the equipment operator's pitching is a part of his fantasy life, corresponding to the song's lyrics about a former high school baseball star who can't stop talking about his glory days. It is telling that even in his fantasy, he loses the game. On *Born in the U.S.A.,* the dreams that lived in Springsteen's earlier songs no longer inspire hope but are consigned to the past, when one was foolish enough to believe in them. There is a continuum in the video from the utterly repetitive and apparently meaningless work of running the pile driver, to the less alienated but still repetitive, lonely, and unsuccessful pitching, to the unambiguous pleasure of the band as it plays. Clearly the band is enjoying its work, yet even this enjoyment is qualified by the fact that the bar patrons don't appear to be listening. There is a stark contrast between this scene and the performance captured in Brian De Palma's video for "Dancing in the Dark," where the star is the object of rapt attention of admiring fans, especially the young Courteney Cox, who gets invited up onstage to dance with him.

The videos for "I'm on Fire" and "Glory Days" give us a Springsteen who looks like someone from the working class, and that look has become part of Springsteen's persona. But the class identification solidified in these images coexists with a national identification announced in the title of the album, *Born in the U.S.A.* The potential conflict between these two identities is paralleled by another conflict that is a consistent feature of the album, a conflict between an upbeat, joyous mood and the pointed critical social commentary of many of the lyrics. "Glory Days" and its video exemplify this conflict, which one can find in earlier songs but which is now intensified. Where songs like "Promised Land" and "Badlands" had insisted on hope and faith in the future in the absence of any support for these beliefs, *Born in the U.S.A.*

offers only the music itself as an antidote to its critique of America. The most powerful instance of this is, of course, the title track itself. Famously, President Ronald Reagan during his 1984 reelection campaign tried to appropriate "Born in the U.S.A.," treating it as a celebration of America and therefore an endorsement of his regime. It could be misread this way, because the song sounds like an anthem and a celebration despite the very uncelebratory picture its lyrics paint:

> Born down in a dead man's town
> The first kick I took was when I hit the ground
> You end up like a dog that's been beat too much
> Till you spend half your life just covering up.

There has been a great deal of discussion over the years of the contradiction between these lyrics on the one hand—and the chorus, which pretty much just repeats the title—and the way the song sounds on the other. The effect of the music on audience reception can be gauged by comparing the acoustic version of "Born in the U.S.A.," recorded solo around the same time as *Nebraska,* where the lyrics are much clearer and the chorus sounds more like a lament than a brag. Those on the Left have tended to see the version released on the album either as evidence that he's not really a progressive or as a mistake—Springsteen's views are correct but the expression of them fails. David Masciotra takes the latter view, when in a detailed reading of the song's lyrics he treats the record's sound as the source merely of a "mistaken" sense of "triumph."[23]

The one possibility almost no one seems to entertain is that the conflict is an intended aesthetic choice. Ann Kaplan, in her book about MTV, observes "the bitter irony common to many songs" on *Born in the U.S.A.,* but she doesn't note that that irony is as much a function of the relation of music to lyrics as it is of lyrics themselves.[24] Moreover, while irony is one trope Springsteen uses on the album, it's a bit too simple to read it as the key to all of its disjunctions. Rather, as Jefferson Cowie has argued, "'Born in the U.S.A.' . . . was consciously crafted as a conflicted, but ultimately indivisible whole. Its internal conflicts gave musical form to contradictions that grew from fissures to deep chasms in the heart of the working-class life during the 70s and their aftermath."[25] One should understand the conflicting moods of music and lyrics as the deliberate yoking of antagonistic elements, in which the meaning of both elements is changed by their juxtaposition. In this way, one could argue that "Born in the U.S.A.," "Glory Days," and "My Hometown" *are* meant as celebrations—not, of course, of the Vietnam War, nostalgia, or the exporting of jobs but of the people who find themselves oppressed by these conditions.

The disjuncture between lyrical content and musical presentation on "Born in the U.S.A." is in fact a common feature of Springsteen's work. It may make many of his songs ineffective as expressions of protest, but it does not necessarily render them politically insignificant. Springsteen was slow to develop a sense of himself politically and clearly didn't intend the song as a work of propaganda.[26] Of course, it's not clear how successful even the most explicit protest songs, like those of the early Bob Dylan or Phil Ochs, have been at spreading their message beyond the already committed. Studies have claimed to show that teenagers often don't listen to the lyrics, suggesting that protest songs are heard as mere entertainment.[27] But art can be political in other ways than spreading the message, helping us to think through political issues just as it can help us think through emotional or metaphysical ones. If both the Right and Left sometimes misread Springsteen's songs, they don't seem to be misread by his fans. Dan Cavicchi's study shows that Springsteen's fans typically understand the critical content of the lyrics of "Born in the U.S.A." but that they are also aware of the track's ambiguity, many of them holding that despite the song's criticism it is still an expression of patriotism.[28]

Most Americans probably identify patriotism with uncritical support for the state, but there is a long tradition that distinguishes love of country from that, and indeed, identifies patriotism with resistance to the state when necessary. In discussing "Born in the U.S.A.," Jack Newfield invoked a distinction, borrowed from George Orwell, between patriotism in this sense and nationalism, the jingoistic identification of state and nation.[29] Nationalism is a system of classifying human beings so that they can be labeled good or bad, but also the habit of identifying one's self with a nation, placing it beyond good and evil; patriotism is a devotion to a particular place and way of life, but it can be a critical devotion and it does not seek to impose itself on anyone else. In practice, of course, these two ideas are not completely separable, since patriotism in the nation-state is always going to be influenced by nationalism. Nevertheless, it is useful to be reminded that love of one's country need not be synonymous with support for the status quo.

As a critical patriot, Springsteen enters into a discourse that the American Left has avoided. The New Left of the 1960s failed to deploy patriotism in its rhetoric, contributing to this movement's lack of appeal to a broad range of Americans, especially those over thirty and those from the traditional working class. This may have helped to drive many in the working class to the Right, into the arms of the Republicans. As Eric Alterman puts it, Springsteen "missed the sixties" and so began with many of the values he learned growing up in that class intact.[30] His songs assume that those values matter, and they reflect his struggle with what it means to be critical of America and yet to continue to believe in the American Dream. While it might be the correct analysis simply to assert that the American Dream is a lie—as "The River" suggests—it is as hard for most Americans to accept this as it would be for the French to believe that they should give up their language and start speaking English. So Springsteen's songs are about what it is like to be trapped in the promised land, or trapped by a promise that is both false and the very ground of one's identity. This is a real dilemma for progressive politics in the United States. Springsteen's work doesn't provide a solution, but it helps us to recognize the problem.

The success of *Born in the U.S.A.* and of *Live/1975–85* (1986) raised new questions for some critics and listeners about Springsteen's authenticity. The idea that he was a product or an instance of industry hype, first articulated by *Newsweek* in 1975, had not in the meantime become widespread. Indeed, *Newsweek*'s own 1985 story described him as "rock and roll's Gary Cooper—a simple man who expresses strong beliefs with passion and unquestioned sincerity."[31] But the record industry had grown enormously since *Born to Run*, when a $1 million album was rare. In the later 1970s, records like Fleetwood Mac's *Rumours* (1977) sold in excess of 10 million copies, and in the 1980s Michael Jackson's *Thriller* (1982) sold *tens* of millions. Like their corporate siblings the movie studios, record companies now saw profits primarily in blockbuster albums, and they promoted likely candidates lavishly. According to Fred Goodman, Columbia heard *Born in the U.S.A.* as blockbuster material and promoted it as such.[32] In this case, the company had guessed correctly. *Born in the U.S.A.* remained on the charts for two years and sold in excess of 18 million copies in the United States. The tour behind the album sold $117 million in tickets, and income from both record and tour far surpassed any of Bruce's earlier successes.

The growth of the record industry and the importance of rock & roll to it contributed to a growing skepticism about artists who attained great popularity and financial success. Many rock fans and critics were now unable to accept such popularity as a genuine achievement—something that Elvis, the Beatles, or the Rolling Stones never had to face. As Robert Christgau had theorized in the wake of punk, the most important rock & roll was now semipopular music.[33] The fact that so many people were buying his records, and that they were heard constantly on more radio stations, made Springsteen suspect to those who defined themselves against mainstream tastes. Because Springsteen had always claimed to be more than a mere entertainer, his success was more troubling than Michael Jackson's. Thus, as Alterman observed, for many leftist critics, any politics in which Springsteen engaged must be "part of a cynical media strategy."[34] *Esquire* published the 1985 version of the 1975 *Newsweek* piece, suggesting the renewed concern about the boss's authenticity but also, appropriately, that that concern was now itself less popular.[35]

Some years later, writers like Goodman and Jim Miller gave a more sophisticated articulation to these suspicions. Goodman insisted that everything about *Born in the U.S.A.*, from the flag on the cover, to the references to Vietnam, to the money donated to local charities during the tour were all cynical marketing ploys, though they are attributed to Jon Landau rather than Springsteen himself.[36] Miller was even more totalizing, asserting that Springsteen became a "fetishized" commodity and a "prefab" token of a "rapturous transcendence, producing a variety of goods that could be purchased and (for the truly idolatrous) reverently collected."[37] That this argument could have been made about Elvis or the Beatles (who inspired much greater degrees of purchasing and collecting) seems not to have occurred to Miller. The fact that he could see it this way is evidence of the passion that the reaction against Springsteen often entailed.

Even those who reacted thoughtfully to Springsteen's new superstardom, however, were sometimes still skeptical. Simon Frith, responding to the sales of the *Live* album, asserted, "Those piles of Springsteen boxes . . . seem less a tribute to rock authenticity than to corporate might."[38] Frith ironically called Bruce Springsteen "the real thing," and he associated the artist with what he calls "1985's New Authenticity movement."[39] According to Frith, "The recurring term used in discussions of Springsteen, by fans, by critics, by fans-as-critics is 'authenticity.' What is meant by this is not that Springsteen is authentic in a direct way—is simply expressing himself—but that he represents 'authenticity.' This is why he has become so important: he stands for core values of rock and roll even as those values become harder and harder to sustain."[40]

Such values are populist and anticapitalist, and Frith believes that it's harder for rock to be that as it becomes more enmeshed in commercialism. Frith explains how and in what ways Springsteen appears authentic: he is the voice of the people, a successor to Woody Guthrie; his image is natural or "raw," expressed both in his style of dress and the plain language of his lyrics; his songs are about working-class people and their struggles under capitalism; he celebrates the ordinary and the everyday. Authenticity exists here in both what Springsteen represents and in the "natural," "real," and "honest" way he represents it. But this honesty turns out to be dishonesty, since it is a construction: "Because the constructed 'Springsteen,' the star, is presented plain, there can never be the suggestion that this is just an act (as Elvis was an act, as Madonna is). There are no other Springsteens, whether more real or more artificial, to be seen."[41] Frith shows how Springsteen is "false," in the sense that he is not what he appears to be, not the working-class man he sings about and seems to portray, but a multimillionaire who lives in a real (as opposed to metaphorical) mansion. In effect, Frith is arguing that a star is by definition inauthentic and that Springsteen is less authentic because he presents himself as having authenticity.

It is obviously true that Bruce Springsteen is not any longer a member of the working class, but by raising the issue in this way Frith demonstrates a misunderstanding of how stars and rock & roll communicate authenticity. *Newsweek* got the matter nearly right when it compared Springsteen to Gary Cooper. Cooper stood for authenticity during Hollywood's golden age, not because he was in real life the same as his star persona, but because the persona was associated with qualities and experiences that were understood as authentic. Cooper is no less authentic—or less "true" or "real"—than an actor like Errol Flynn, who did not claim authenticity. But perhaps most important, Springsteen's audience never shared Frith's qualms.

According to June Skinner Sawyers, Springsteen contrasts with Dylan, in that "unlike the bard from Hibbing, Minnesota . . . he exudes sincerity, not cynicism."[42] The *Seattle Times* called *Tunnel of Love* "as genuine a statement as any rocker has ever made and one of the most truthful LPs in rock history."[43] To be Bruce Springsteen is, apparently, to be transparent to one's audience.

In his fans' view, it would appear that Bruce has no persona, merely his authentic self, but to Frith Bruce is merely a persona that is mistaken for something real. The question of persona seems at first to be grounded in the very epistemology on which Frith relies, since, if Springsteen were authentic, this argument goes, he would not have a persona but simply a self. My view is something like the reverse of this position: the fact that a public persona always exists at some distance from the private self means that a persona will always give rise to questions of truth or authenticity, and it is impossible to escape these questions. One does not stop wondering about the "the real Bowie" merely because one knows that he is not identical to Ziggy Stardust. In any case, questions about Springsteen's authenticity have more recently subsided, as the response to *The Rising* shows.

The Rising

The albums that followed *Born in the U.S.A.* and the *Live* box in the main lack the former's duality of music and lyrics and did not approach its sales success. *Tunnel of Love* and the two albums released simultaneously in 1992, *Human Touch* and *Lucky Town,* were read as deeply personal, or even autobiographical, albums. They didn't further develop Springsteen's working-class identity, but they did make him seem even more authentic by revealing his own emotions and experiences. The release of *Tunnel of Love* coincided with the dissolution of his marriage to Julianne Phillips, and the beginning of his relationship with E Street Band member Patti Scialfa. Even though the songs were written before his marital troubles began, the content of the record made it widely perceived to be the artist's commentary on these specific events. The E Street Band was not used in recording *Tunnel of Love,* and, though Springsteen did tour with them behind that album, he declared himself a solo artist when it ended. That breakup, coupled with the long silence between *Tunnel of Love* and the later pair of albums and Springsteen's acknowledgment that he had sought help from a psychiatrist in the interim made fans listen to the new albums as reports on the artist's life.

The personal focus is replaced with a political one on *The Ghost of Tom Joad* (1995), a spare but emotionally powerful album that strikes one as being engaged as the more distanced *Nebraska* did not. The title and title track refer to the hero of John Steinbeck's 1939 novel, *The Grapes of Wrath.* Henry Fonda portrayed him in John Ford's film adaptation, and he was the subject of Woody Guthrie's song "Tom Joad," from *Dust Bowl Ballads* (1940). Tom departs in each version, telling his aged mother as he runs off to escape the police that she can find him wherever people are oppressed. Springsteen, like Guthrie, echoes "Joe Hill" and makes Joad's exit lines more explicitly political: "Wherever somebody's strugglin' to be free/Look in their eyes Mom you'll see me." "The Ghost of Tom Joad" implies that the 1990s are much like the 1930s: "Hot soup on a campfire under the bridge/Shelter line stretchin' 'round the corner/Welcome to the new world order." The last line is an ironic invocation of American triumphalism at the end of the Cold War. The chorus picks up on another symbol of American optimism, one that Springsteen celebrated often in his early recordings: "The highway is alive tonight/But nobody's kiddin' nobody about where it goes." It's certainly not "that place where we really want to go" and can "walk in the sun," as *Born to Run* had promised. Rather than an anthem, the song is slow and mournful. Mourning is appropriate, since Tom Joad is now a ghost and it is unclear whether the struggle he represents is alive or dead. Still, it was now unambiguous where Bruce stood on the merits of that struggle.

In 1999, Springsteen reunited with the E Street Band for a major tour. The tour was not associated with a new album, and the first one to come out of the reunion was a live recording. Springsteen did write one new song during the period that generated significant media attention. "American Skin (41 Shots)" was a foray into topical songwriting of the sort Dylan did in his early years but which Springsteen had previously avoided. The song deals with the police killing in February 1999 of Amadou Diallo, an unarmed African immigrant in the Bronx. The victim, standing in the doorway to his own apartment building, had been told to halt, but he reached for his wallet, which the cops took to be a gun. They fired forty-one shots at him. A subsequent investigation failed to find anything criminal in Diallo's killing. Springsteen's song asserts, "It ain't no secret . . . You can get killed just for living in your American skin." In the wake of the song's initial performance in Atlanta, Springsteen was for the first time the subject of attacks by the Right and its media, such as Rupert Murdoch's *New York Post*. When he performed it at Madison Square Garden, members of the audience who were thought to be New York police booed him. Their reaction to the song was predictable, but their presence at the concert revealed that Springsteen did have working-class fans. Moreover, the controversy was short-lived.

Bruce Springsteen's importance to his fans, and his special meaning to those in New York and New Jersey, became apparent in the wake of the attack on the World Trade Center on September 11, 2001. In the weeks following the attack, the *New York Times* published special obituaries of all of the victims, and Springsteen's name was repeatedly mentioned in them. Like many others, Springsteen was moved by their stories, but because he meant so much to many of them, he was also inspired to seek out their families and ultimately to write songs about their experiences. The result was *The Rising*, a commemoration of the terrorist attacks that was his first studio album with the E Street Band since 1987. Perhaps not surprisingly, the album is, to some extent, a reprise of the sound and the aesthetics of *Born in the U.S.A.* and earlier recordings.

Traditionally, commemorative art is conservative art in both senses: it is formally conventional and it glorifies the status quo. While most memorial sculpture, music, and poetry serves nationalist and militarist ends, there are some examples to the contrary. Maya Lin's Vietnam War Memorial may have been so controversial because it was formally unconventional, but it was also criticized because, lacking in explicit heroic iconography, it seemed to many a protest against the war. Benjamin Britten's *War Requiem,* while fairly conventional musically, used the antiwar poetry of Wilfred Owen to make its stance clear. The *Requiem* was performed for the first time in 1962 at the opening of the rebuilt Coventry Cathedral, a building destroyed by a deliberate German attack on a purely civilian target. The performance celebrated the rebuilding, and the work was "an immediate critical and popular success and seemed to give people something that they wanted and *needed* to hear."[44] Occurring twenty years after the atrocity, the performance was doubtless better received than it would have been when the war was fresher in people's minds. By 1962, opposition to war could be heard without it sounding like a repudiation of the heroism and sacrifice of that particular war. Moreover, in using the requiem mass, Britten memorialized the dead in a politically neutral and culturally acceptable manner. The result, I think, is that, like Lin's sculpture, the *War Requiem* is an ambiguous statement.

The Rising differs from the two previous examples in several respects. For one thing, it was released less than a year after the attacks, meaning that the events were still raw and, maybe more important, not yet subject to a long enduring ideological inscription. Indeed, the "war on terror" that the attacks precipitated was in a very early stage when the album was released. This might have allowed Springsteen to make a more effective intervention than the other memorialists I've mentioned, but it may also have made it difficult to decide just what the event meant to the public—and hence how to address that public. Secondly, while both public sculpture and classical music are traditional genres for commemorative art, popular music is not. *The Rising* is pretty conventional in rock terms, but rock & roll has not previously been regarded as an art form suitable for such purposes. That *The Rising* successfully played this role is demonstrated by the fact that the album sold more than a half a million copies in its first week. And *Time* gave the album a cover story emphasizing Springsteen's empathy and the album's "message of hope."[45] Compared to the leading example of classical music devoted to 9/11, John Adams's *On the Transmigration of Souls*, *The Rising* has had a far greater public profile, in addition to the obvious fact that as popular music it was also heard by many more listeners. Although there were some negative reviews here and there, in general *The Rising* was not so much well received as welcomed with open arms. Like the first listeners to the *War Requiem*, many Americans seemed to need what *The Rising* offered.

Trying to determine what exactly it does offer is a bit more complicated than the *Time* story makes it sound. Like the works of Lin and Britten, *The Rising* does not indulge in the patriotism of most public commemorative art, and of most of the commemorations of 9/11 in particular. On the other hand, the album's overt statements are a good deal less clear than the lyrics of the *War Requiem*. The album's opening track, "Lonesome Day," includes the lines, "A little revenge and/this too shall pass," suggesting Springsteen's rejection of that response. "Worlds Apart" gestures toward a more internationally contextualized view of the events, using the situation of lovers divided by cultural differences to stand for the larger divisions between the Western and Muslim worlds.

On the whole, however, *The Rising* is not an overtly political album but one that seeks to explore the emotions that the attack produced in those most touched by it. It's a mark of Springsteen's talent as a songwriter—but, also, as I will suggest below, of the way the songs are arranged and produced— that he could do this without undue sentimentality. The songs often seem to be fragments taken from the minds of the grieving. This may be because Springsteen interviewed spouses and partners of victims and read the *New York Times* bios with great interest. Most of the songs, as on *Nebraska*, are not sung from the singer's perspective but rather that of someone involved in the attack. The most common motif is the power of the memory of a loved one to inspire hope despite his or her death. So, "Countin' on a Miracle" tells us,

"Your kiss was taken from me/Now all I have is this . . . / Your kiss, your kiss,/your touch, your touch."

The paradox that the dead are still with those they have left behind is an aspect of grieving. Other songs, however, suggest that for Springsteen transcendence is not merely a trick of the mind. "My City of Ruins" and "Lonesome Day" invoke prayer, while "Paradise" and "Further On (Up the Road)" concern the possibility of an afterlife. It has been argued in the Catholic magazine *America* that the "rising" mentioned in the title track is meant to connect an emergency worker's ascent in the tower to the resurrection of Jesus—a point supported by a reference to Mary.[46] But *The Rising* is not, finally, a religious album; rather, it acknowledges religion's role in our culture. That is, religion remains a solace many turn to in the face of loss. "You're Missing" addresses, if only obliquely, the obvious problem many find with religion in the face of tragedy. "God's drifting in/heaven, devil's/in the mailbox/I got dust on my/shoes, nothing/but teardrops." And neither "Paradise" nor "Further On" depicts the afterlife as a reward or unambiguous solace. "Paradise" describes the dead beloved's eyes as "empty as paradise." The singer of "Worlds Apart" articulates a carpe diem rejection of the afterlife: "We've got this/moment now to/live, then it's all/just dust and dark." Religion is not the main source of the hope that is the album's dominant message. It is hard to discover a rational source for that hope in the lyrics. Rather, as on songs like "Badlands" and "Promised Land," it seems to be a matter of faith, not so much in God, but in the future—in the belief that things will get better.

Not every song on the album is hopeful. "You're Missing" presents the absurdity, the cognitive scandal of the sudden loss of a spouse or partner. The lyrics name the ordinary objects of family life that remain, leading to the refrain, "Everything is Everything/But you're missing." "Nothing Man" is even bleaker. The singer, an apparent survivor, feels anything but happy with being alive. He invokes his apparently living lover to "give me your kiss/Only understand/I am, the nothing man." The odd punctuation here—with a comma after "am" in the last line, suggests a sort of opposition of existence and nonexistence within the singer's person. Moreover, his courage comes from "The pearl and silver/Restin' on my night table," and the next line doesn't make it clear whether he wants to end his life or not: "It's just me Lord, pray I'm able."

Both of these darker songs are slow in tempo and are arranged with relatively spare instrumentation. While not quite as stripped down as the tracks on *Nebraska,* these songs are more like those than they are like most of the others on *The Rising.* As befits its advertised status as his first studio album with the E Street Band since *Born in the U.S.A., The Rising* is full of anthemic, up-tempo rockers. And just like on the title track of the earlier album, the lyrics and production don't always seem to fit with each other. This is true of "Lonesome Day," "Into the Fire," "Waiting on a Sunny Day," "Mary's Place," "The Rising," and "My City of Ruins." On many, if not all, of these tracks it is as if hope is asserted musically despite the lack of grounds for it in the lyrics. "Mary's Place" is the best example, where the lyrics ask in the middle of a call to party, "Tell me how do you / live broken-hearted." This odd combination of music and lyrics is a return to the aesthetics of "Born in the U.S.A."

Keeping the commemorative works of Lin and Britten in mind, such a commemoration need not be inherently regressive, but the politics of *The Rising* are necessarily ambiguous—and perhaps this time they were intended to be so. The polarized political responses to 9/11 make it difficult for a memorial work not to be a simple expression of right-wing nationalism and militarism. Indeed, many on the Left seem to find such memorials inevitably to be right-wing propaganda. So, for them, "Into the Fire," a celebration of the heroism of firefighters, cops, and other emergency workers, sounds like a celebration of the state itself. One must wonder whether these people think that, come the revolution, there will be no more fires. The progressive aspect of *The Rising* mainly lies not in its gestures toward a nonaggressive response to the attack but in its evocation of social bonds. That's what successful public art must do. I'm not arguing that the album brought us together but that its content and existence instance those forces that hold us together despite their degradation by unrestrained capitalism. As we should have learned from the war in Iraq, no people, no matter how oppressed, will cheer the destruction of their own world. This makes an explanation of the event almost impossible, and, when that explanation appears, as with Noam Chomsky, to justify the attackers, it will not make emotional sense to most people, regardless of its rationality.[47]

It is hard to remember the last *album* that seemed this culturally significant. One is almost inclined to go back to the Beatles to find one of similar standing, though clearly this is an overstatement. However, the record's significance as an album is a recognition of changing practices in the reception of popular music. More and more listeners are interested in songs that they download, rather than albums that they purchase. The idea that emerged with records like *Revolver, Sgt. Pepper's,* and others of that era, that an album could be a major cultural intervention, has largely been lost. I think this is as much the result of the changing status of rock as it is of changing technology. In the 1960s, rock, despite being sold by large corporations, was culturally and politically challenging. For many, it was an expression of revolt against the system that had given us war, racism, and poverty. In order to play that role, the music could not seem to belong to the public at large. It was the property of youth, the rock communion—as Simon Frith has suggested. What the success of *The Rising* demonstrates is that rock is now the property of the public as a whole. While many who listen to it still doubtless experience identification with the revolts of the past, the music no longer is part of a subculture, much less a counterculture. The cultural valence of rock & roll has shifted; it is now as mainstream as any element of mass culture.

The politics of this change are ambiguous. Springsteen became increasingly political over the course of his career, but he never has written songs as confrontational as those of the Clash. To conclude, we might want to consider the contrasting ways class figured in these two acts. The Clash celebrated resistance and refusal but did not celebrate working-class culture or life. Springsteen has celebrated working-class life and has adopted its traditional styles. Unlike almost any rock star since Elvis, Springsteen has continued to assert a working-class identity. This is unusual, not only among rock stars, but among successful Americans, most of whom shed their class roots as soon as they can. Springsteen leaves himself open to the criticism that he is turning class into an identity politics, but we should keep in mind that Marx himself understood class as being, in part, a matter of identity. While working-class identity has traditionally been strong in Britain, it has been weak in the United States. Springsteen's work may not change this, but he should not be criticized for trying.

Since *The Rising,* Springsteen's identification with the working class and with progressive politics has only grown stronger. Springsteen performed fund-raising concerts for John Kerry in 2004. In 2005, he released *Devils and Dust,* a mainly acoustic album in the vein of *The Ghost of Tom Joad.* The following year brought *We Shall Overcome: The Seeger Sessions,* a collection of folk songs associated with Pete Seeger, a major figure of the folk revival of the 1950s. Michael Denning identified him as the "link" between folk artists such as Woody Guthrie and Leadbelly, who emerged from the Depression of the 1930s, and Dylan, Joan Baez, and other new folksingers of the early 1960s.[48]

Seeger and Springsteen performed at the 2008 preinauguration concert for Barack Obama. Titled "We Are One," the concert was a remarkable moment, given the history of many of the performers, who probably never imagined themselves celebrating a presidential inauguration. Seeger led the performers and audience in singing Woody Guthrie's "This Land Is Your Land," and they included the two rarely performed verses that make the song's politics explicit. Though Lyndon Johnson once suggested it ought to be the national anthem and it is often included in collections of patriotic songs, "This Land Is Your Land" was written as a left-wing response to Irving Berlin's "God Bless America." While the song's three most commonly performed verses uncontroversially celebrate the American landscape, the additional verses make the song's politics clear. The first evokes the Depression, describing hungry people at the relief office and wondering *if* "this land was made for you and me." The next verse is more radical, questioning the very idea of private property. Guthrie was a communist sympathizer, and Seeger and his band, the Weavers, had been blacklisted during the 1950s because of their association with the party. Although Seeger's reputation began to be revived in the 1960s, with his contributions to the civil rights and antiwar movements, and he went on to become strongly associated with environmentalism as well, the significance of his invitation to perform at a presidential inauguration should not be diminished. At the concert Seeger and Springsteen symbolized not only the coming together of the Old Left and the New Left but also the end of the isolation of the American Left in general.

Despite the genuinely progressive meaning of this moment, Obama failed to offer a new New Deal, and the hope it announced gave way, if not to despair, then grim determination on Springsteen's 2012 *Wrecking Ball,* which addresses what *New York Times* columnist Paul Krugman has persuasively argued is the second Great Depression.[49] It is striking how little the recent economic crisis has found expression in popular music, and Springsteen's willingness to address the human cost of inequality continues to set him apart.[50] Springsteen's persona identifies with those who are on the losing end of capitalism's increasingly unrestrained war of the rich against everyone else. Nevertheless, I think Masciotra claims too much when he attributes to Springsteen's oeuvre "a progressive political vision," which would be perhaps too much to expect of any popular musician.[51] The blame for the current absence of such a vision in contemporary American politics must lie elsewhere. Springsteen's influence is better understood as an authority that, in part, derives from the fact that, despite his recent support of Democratic presidential candidates John Kerry and Barack Obama, he is not primarily understood as a partisan. Notwithstanding the power of this authority and the fact he continues to command broad attention and respect from the media, Springsteen is no longer selling records like he did in the mid-1980s. As I will suggest in the conclusion, it looks as though the moment of the politically significant rock star may well be nearing an end.

WHERE HAVE ALL THE ROCK STARS GONE?

The stars I've discussed in this book were and remain cultural icons. These performers and others of their era had broad cultural currency; they had meaning for people who did not like, or even hear, their music. They embodied currents of cultural change that emerged in the 1950s and became dominant in the 1960s. Is there any figure who has emerged recently in popular music of whom this can be said? This is not meant as one of those laments about artistic decline, in which the younger generation is compared unfavorably to the great achievements of the past ones. I have no doubt that more recent generations of performers are more skilled and at least as talented as their musical forebearers. Rather, my point is that the cultural position of popular music and its stars has been diminished.

Some of this change has to do with social conditions not directly related to either the production or consumption of popular music and its performers. I hope I have convinced the reader that rock stars contributed to the changes that we associate with the 1960s: the breaking down of hierarchies of race and gender; the new patterns of courtship, love, and marriage; the reintroduction of leftist political perspectives into popular consciousness. But rock & roll hardly caused these changes all by itself. Even the development of a politicized youth culture, perhaps the change most strongly dependent on the music, emerged out of manifold forces and conditions, among them Cold War rhetoric and youth's increasing purchasing power. The ferment of the 1960s was largely over by the 1980s, and, while many of the changes that grew out of the 1960s remain incomplete, the early years of the new millennium have not seen young people associated with new movements for social change. If the Occupy movement (or was it a moment?) is an exception, we might ask where its impact in popular culture has been felt. While that impact might still come, it is possible that the economic conditions that gave rise to Occupy are not those likely to support cultural innovation. The 1950s and 1960s were defined by prosperity. Thus, we might

conclude the time is not ripe for stars to take on the kind of cultural significance that those I've discussed here attained.

Other changes have to do specifically with patterns of production, distribution, and consumption of music. The continuing decline in CD sales, the
shift to music downloads, and the increasing difficulty of getting consumers
to pay for music have changed the character of the music business and have
contributed to (but are also partly a result of) a major shift in the way the pop
audience experiences music. Between 1999 and 2009, music sales declined by
half.[1] The industry blames illegal downloads and file sharing, and clearly this
accounts for some of the change. Older buyers, especially baby boomers, have
increased their music market share, while the younger demographics' shares
have decreased. In other words, the young, the group the industry previously
counted on to fuel music sales—and at whom promotional strategies continued to be aimed—are no longer buying as much music.[2] Those who do buy
music are purchasing albums on CD less and less. CD sales in the United
States dropped by 20 percent in 2010, and there was a continued decline in
2011 of 4.8 percent, when for the first time the value of digital music sales
exceeded those of physical sales.[3]

This change in purchasing behavior needs to be understood in the context
of changes in listening behavior. Where at one time, listening to recorded
music was often a social activity, with the advent of the iPod it has become
an intensely private pastime. Despite the decline of music purchases by
young people, popular music continues to be significant for adolescents.
Many college students seem attached to their iPods as if they were life-
support systems. Yet the prevalence of iPods illustrates one reason why popular music has lost its centrality. The 1960s equivalent technology to the iPod
was the car radio, but the radio was public, while an iPod is private. Not only
did young people ride around listening in groups, but everyone listening to a
station—or, indeed, during the heyday of the top 40, to almost any station—
heard the same records. Now, each listener creates his or her own playlist,
taking individual songs and typically ignoring their presentation within an
album. With the decline of radio as a major medium for the exposure of new
artists and songs, the music market has become fragmented. Young people
no longer have a common music culture that defines them against their parents. Rather, they may participate in a particular music culture that exists
together with others in which their peers participate, or they may simply
pick up tracks more or less randomly. Thus, individual listeners tend to be

increasingly isolated users of music, despite social networking tools such as Apple's Ping or Facebook.

Although one statistic shows that individual unit sales are higher than ever before, album sales in all forms continue to decline, with fewer blockbuster recordings.[4] Only thirteen albums sold a million copies in 2010.[5] The shift from albums to tracks is not only an obvious economic loss to the industry but also a significant change in the relationship between audience and artist. In the days of the LP, the album and its packaging allowed purchasers to get to know (or feel as if they got to know) the artist. Downloading a track provides far less of a sense of the producer, turning every artist into the equivalent of the one-hit wonder. It is true that, prior to 2009 and the recession, proceeds from live performance had grown significantly since the mid-1990s. But even this phenomenon reveals the dependence of the industry on older audiences and older acts.[6] It is symptomatic of the current popular music scene that the Rolling Stones' 2006 tour was the largest grossing such event up to that time, to be topped in 2011 by U2's 360 tour. Mick Jagger remains a bigger celebrity than any performer who has emerged in the last twenty years.

The conditions specific to the music industry need to be understood in the context of the decline of a genuine mass audience for any medium. What we have long considered to be mass culture has become increasingly a collection of niche cultures. The movies and radio, which had been mass media before World War II, began to lose audience to television in the 1950s, and they responded with the first wave of niche marketing—to youth. Television became the most dominant mass medium of all time by the late 1950s, but by the 1970s, cable began to produce audience fragmentation, which has continued apace as the three broadcast television networks became the 100-plus channels of digital cable or satellite TV. The same fragmentation affected print as early as the late 1960s, when mass-circulation magazines like *Life* gave way to special interest periodicals, and has continued until the present, when people are increasingly reading a plethora of blogs instead of a newspaper their neighbors are also likely to read.

Music was dependent to a great degree on these other media for mass-audience exposure, first with radio and later television, with the movies providing powerful, if secondary, exposure. The rise of rock stardom was enabled by the allied media. The mass-print media, which had provided movie stars their primary offscreen connection to the audience, also gave rock fans the most detailed information about the stars' lives offstage. The decline of mass culture means not only that the music reaches smaller groups of listeners but also that performers are less likely to find themselves magnified into stars. Because stars are less visible, their economic clout is much reduced. Young listeners are much less likely to purchase new songs merely because they were recorded by a particular artist, and so the decline of the music star system contributes to the decline in music sales.

Popular music never equaled the mass reach of movies or television, but it may have had its peak mass audience later, in the 1980s, with megaselling albums such as Michael Jackson's *Thriller*. One might equally suggest that these blockbuster records and the mentality they produced in the industry are properly understood in parallel with the similar phenomenon in Hollywood, whereby the enormous sales of a few products tended to mask a decline in the frequency of purchase and experience. Beginning in the late 1990s, however, even the blockbuster strategy failed, and sales declined as the market continued to fragment.

Still, the music industry was also involved in niche marketing much earlier than the other media, with specialized segments going back to the dawn of commercial recording. However, as Elijah Wald has argued, prior to the emergence of rock & roll as the dominant product category, popular music was characterized by a diversity of styles of performance that were heard by a mass audience. What these diverse styles tended to share were songs, which remained the industry's main product until perhaps as late as the 1960s.[7] Thus, up through the 1950s, songwriters—Berlin, the Gershwins, Porter, and so on—had a greater reach than all but a few artists, such as Enrico Caruso or Bing Crosby. On these grounds, it might be argued that popular music lacked a robust star system until the rise of rock & roll. It was then that the experience of music became increasingly dependent on a bond with a performer who was understood as the author of his or her own songs.

I offer this history in order to suggest that the period of popular music beginning in the 1950s with rock & roll, which critics and the industry have accepted as the norm, is in fact just one moment in a continually changing formation. Thus, gurus of a new music business or Internet utopia are right when they caution doomsayers that music will not disappear even if CDs do. But because the experience of music has never been the pure appreciation of the sound apart from a performance context, this change will mean that the listening will change even if the music itself remains the same. In the era of mass culture—what Max Horkheimer and Theodor Adorno described under the heading of the "culture industry"—the various mass media magnified each other.[8] The profits produced from sales to a mass market made the culture industries invest heavily in promotion, and such publicity was a significant condition for the star system in both film and music. Under the new music economics, where niche rather than mass marketing is the rule, heavy investment in promotion no longer makes sense. Indeed, investment of any kind in any particular act must be curtailed, since the likely returns are smaller.

Fortunately for musicians, the costs of recording and distributing music have become radically cheaper. Where at one time, record company resources were necessary to make top-quality recordings, current technology means that high-quality recordings can be made by almost anyone. The Internet, of course, has solved the problem of distribution. The result is that, despite falling music sales, there are more recordings available. Because these recordings are not supported by mass publicity, however—or reflected in mass media—they reach fewer and fewer people. Under these conditions, the beginnings of what has been called by Peter Spellman "patronage from the masses" or "crowdfunding" have emerged.[9] Under this model, instead of selling products or performances, musicians are supported by direct contributions from fans.

The Internet is at the heart of this as well, and the new patronage began by artists using it to reach fans to ask for support. Within the last five years, at least three different patronage sites have appeared: Artists Share, Sellaband, and Slice the Pie. Artists Share offers fans greater access to an artist's music and the creation of that music in return for a small donation. The greater the donation, the greater degree of access a fan will have. Sellaband allows performers to produce a CD through direct contributions from fans. A band must reach the goal of $50,000 to have the CD recorded and distributed, with distribution arranged through Amazon.com. The donations by "believers," as they are called, are not pure charity, however. Believers are investors who receive a percentage of profits from the CD's sales and are entitled to a share of the site's ad revenue. Slice the Pie calls itself "the music stock market." Users are paid a small amount for each review they contribute based on how accurately the review reflects the tastes of other investors. In effect, this turns each audience member into an A&R person, and the "review" into a scouting report. The site also allows participants to invest in a band and profit if its "stock" rises. Bands that reach a certain threshold of approval get to make a

CD, which their investors receive along with other access privileges, at the band's discretion.

The rhetoric of these crowdfunding services and of the champions of this new model of music commerce like Spellman, Dave Kusek (another Berklee administrator), and Internet prophet, Yochai Benkler, is couched in terms of democracy, meritocracy, community, and artistic freedom. These promoters have different ideologies, which bespeak the ambiguous economic implications of the new patronage. Spellman's rhetoric is clearly neoliberal, and his populism reminds one a bit of the Tea Party in his antipathy to the record companies, combined with a championing of economic freedom. He uses the words *community, audience,* and *fans,* interchangeably with *customers.* Kusek asserts that music is entertainment and bands are entertainers—not artists.[10] Benkler, on the contrary, imagines the failure of copyright protection of musical property to push popular music in the direction of not-for-profit activities such as classical music performances or the academic disciplines of the humanities. He sees the Internet as distancing music from the usual model of commodity exchange and returning it to older models of fee-for-service (for performances) and pro bono. This is not only because the music the artist produces will not earn a significant return when sold as a commodity but also because fans' donations are genuinely charitable in their intent and effect.[11] Spellman and Benkler each capture an aspect of the changes in the music economy, and the latter is helpful in reminding us that even under late capitalism, nonconforming economic activities continue to exist. But, in the long run, I see the neoliberal model as more likely to prevail, producing not, as Kusek has claimed, a new musical middle class but a new musical underclass, as more bands are able to eke out a living, but just barely.

Despite their differing ideologies, both Spellman and Benkler speak of the opportunities available when artists are freed from the domination of the record companies. While it is certainly the case that record companies' "gate keeping" has traditionally been restrictive, and the overhead associated with these businesses has meant that artists have received a tiny percentage of the revenue their work has generated, the companies did offer numerous services to artists, many of which under the new model have devolved back to the artists themselves. For example, in order to raise money on one of the new patronage sites, bands have to promote themselves. As Spellman reveals, crowdfunding is in fact akin to outsourcing, and it reminds one of what

Andrew Ross has observed about the trap that knowledge workers fall into of ever-expanding labor justified by one's devotion to the work.[12]

Moreover, since most new patronage schemes involve some form of increased access, artists would seem simply to have exchanged a few masters for many. Under the old system, established stars at least had the freedom to experiment, knowing that one poorly selling record would not mean the end of their contract. Under crowdfunding, the fans must be kept satisfied or they will stop contributing. And access often includes intervention into the creative process. The jam band Umphrey's McGee, for example, offers small groups of fans concerts where they can text themes or ideas to the band around which it will improvise.[13] This kind of audience interaction may be satisfying to the band, but one could imagine it feeling tyrannical to many artists. Offering increased access itself requires time investments in responding to fans' communications and desires. Singer-songwriter Jonathan Coulton allows anyone to use his recordings as the basis for their own works in any medium, which has helped him to build a paying audience for his music, but he says he spends countless hours emailing with fans about their long-distance collaborations.[14]

After these special access concerts, Umphrey's McGee hangs out with the audience, sharing beers and conversation. To me this epitomizes the upside and the downside of the fan experience under the new model. The upside is that fans have always fantasized about getting to hang out with their idols. Jann Wenner started *Rolling Stone* in order to meet rock stars. But what if the musicians you are hanging out with aren't rock stars but just musicians? Is it still a thrill when you have just spent the last hour telling these guys what to play? Stardom is partly defined by fans' imaginary personal relationships with stars. What happens when they start having actual relationships with them? On the upside, they get a certain degree of recognition from the star; on the downside, they are in an actual relationship, with all of the complications that that involves, including the inevitable disappointments that real—rather than imaginary—relationships entail.

For the artist, the new music economy has meant that it is harder and harder to attain recognition beyond his or her niche. The new patronage model institutionalizes and further narrows the niche to those fans willing to pay more than the cost of a track or CD—or to pay without the certainty of receiving a product in return. One could argue that the term "popular music" has become outdated because no style of music reaches a broad enough audience. My undergraduate students all typically know the music of my college cohort—the Beatles, Eric Clapton, Joni Mitchell, Led Zeppelin, and so on—but it is often difficult to find more than a few who are familiar with the same current releases. As a result of this audience fragmentation, popular music and its performers have lost the cultural centrality they once enjoyed, and that means that fewer people are interested enough to pay for the product.

This is not to say that music celebrities now fail to inspire great devotion in their fans. Celebrity has, if anything, become a larger element of popular culture since the 1960s, and the music industry continues to produce it. Yet increasingly, performers seem less to be stars and more to be mere celebrities. The dream of those entering the business since the 1950s has been to become a star, the creation of which was also the aim of the record companies, whose A&R and publicity apparatuses were designed with this goal in mind. But now, as even the most popular music reaches a smaller and smaller fraction of the total audience, the position of the star has, in effect, been eliminated.

Perhaps the bigger issue is that even the music of chart toppers reaches a small fraction of the total audience. Paradoxically, however, as popular music has reached a smaller audience, it has become more pop in form. Those whose recordings now top the charts usually seem to be of the least cultural significance, because their music typically takes no risks. One might argue that Michael Jackson's shift from the rock & roll persona of his years with the Jackson Five to his solo incarnation as the "King of Pop," mark the moment when the pendulum of popular taste began swinging away from the innovation and radicalism of rock toward the familiarity and safety of pop. With the rise of *American Idol* as America's most popular television show after 2002, the new triumph of pop was confirmed. Chart-topping performers going back to Britney Spears and continuing through Lady Gaga and Adele are best understood as entertainers, even though they borrow from the tradition of rock & roll theatrics and may on occasion push the boundaries of decorum.

To some extent, the cultural practices associated with rock & roll remain in place. These range from matters of the place of music within culture to formal characteristics of music. Despite the reversion to a pop sensibility, most new acts work in one of the variants of guitar-based rock & roll that had emerged by the early 1970s or one of the later offshoots of rock, including hip-hop and various forms of dance music. The rise of the rock stars in the

1960s meant that popular music would be treated differently afterward, and it continues to receive more serious treatment than it did in the prerock era. The new pop is not, therefore, a mere repetition of your great-grandfather's music or style, but it may be equally inconsequential. The age of silly love songs and lavish display has returned. Hence, while lots of people know who Lady Gaga is, I suspect most don't think of her as representing anything beyond sheer spectacle itself. The media remain inclined to assume that popular musicians have something to say about serious matters—and some of them do. But the fragmentation of mass culture has meant that they are able say it to smaller and smaller fractions of the population.

Bono, whose political advocacy in the courts of real-world power has expanded his reach, may have been the last rock star to capture the imagination of a broad spectrum of the public. But even this case reveals a change. Bono's advocacy, in which he presents himself as an equal of diplomats and captains of industry, does not seem to be of a piece with his role in U2, the way, say, John Lennon's antiwar activism seemed perfectly consistent with his role in the Beatles.

The fate of hip-hop may be the best illustration of the increasing marginalization of popular music and its impact on American culture. Hip-hop is arguably the last great innovation in popular music, the successor to ragtime, jazz, R&B, and rock & roll. All of them emerged out of African American culture to change the tastes of Americans of all races. Hip-hop also attracted a large audience of young white listeners, but it did not come to dominate the way its predecessors had. Though several aspects of hip-hop may have made it a more difficult taste to acquire—one could mention the absence of melody and harmony and the often violent and misogynistic lyrics—I would argue that the fragmentation of the market, which was already well under way in the late 1980s, has been a bigger factor. Most Americans didn't hear the music routinely, so it remained foreign to their ears. Earlier hip-hop stars like Grandmaster Flash and Public Enemy were at least as critical of American society as Dylan ever was, and they led some commentators to imagine hip-hop artists as politically efficacious organic intellectuals.[15] But in the last ten years or so, even though hip-hop artists like Jay-Z are popular music's most innovative contributors, the form has become less political and its performers seem less culturally central.[16] In a different market, hip-hop stars might have become leaders like James Brown. As it is, popular music appears to be headed back to the margins of cultural life, and that is a loss for all us.

Preface

1. By *icon,* I intend a now common, popular usage, which the *Oxford English Dictionary* has defined as "a person or thing regarded as a representative symbol, esp. of a culture or movement," "icon, n." *OED Online,* Dec. 2012, Oxford University Press, www.oed.com/view /Entry/90879?redirectedFrom=icon.

2. Matthew Weiner, "Lady Lazarus," *Mad Men,* season 5, episode 8, May 6, 2012.

3. Peter Wicke, *Rock Music: Culture, Aesthetics and Sociology* (Cambridge: Cambridge University Press, 1990), 105.

4. Dick Hebdige, *Subculture: The Meaning of Style* (London: Methuen, 1979); Lawrence Grossberg, "Another Boring Day in Paradise," in *Dancing in Spite of Myself: Essays on Popular Culture* (Durham, NC: Duke University Press, 1997), 37.

5. Grossberg, "Another Boring Day in Paradise," 31.

6. Ibid., 45–49, and Lawrence Grossberg, "Is Anybody Listening? Does Anybody Care?: On 'The State of Rock,'" in *Dancing in Spite of Myself,* 113. My reading of rock stardom assumes the idea of "us vs. them" is part of rock stars' personas but that their stardom demonstrates their cultural inclusion.

7. Arthur Marwick, *The Sixties: Cultural Transformation in Britain, France, Italy and the United States, c. 1958–c. 1974* (New York: Oxford University Press, 2000), 26.

8. Lawrence Grossberg, "'I'd Rather Feel Bad Than Not Feel Anything at All': Rock and Roll, Pleasure and Power," in *Dancing in Spite of Myself,* 77.

CHAPTER 1: Reflections on Stardom and Its Trajectories

1. Robert Greenfield, *A Journey through America with the Rolling Stones* (London: Helter Skelter, 2001 [1974]), 83.

2. Daniel Herwitz, *The Star as Icon: Celebrity in the Age of Mass Consumption* (New York: Columbia University Press, 2008), 1–22.

3. Daniel J. Boorstin, *The Image: A Guide to Pseudo-Events in America* (New York: Random House, 1961), 57.

4. Ibid., 49.

5. P. David Marshall, *Celebrity and Power: Fame in Contemporary Culture* (Minneapolis: University of Minnesota Press, 1997), 11. See also Chris Rojek, *Celebrity* (London: Reaktion, 2001).

6. On fame as a distinct category, see Leo Braudy, *The Frenzy of Renown: Fame and Its History* (New York: Vintage, 1997 [1986]).

7. Fred Inglis, *A Short History of Celebrity* (Princeton: Princeton University Press, 2010), 8.

8. Boorstin, *The Image,* 63.

9. Judith Butler, *Gender Trouble: Feminism and the Subversion of Identity* (New York: Routledge, 1990), 185–93.

10. Inglis, *A Short History of Celebrity,* 40–41.

11. Marcel Proust, *Remembrance of Things Past,* vol. 1, trans. C. K. Scott Moncrieff and Terence Kilmartin (New York: Random House, 1981), 80.

12. Denise Scott Brown, "Room at the Top?: Sexism and the Star System in Architecture," in *Architecture: A Place for Women,* ed. Ellen Perry Berkeley (Washington, DC: Smithsonian Institution Press, 1989), 237–45, and David Shumway, "The Star System in Literary Studies," in *The Institution of Literature,* ed. Jeffrey J. Williams (Albany: State University of New York Press, 2000), 173–201.

13. Richard Dyer, *Stars,* new edition (London: BFI, 1998), 20.

14. Marshall, *Celebrity and Power,* 234.

15. Roland Barthes, "The Face of Garbo," in *Mythologies,* trans. Annette Lavers (New York: Hill and Wang, 1972), 56.

16. Budd Schulberg quoted in Brown, "Room at the Top?," 241.

17. Joshua Gamson, *Claims to Fame: Celebrity in Contemporary America* (Berkeley: University of California Press, 1994), 145–47.

18. Jackie Stacey, *Star Gazing: Hollywood Cinema and Female Spectatorship* (London: Routledge, 1994).

19. Brown, "Room at the Top?," 241.

20. Richard Schickel, *Intimate Strangers: The Culture of Celebrity in America* (Chicago: Ivan Dee, 2000 [1985]), 25.

21. Richard deCordova, *Picture Personalities: The Emergence of the Star System in America* (Urbana: University of Illinois Press, 2001), 51.

22. Samantha Barbas, *Movie Crazy: Fans, Stars, and the Cult of Celebrity* (New York: Palgrave MacMillan, 2001), 21–22.

23. Walter Benjamin, "The Work of Art in the Age of Mechanical Reproduction," in *Illuminations,* trans. Harry Zohn (New York: Schocken, 1960), 221.

24. Herwitz, *The Star as Icon,* 59–78.

25. See Greil Marcus, *Dead Elvis: A Chronicle of a Cultural Obsession* (New York: Doubleday, 1991).

26. Steven J. Ross, *Hollywood Left and Right: How Movie Stars Shaped American Politics* (Oxford: Oxford University Press, 2011), 363–407.

27. Gamson, *Claims to Fame,* 32.

28. Dyer, *Stars,* 35.

29. Barbas, *Movie Crazy,* 36.

30. Ibid., 35–36.

31. Ross, in *Hollywood Left and Right,* calls Chaplin "the first political movie star" (11). The subtitle, *How Movie Stars Shaped American Politics,* might suggest a disagreement between us, but I see his book as largely supporting my interpretation. Chaplin and Edward G. Robinson are the only prewar stars Ross features, and much of the Robinson chapter deals with his being smeared as a communist after the war. In any case, Ross's focus is on stars' (and moguls') involvement in actual politics, while my concern is the political valence of stars' personas.

32. DeCordova, *Picture Personalities,* 110.

33. Lary May, *The Big Tomorrow: And the Politics of the American Way* (Chicago: University of Chicago Press, 2000), 175–213.

34. Quoted in ibid., 177.

35. Garry Wills, *John Wayne's America* (New York: Simon & Schuster, 1997), 193.

36. Ibid., 148.

37. Ibid., 149.

38. Richard Dyer, "Monroe and Sexuality," in *Heavenly Bodies: Film Stars and Society,* 2nd ed. (London: Routledge, 2004), 24.

39. Quoted in ibid., 30.

40. Leerom Medovoi, *Rebels: Youth and the Cold War Origins of Identity* (Durham, NC: Duke University Press, 2005), 3.

41. Ibid., 177–86.

42. David R. Shumway, "Rock & Roll as a Cultural Practice," *South Atlantic Quarterly* 90 (Fall 1991): 753–69.

43. Thus, following Anthony DeCurtis, who in the title of his collection, *Present Tense: Rock & Roll and Culture* (Durham, NC: Duke University Press, 1992), invented a solution to this typographic problem, I use "rock & roll" throughout this volume.

44. For a good example of this strategy, see Robert Palmer, "When Is It Rock and When Is It Rock & Roll?: A Critic Ventures an Answer," *New York Times*, Aug. 6, 1978, rpt. in *Blues & Chaos: The Music Writing of Robert Palmer*, ed. Anthony DeCurtis (New York: Scribner, 2009), 13–18.

45. *Elvis '56*, prod. Alan Raymond and Susan Raymond (Media Home Entertainment, 1987), videocassette (VHS).

46. Linda J. Sandahl, *Rock Films: A Viewer's Guide to Three Decades of Musicals, Concerts, Documentaries and Soundtracks, 1955–1986* (New York: Facts on File, 1987).

CHAPTER 2: Watching Elvis

1. Gary R. Edgerton, *The Columbia History of American Television* (New York: Columbia University Press, 2007), 103, 107.

2. Lynn Spigel, *Make Room for TV: Television and the Family Ideal in Postwar America* (Chicago: University of Chicago Press, 1992), 101.

3. Robert Lowell, "Memories of West Street and Lepke," in *Life Studies* (New York: Farrar, Straus, 1956).

4. Thomas Doherty, *Cold War, Cool Medium: Television, McCarthyism, and American Culture* (New York: Columbia University Press, 2003).

5. Brian Ward, *Just My Soul Responding: Rhythm and Blues, Black Consciousness, and Race Relations* (Berkeley: University of California Press, 1998), 2.

6. Ibid., 19.

7. Ibid., 105.

8. Ibid., 109.

9. Eric Lott, *Love and Theft: Blackface Minstrelsy and the American Working Class* (New York: Oxford University Press, 1993), 103.

10. James Gilbert, *A Cycle of Outrage: America's Reaction to the Juvenile Delinquent in the 1950s* (New York: Oxford University Press, 1986).

11. Leerom Medovoi, *Rebels: Youth and the Cold War Origins of Identity* (Durham, NC: Duke University Press, 2005), 29.

12. Barbara Ehrenreich, Elizabeth Hess, and Gloria Jacobs, *Re-Making Love: The Feminization of Sex* (Garden City, NY: Doubleday, 1986), 11.

13. Beth L. Bailey, *From Front Porch to Back Seat: Courtship in Twentieth-Century America* (Baltimore: Johns Hopkins University Press, 1988), 98.

14. Ibid., 104.

15. On the postwar ideological effort to return women to traditional roles, see Betty Friedan, *The Feminine Mystique* (New York: Dell, 1963).

16. Bailey, *From Front Porch to Back Seat*, 105.

17. Marjorie Garber, *Vested Interests: Cross-Dressing and Cultural Anxiety* (New York: Routledge, 1992).

18. Ibid., 368.

19. Ibid., paraphrasing Albert Goldman, *Elvis* (New York: McGraw-Hill, 1981).

20. Garber, *Vested Interests*, 368, quoting Goldman, *Elvis*. Garber doesn't seem to understand the cultural significance of the insults Goldman directs at Elvis's masculinity. Such insults are a staple of working-class-male culture and an expression of homophobia. She writes as if Goldman were also celebrating transvestism, when his goal is in fact to castrate Elvis, to deprive him of his cultural power.

21. Nancy Henley, *Body Politics: Power, Sex, and Nonverbal Communication* (Englewood Cliffs, N J: Prentice-Hall, 1977), 160–66.

22. Laura Mulvey, "Visual Pleasure and Narrative Cinema," in *Feminism and Film Theory,* ed. Constance Penley (New York: Routledge, 1988), 57–68. In "Afterthoughts on 'Visual Pleasure and Narrative Cinema' Inspired by King Vidor's Duel in the Sun (1946)," in *Feminist Film Theory: A Reader,* ed. Sue Thornham (New York: New York University Press, 1999), 122–30, Mulvey discusses how female spectators respond to being positioned to identify with male protagonists, but she does not discuss the female gaze. While the "female gaze" has been the topic of numerous scholarly articles, it has not been discussed with regard to rock performers. As might be obvious, my citation of Mulvey is not meant to invoke the details of her larger argument rooted in Lacanian psychoanalysis.

23. John Berger et al., *Ways of Seeing* (London and Middlesex: BBC and Penguin, 1972), 47. But see Richard Leppert, *The Nude: The Cultural Rhetoric of the Body in the Art of Western Modernity* (Boulder, CO: Westview, 2007), 8–15, for some important qualifications to Berger and Mulvey.

24. Steve Neale, "Masculinity as Spectacle: Reflections on Men and Mainstream Cinema," *Screen* 24, no. 6 (1983): 15. See Jackie Byars, *All that Hollywood Allows: Re-reading Gender in 1950s Melodrama* (Chapel Hill: University of North Carolina Press, 1991), for an extended discussion of gender in 1950s melodramas that supports Neale's position.

25. Mulvey, "Visual Pleasure and Narrative Cinema."

26. Miriam Hansen, "Pleasure, Ambivalence, Identification: Valentino and Female Spectatorship," *Cinema Journal* 25, no. 4 (1986): 12–13.

27. Gaylyn Studlar, "Valentino, 'Optic Intoxication,' and Dance Madness," in *Screening the Male: Exploring Masculinities in Hollywood Cinema,* ed. Steven Cohan and Ina Rae Hark (London: Routledge, 1993), 23–45.

28. Jon Savage, "The Enemy Within: Sex, Rock, and Identity," in *Facing the Music,* ed. Simon Frith (New York: Pantheon, 1988), 144.

29. Ibid.

30. Sue Wise, "Sexing Elvis," in *On Record: Rock, Pop, and the Written Word,* ed. Simon Frith and Andrew Goodwin (New York: Pantheon, 1988), 395, 397.

31. Henley, *Body Politics,* 167.

32. Peter Guralnick, *Last Train to Memphis: The Rise of Elvis Presley* (Boston: Little, Brown, 1994), 284.

33. Jack Gould, "TV: New Phenomenon," *New York Times,* June 6, 1956, 67.

34. Quoted in Ward, *Just My Soul Responding,* 110.

35. Ibid., 107.

36. Marc Weingarten, *Station to Station: The History of Rock 'n' Roll on Television* (New York: Simon & Schuster, 2000), 29.

37. Steven Cohan, "'Feminizing' the Song-and-Dance Man: Fred Astaire and the Spectacle of Masculinity in the Hollywood Musical," in *Screening the Male,* 46–69.

38. This is not to say that athletes cannot present themselves as objects of the sexual gaze, as tennis stars Andre Agassi or Anna Kournikova have done. Moreover, as male bodies have become more often the object of the sexual look in the culture at large, male athletes have increasingly been understood as such objects.

39. Henry Glover quoted in Nick Tosches, *Unsung Heroes of Rock 'n' Roll* (New York: Scribner's, 1984), 37.

40. Robert Henry quoted by Margaret McKee and Fred Chisenall, *Beale Black & Blue,* quoted in Greil Marcus, *Dead Elvis: A Chronicle of a Cultural Obsession* (New York: Doubleday, 1991), 57.

41. Wynonie Harris quoted in Tosches, *Unsung Heroes of Rock 'n' Roll,* 40.

42. Charlie Gillett, *The Sound of the City: The Rise of Rock and Roll* (New York: Dell, 1972), 139.

43. Peter Guralnick, "Elvis Presley," in *The Rolling Stone Illustrated History of Rock & Roll,* 3rd ed., ed. Anthony DeCurtis, James Henke, and Holly George-Warren (New York: Random House, 1992), 26.

44. Greil Marcus, *Mystery Train: Images of America in Rock 'n' Roll Music* (New York: Dutton, 1976), 204.

45. Guralnick, "Elvis Presley," 21.

46. *Elvis '56,* prod. Alan Raymond and Susan Raymond (Media Home Entertainment, 1987), videocassette (VHS).

47. Wise, "Sexing Elvis," 395.

48. Ibid., 397.

49. Simon Frith, *Music for Pleasure: Essays in the Sociology of Pop* (New York: Routledge, 1988), 167.

50. T. H. Lhamon, *Deliberate Speed: The Origins of Cultural Style in the American 1950s* (Washington: Smithsonian Institution Press, 1990), 92–96.

51. Eliot Cohen quoted in Medovoi, *Rebels,* 27.

52. Ibid.

53. Thomas Doherty, *Teenagers and Teenpics: The Juvenilization of American Movies in the 1950s* (Boston: Unwin Hyman, 1988).

54. Todd Gitlin, *The Sixties: Years of Hope, Days of Rage* (New York: Bantam, 1987), 43.

CHAPTER 3: James Brown

1. James Brown with Bruce Tucker, *James Brown: The Godfather of Soul* (New York: Thunder's Mouth, 1997 [1986]). James Brown, *I Feel Good: A Memoir of a Life of Soul* (New York: New American Library, 2005).

2. Gerri Hirshey, *Nowhere to Run: The Story of Soul Music* (New York: Times, 1984), 61.

3. Nelson George, *The Death of Rhythm and Blues* (New York: Plume, 1988), 70, 83.

4. Peter Guralnick, *Sweet Soul Music: Rhythm and Blues and the Southern Dream of Freedom* (Boston: Little, Brown, 1986), 220.

5. Rob Bowman, *Soulsville, U.S.A.: The Story of Stax Records* (New York: Schirmer, 1997), 49.

6. Suzanne E. Smith, *Dancing in the Streets: Motown and the Cultural Politics of Detroit* (Cambridge: Harvard University Press, 1999), 118.

7. Guralnick, *Sweet Soul Music,* 220.

8. Brown, *I Feel Good,* 46.

9. Brown, *The Godfather of Soul,* 1.

10. Brown, *I Feel Good,* 58.

11. Brown, *The Godfather of Soul,* 28.

12. Ibid., 65.

13. Guralnick, *Sweet Soul Music,* 225.

14. Brown, *I Feel Good,* 67.

15. LeRoi Jones, *Blues People: Negro Music in White America* (New York: HarperCollins, 2002 [1963]), 169.

16. Brown, *James Brown,* 109.

17. Alan Leeds, interview, "Respect," written, produced, and directed by David Espar, episode 4, *Rock and Roll* (South Burlington, VT: WGBH, 1995), videocassette (VHS).

18. Brown, *I Feel Good,* 76.

19. Hubert Saal, "Mr. Dynamite," *Newsweek,* July 1, 1968, 98.

20. Robert Palmer, "James Brown," in *The Rolling Stone Illustrated History of Rock & Roll,* 3rd ed., ed. Anthony DeCurtis, James Henke, and Holly George-Warren (New York: Random House, 1992), 166.

21. Bill Wyman with Ray Colman, *Stone Alone: The Story of a Rock 'n' Roll Band* (New York: Signet, 1991), 268.

22. Cynthia Rose, *Living in America: The Soul Saga of James Brown* (London: Serpent's Tail, 1990), 32.

23. Brown, *I Feel Good,* 46.

24. Guralnick, *Sweet Soul Music,* 235.

25. Quoted in ibid.

26. Ibid.

27. Brown, *James Brown,* 130.

28. Ibid., 133.

29. James Brown, "Please, Please, Please," *The T.A.M.I. Show,* prod. Lee Savin, dir. Steve Binder (1964; New York: Shout Factory, 2009), DVD.

30. Stephen Davis, *Old Gods, Almost Dead: The 40-Year Odyssey of the Rolling Stones* (New York: Broadway, 2001), 104.

31. Palmer, "James Brown," 168.

32. David Brackett, *Interpreting Popular Music* (Berkeley: University of California Press, 2000), 144–45.

33. Ibid., 145.

34. Alexander Stewart, "'Funky Drummer': New Orleans, James Brown and the Rhythmic Transformation of American Popular Music," *Popular Music* 19 (2000): 309.

35. Brown, *I Feel Good,* 71.

36. Ibid., 79–80.

37. Stewart, "'Funky Drummer,'" 304.

38. Brown, *I Feel Good,* 79.

39. Rickey Vincent, *Funk: The Music, the People, and the Rhythm of the One* (New York: St. Martin's, 1996), 74.

40. Michael Eric Dyson, "The Culture of Hip-Hop," in *That's the Joint!: The Hip-Hop Studies Reader,* ed. Murray Forman and Mark Anthony Neal (New York: Routledge, 2004), 67.

41. LeRoi Jones, quoted in Guralnick, *Sweet Soul Music,* 221; LeRoi Jones, *Black Music* (New York: Morrow, 1967), 185.

42. David Levering Lewis quoted in Guralnick, *Sweet Soul Music,* 240.

43. Ron Welburn quoted in Guthrie P. Ramsey, *Race Music: Black Cultures from Bebop to Hip-Hop* (Berkeley: University of California Press, 2003), 154.

44. William Van Deburg, *New Day in Babylon: The Black Power Movement and American Culture, 1965–1975* (Chicago: University of Chicago Press, 1992), 9.

45. Brown, *James Brown,* 187.

46. R. J. Smith, *The One: The Life and Times of James Brown* (New York: Gotham, 2012), 192–94, correctly observes that there is no way to know if Brown's performance actually did prevent a riot, since a negative can't be proved, but he shows that Brown was given credit for doing so, not only in the press, but also by leaders up to and including President Lyndon Johnson.

47. "James Brown Entertains the Troops," *Ebony* 23 (Aug. 1968): 94.

48. Saal, "Mr. Dynamite," 98.

49. James Brown quoted in ibid.

50. Ward, *Just My Soul Responding,* 392.

51. *Look,* Feb. 18, 1969, cover.

52. Thomas Barry, *Look,* Feb. 18, 1969, 56.

53. Vincent, *Funk,* 83–84.

54. Ibid., 78.

55. Smith, *The One,* 219.

56. Palmer, "James Brown," 168.

57. Brown, *James Brown,* 228.

58. Ibid., 229.

59. James Brown, interview in *Details,* July 1991, 56, quoted in Ward, *Just My Soul Responding,* 392.

60. Brackett, *Interpreting Popular Music,* 124.

61. Brown, *I Feel Good,* 206.

62. Dyson, "The Culture of Hip-Hop," 67.

63. Gerri Hirshey, "Funk's Founding Father," *Rolling Stone,* Jan. 25, 2007, 40.

64. Vincent, *Funk,* 8.

CHAPTER 4: Bob Dylan

1. Robert Hunter quoted in Blair Jackson, *Garcia: An American Life* (New York: Penguin, 1999), 134. Don Heckman, "Once Gable Was King—Now It's Bob Dylan," *New York Times,* Sept. 12, 1971: HF1+. There is one book-length study focusing on Dylan through the lens of stardom, Lee Marshall, *Bob Dylan: The Never Ending Star* (Cambridge: Polity, 2007). Perhaps because Marshall makes no distinction between stardom and celebrity, he fails to provide a clear picture of Dylan's persona in the 1960s; however, the book offers the best account we have of the "never-ending tour" persona of the 1990s and later. Sean Wilentz, *Bob Dylan in America* (New York: Doubleday, 2010), does not explicitly address issues of stardom or persona, but by depicting his subject in a series of different historical contexts he enriches our sense of Dylan's cultural meaning.

2. Clinton Heylin, *Bob Dylan: Behind the Shades* (New York: HarperCollins, 2001), 206.

3. Robert Shelton, *No Direction Home: The Life and Music of Bob Dylan* (New York: Da Capo, 1997), 302.

4. Thus, I think Loren Glass, in "Buying In, Selling Out: From Literary to Musical Celebrity in the United States," *Hedgehog Review* 7, no. 1 (Spring 2005), overrates Dylan's "resistance to his audience(s)" (34). Dylan resisted the folk audience in order to capture the much bigger rock audience.

5. See ibid., 29, which argues that Dylan represents the shift of the bohemian from the literary to the musical field.

6. John Bauldie, liner notes, *Bootleg Series,* vols. 1–3 (New York: Sony Music, 1991), 1.

7. For an insightful reading of this film, see David Yaffe, *Bob Dylan: Like a Complete Unknown* (New Haven: Yale University Press, 2011), 31–58.

8. Anthony Scaduto, *Bob Dylan* (London: Helter Skelter, 1996 [1971]), 45.

9. Bob Dylan, quoted in Shelton, *No Direction Home,* 90.

10. David Hajdu, *Positively 4th Street: The Lives and Times of Joan Baez, Bob Dylan, Mimi Baez Fariña and Richard Fariña* (New York: Farrar, Straus, 2001), 73.

11. Bob Dylan, quoted in Shelton, *No Direction Home,* 90.

12. Ibid., 193.

13. On early imitators of Woody Guthrie, see Joe Klein, *Woody Guthrie: A Life* (New York: Knopf, 1980).

14. Greil Marcus, *Invisible Republic: Bob Dylan's Basement Tapes* (New York: Holt, 1997).

15. "Let Us Now Praise Little Men," *Time,* May 31, 1963: 40.

16. "I Am My Words," *Newsweek,* Nov. 4, 1963, 95.

17. Ellen Willis, "The Sound of Bob Dylan," *Commentary,* Nov. 1967, 71.

18. Heylin, *Bob Dylan: Behind the Shades,* ix; *I'm Not There,* dir. Todd Haynes (Weinstein Company, 2007), DVD.

19. Hajdu, *Positively 4th Street,* 73.

20. Rob Wilson, "Becoming Jeremiah inside the Wilderness of the US Empire: On the Trickster Poetics and Visionary Masks of the Poet, Bob Dylan." Unpublished dialogue between videographer Linda Ching and Wilson. Honolulu, 2003.

21. Raymond Williams, *Keywords: A Vocabulary of Culture and Society,* rev. ed. (New York: Oxford University Press, 1983), 41.

22. W. J. T. Mitchell, "Art," in *New Key Words,* ed. Tony Bennett, Lawrence Grossberg, and Meaghan Morris (Malden, MA: Blackwell, 2005), 6.

23. Clement Greenberg, "Avant-Garde and Kitsch," *Partisan Review* 6 (Autumn 1939): 34–49.

24. Michael Kammen, *American Culture, American Tastes: Social Change and the 20th Century* (New York: Knopf, 1999), 95–100.

25. Bob Dylan, *Chronicles,* vol. 1 (New York: Simon & Schuster, 2004). "Apparently" is all one can say, because one cannot be sure what in *Chronicles* is fact and what is fiction.

26. Ibid., 269.

27. *No Direction Home,* dir. Martin Scorsese (Paramount Home Video, 2005), DVD.

28. Dylan, *Chronicles,* 287.

29. Ibid., 269–70.

30. Elijah Wald, *How the Beatles Destroyed Rock 'n' Roll: An Alternative History of American Popular Music* (New York: Oxford University Press, 2009), 184.

31. Sean Wilentz, liner notes, *Bob Dylan Live 1964* (New York: Sony BMG Music, 2004), 5.

32. Bob Dylan quoted in Nat Hentoff, "The Crackin', Shakin', Breakin' Sounds," *New Yorker,* Oct. 24, 1964, 65.

33. Irwin Silber, "An Open Letter to Bob Dylan," *Sing Out,* Nov. 1964, quoted in Mike Marqusee, *Wicked Messenger: Bob Dylan and the 1960s* (New York: Seven Stories, 2005), 104.

34. Marqusee, *Wicked Messenger,* 111–13.

35. Ibid., 113.

36. Bob Dylan, quoted in Cameron Crowe, liner notes, *Biograph* (New York: Columbia Records, 1985).

37. Marqusee, *Wicked Messenger,* 127.

38. Nick Bromell, *Tomorrow Never Knows: Rock and Psychedelics in the 1960s* (Chicago: University of Chicago Press, 2000), 131, quoting Greg Calvert, national secretary of Students for a Democratic Society. Bromell attributes this shift to the influence of LSD, which Dylan apparently started using in the spring of 1964. Whether or not this explanation is correct, the result remains the same. The singer of these songs is now someone special, sensitive, and autonomous—i.e., an artist.

39. Dylan, *Chronicles,* 115.

40. Ibid.

41. "Let Us Now Praise Little Men," *Time,* May 31, 1963: 40; "I Am My Words," *Newsweek,* Nov. 4, 1963, 94.

42. Greil Marcus, *Like a Rolling Stone: Bob Dylan at the Crossroads* (New York: Public-Affairs, 2005), 35–45.

43. Bruce Springsteen quoted in ibid., 94.

44. Marqusee, *Wicked Messenger,* 163.

45. Christopher Ricks, *Dylan's Visions of Sin* (New York: Ecco, 2004).

46. Keir Keightley, "Reconsidering Rock," in *The Cambridge Companion to Rock and Pop* (Cambridge University Press, 2001), 131.

47. Ray Colman, "Beatles Say—Dylan Shows the Way," *Melody Maker,* Jan. 9, 1965, 3, rpt. in *The Bob Dylan Scrapbook, 1956–1966* (New York: Simon & Schuster, 2005), 39.

48. Thomas Meehan, "Public Writer No. 1?" *New York Times Magazine,* Dec. 12, 1965, 44–45.

49. Jules Siegel, "Well, What Have We Here?" *Saturday Evening Post,* July 30, 1966, 33.

50. Willis, "The Sound of Bob Dylan," 77.

51. Meehan, "Public Writer No. 1?," 44.

52. Karen Murphy and Ronald Gross, "All You Need Is Love," *New York Times Magazine,* Apr. 13, 1969, 42.

53. Marqusee, *Wicked Messenger,* 208.

54. Heylin, *Bob Dylan: Behind the Shades,* 269.

55. "Basic Dylan," review of *John Wesley Harding,* by Bob Dylan, *Time,* Jan. 12, 1968, 50.

56. Mike Jahn, "Self-Portrait of the Artist as an Older Man," review of *John Wesley Harding,* by Bob Dylan, *Saturday Review,* May 11, 1968, 63–64.

57. Ralph Gleason quoted in Shelton, *No Direction Home,* 299; Joe Morganstern, review of *Don't Look Back, Newsweek,* Aug. 21, 1967, 65.

58. Bob Spitz, *Dylan: A Biography* (New York: McGraw-Hill, 1989), 384.

59. D. A. Pennebaker, interview in Scorsese, *No Direction Home.*

60. Clinton Heylin, *Bob Dylan: The Recording Sessions, 1960–1994* (New York: St. Martin's, 1995): 57.

61. Ibid.; Marcus, *Invisible Republic.*

62. Mick Jagger, interview, *25 X 5: The Continuing Adventures of the Rolling Stones,* prod. Andrew Solt (CBS Music Video Enterprises, 1989), videocassette (VHS).

63. Todd Gitlin, *The Sixties: Years of Hope, Days of Rage* (New York: Bantam, 1987), 29.

64. John Cunnick quoted in Bromell, *Tomorrow Never Knows,* 1.

65. Ibid., 5.

66. Greil Marcus quoted in ibid., 13.

67. Simon Frith, "Afterword: Making Sense of Video," in *Music for Pleasure: Essays in the Sociology of Pop* (New York: Routledge, 1988), 213.

68. Simon Frith, "Something to Be—John Lennon," in *Music for Pleasure,* 74–75.

69. Gitlin, *The Sixties;* Charles Kaiser, *1968 in America: Music, Politics, Chaos, Counterculture, and the Shaping of a Generation* (New York: Weidenfeld & Nicolson, 1988).

70. James Miller, *Democracy in the Streets: From Port Huron to the Siege of Chicago* (Cambridge: Harvard University Press, 1994), 238, 254.

71. Richard Flacks quoted in ibid., 161.

CHAPTER 5: The Rolling Stones

1. In the 1960s, the Stones were sometimes embraced by the New Left. Peter Wicke, *Rock Music: Culture, Aesthetic and Sociology* (Cambridge: Cambridge University Press, 1990), quotes a 1967 manifesto by San Francisco students welcoming the Stones as comrades in struggle. Tony Sanchez, *Up and Down with the Rolling Stones* (New York: Signet, 1980 [1979]), 127–28, describes Mick Jagger's brief participation in an antiwar demonstration, which he left after being recognized and feeling himself to be a distraction. Sanchez describes this as the origin of "Street Fighting Man." See John Platoff, "John Lennon, 'Revolution,' and the Politics of Musical Reception," *Journal of Musicology* 22, no. 2 (2005): 241–67, for an account of how "Street Fighting Man" was embraced despite its lyrics, while the Beatles' "Revolution" was

rejected because of lyrics that say pretty much the same thing. Barry Faulk, *British Rock Modernism, 1967–1977: The Story of Music Hall in Rock* (Farnham: Ashgate, 2010), 101, thinks Jagger held an "activist ideal" in 1968 from which he later moved away. In general, however, the Stones have not recently been explicitly cited as progressive, but many paeans to punk have made the same mistake. I would exempt analyses like Dick Hebdige, *Subculture: The Meaning of Style* (London: Methuen, 1979), here because he specifies very particular subcultural contexts in which he believes punk was politically significant.

2. Mick Jagger, interview in *Gimme Shelter,* dir. Albert Maysles, David Maysles, and Charlotte Zwerin (1970; Criterion Collection, 2004), DVD.

3. Tom Donahue, "The Rolling Stones / B.B. King: Oakland Coliseum, California," *Cashbox,* Nov. 22, 1969, www.rocksbackpages.com/article.html?ArticleID=2311&Search Text=tom+donahue.

4. Michael Lydon, *Rock Folk: Portraits from the Rock 'n' Roll Pantheon* (New York: Dell, 1973), 157.

5. Stanley Booth, *The True Adventures of the Rolling Stones* (Chicago: Chicago Review, 2000 [1984]), 29.

6. Mick Jagger quoted in ibid., 31.

7. Thus Elijah Wald, *How the Beatles Destroyed Rock 'n' Roll: An Alternative History of American Popular Music* (New York: Oxford University Press, 2009), 2–4, likens the Beatles to Paul Whiteman, a leader of a jazz orchestra in the 1920s who made jazz palatable for white audiences. On how the Beatles achieved high-culture status, see Bernard Gendron, *Between Montmartre and the Mudd Club: Popular Music and the Avant-Garde* (Chicago: University of Chicago Press, 2002), 161–224.

8. I'm not writing a chapter on the Beatles here because so much has already been written about them—no one doubts their iconic status—and, paradoxically, also because the task of understanding their cultural significance requires more space than I can devote to one star.

9. Bill Wyman with Ray Colman, *Stone Alone: The Story of a Rock 'n' Roll Band* (New York: Signet, 1991), 163.

10. Keith Richards with James Fox, *Life* (New York: Little, Brown, 2010), 127.

11. *Northern Beat Scene,* 1963, quoted in ibid., 177.

12. G. Stanley Hall, *Adolescence: Its Psychology and Its Relation to Physiology, Anthropology, Sociology, Sex, Crime, Religion, and Education* (New York: Appleton, 1904).

13. Edgar Z. Friedenberg, *Coming of Age in America* (New York: Vintage, 1967), 3.

14. Edgar Z. Friedenberg, *The Vanishing Adolescent* (Boston: Beacon, 1959), 12.

15. Erik H. Erikson, *Childhood and Society* (New York: Norton, 1950); Erik H. Erikson, *Young Man Luther* (New York: Norton, 1958).

16. Leerom Medovoi, *Rebels: Youth and the Cold War Origins of Identity* (Durham, NC: Duke University Press, 2005), 6.

17. Bobby Keys quoted in Robert Greenfield, *A Journey through America with the Rolling Stones* (London: Helter Skelter, 2001 [1974]), 176–77.

18. Stephen Davis, *Old Gods, Almost Dead: The 40-Year Odyssey of the Rolling Stones* (New York: Broadway, 2001), 103.

19. Nat Hentoff quoted in Wyman, *Stone Alone,* 324.

20. Ed Sullivan quoted in ibid.

21. Ibid., 325, 263.

22. Sheila Whiteley, "Little Red Rooster v. the Honky Tonk Woman: Mick Jagger, Sexuality, Style and Image," in *Sexing the Groove: Popular Music and Gender* (London: Routledge, 1997), 78–79.

23. Michel Foucault, *The History of Sexuality,* vol. 1: *An Introduction,* trans. Robert Hurley (New York: Pantheon, 1978), 3–13.

24. Leslie Fiedler, *Love and Death in the American Novel,* rev. ed. (Briarcliff Manor, NY: Stein & Day, 1966).

25. Andrew Oldham quoted in James Miller, *Flowers in the Dustbin: The Rise of Rock and Roll, 1947–1977* (New York: Simon & Schuster, 1999), 200.

26. Whiteley, "Little Red Rooster v. the Honky Tonk Woman," 67.

27. Ibid., 77.

28. Robert Christgau, "The Rolling Stones," in *The Rolling Stone Illustrated History of Rock & Roll,* 3rd ed., ed. Anthony DeCurtis, James Henke, and Holly George-Warren (New York: Random House, 1992), 242.

29. Ibid., 246.

30. Mark Edmundson, *The Fine Wisdom and Perfect Teachings of the Kings of Rock and Roll: A Memoir* (New York: HarperCollins, 2010), 20.

31. Michael Lydon, *Rock Folk,* 171–72.

32. Robert Greenfield, *Exile on Main Street: A Season in Hell with the Rolling Stones* (New York: Da Capo, 2006), 26.

33. David Dalton, *The Rolling Stones: The First Twenty Years* (New York: Knopf, 1981), 143.

34. Wyman, *Stone Alone,* 338.

35. Greenfield, *A Journey through America,* 83.

36. Dalton, *The Rolling Stones,* 143.

37. Davis, *Old Gods, Almost Dead,* 364.

38. Greenfield, *A Journey through America,* 166.

39. Wyman, *Stone Alone,* 468; Tony Sanchez, *Up and Down with the Rolling Stones* (New York: Signet, 1980 [1979]).

40. Greenfield, *A Journey through America,* 49.

41. Ibid., 129.

42. Sanchez, *Up and Down with the Rolling Stones,* 306.

43. Greenfield, preface to the 1997 edition, *A Journey through America,* 7.

44. Sanchez, *Up and Down with the Rolling Stones,* quoting Keith Richards, 313.

45. Booth, *The True Adventures of the Rolling Stones,* 348–76.

46. Ibid., 385.

47. "Stones Rule the Road," *Rolling Stone,* Jan. 25, 2007, 12.

48. Leerom Medovoi, *Rebels: Youth and the Cold War Origins of Identity* (Durham, NC: Duke University Press, 2005), 3.

CHAPTER 6: The Grateful Dead

1. Jerry Garcia, interview with Jim Henke, *Rolling Stone,* Oct. 31, 1991, 37.

2. George Will, "About that 'Sixties Idealism,'" *Newsweek,* Aug. 21, 1995, 72.

3. Dennis McNally, *A Long Strange Trip: The Inside History of the Grateful Dead* (New York: Broadway, 2002), 3.

4. Bob Weir, interview in David Gans and Peter Simon, *Playing in the Band: An Oral and Visual Portrait of the Grateful Dead,* 2nd ed. (New York: St. Martin's, 1995), 191.

5. Jerry Garcia quoted in Blair Jackson, *Garcia: An American Life* (New York: Penguin, 1999), 204.

6. McNally, *A Long Strange Trip,* 3; Simon Frith, "Rock and the Politics of Memory," in *The 60s without Apology,* ed. Sohnya Sayers et al. (Minneapolis: University of Minnesota Press, 1984), 65.

7. Phil Lesh, *Searching for the Sound: My Life with the Grateful Dead* (New York: Little, Brown, 2005), 112.

8. Ralph Gleason, *The Jefferson Airplane and the San Francisco Sound* (New York: Ballantine, 1969), 80.

9. Gene Sculatti, "San Francisco Bay Rock," *Crawdaddy!,* 1966, www.rocksbackpages.com /article.html?ArticleID=1765.

10. Michael Lydon, "Has Frisco Gone Commercial?," *New York Times,* Nov. 24, 1968, H3.

11. Frith, "Rock and the Politics of Memory," 61–62.

12. Ibid., 69.

13. Ibid., 59.

14. Alice Echols, *Shaking Ground: The 60s and Its Aftershocks* (New York: Columbia University Press, 2002), 18.

15. Warren Hinckle, "May the Baby Jesus Open Your Mind and Shut Your Mouth: The Hippies," *Ramparts,* Mar. 1967, quoted in Jackson, *Garcia,* 119.

16. Jerry Garcia quoted in Jackson, *Garcia,* 191.

17. McNally, *A Long Strange Trip,* 127.

18. Joel Slevin, introduction, *Summer of Love: The Inside Story of LSD, Rock & Roll, Free Love, and High Times in the Wild West* (New York: Penguin, 1994), n.p.

19. *Monterey Pop,* dir. D. A. Pennebaker (1967; Santa Monica, CA: Criterion, 2006), DVD.

20. *Anthem to Beauty,* dir. Jeremy Marre (1997; New York: Eagle Vision, 2005), DVD.

21. Dan Healy quoted in ibid.

22. Jeff Kisseloff, *Generation on Fire: Voices of Protest from the 1960s; An Oral History* (Lexington: University Press of Kentucky, 2007), 137.

23. Peter Berg quoted in ibid., 144.

24. Ibid., 146.

25. Tom Wolfe, *The Electric Kool-Aid Acid Test* (New York: Bantam, 1969), 211.

26. Jerry Garcia, interview in *Anthem to Beauty.*

27. Frith, "Rock and the Politics of Memory," 65.

28. Arthur Marwick, *The Sixties: Cultural Transformation in Britain, France, Italy and the United States, c. 1958–c. 1974* (New York: Oxford University Press, 2000), 26.

29. Wolfe, *The Electric Kool-Aid Acid Test,* 223.

30. Mickey Hart, interview in *Anthem to Beauty.*

31. Simon Frith, "Grateful Dead: *Vintage Dead; Historic Dead,*" *Cream,* June 1972, www .rocksbackpages.com/article.html?ArticleID=3395.

32. Todd Gitlin, *The Sixties: Years of Hope, Days of Rage* (New York: Bantam, 1987), 195–97.

33. Robert Hunter quoted in Mikal Gilmore, "The New Dawn of the Grateful Dead," *Rolling Stone,* July 30, 1987, 50. Attributing the phrase "Up against the wall"—a New Left and Black Power slogan—to the Jefferson Airplane suggests that Hunter had been out of touch with contemporary radical politics.

34. Jerry Garcia quoted in Jackson, *Garcia,* 191.

35. McNally, *A Long Strange Trip,* 174.

36. Walter Medeiros, "Mapping San Francisco, 1965–1967: Roots and Florescence of the San Francisco Counterculture," in *Summer of Love: Psychedelic Art, Social Crisis and Counterculture in the 1960s* (Liverpool: Liverpool University Press, 2005), 308.

37. McNally, *A Long Strange Trip,* 118.

38. Gans and Simon, *Playing in the Band,* 78–79.

39. *Tie-Died: Rock 'n' Roll's Most Deadicated Fans,* dir. Andrew Behar (1995; New York: Fox Lorber Films, 1999), DVD.

40. Ibid.

41. Ibid.

42. Mikal Gilmore quoted in Gans and Simon, *Playing in the Band,* 204–5.

43. *Tie-Died.*

44. Phil Lesh quoted in Gans and Simon, *Playing in the Band,* 165.

45. Jerry Garcia quoted in Jackson, *Garcia,* 191.

46. Robert Hunter, *A Box of Rain: Lyrics 1965–1993* (New York: Penguin, 1993), 35.

47. Jackson, *Garcia,* 241.

48. Lesh, *Searching for the Sound,* 112.

49. Charles Kaiser, *1968 in America: Music, Politics, Chaos, Counterculture, and the Shaping of a Generation* (New York: Weidenfeld & Nicholson, 1988), 192.

50. McNally, *A Long Strange Trip,* 159.

51. Jerilyn Lee Brandelius, *Grateful Dead Family Album* (New York: Warner, 1989).

52. Steven Stolder, "Grateful Dead Cut Staff," *Rolling Stone,* Oct. 19, 1995, 24.

53. David Gans, interview in *Anthem to Beauty.*

CHAPTER 7: Joni Mitchell

1. Loren Glass misunderstands this when he credits Dylan with shifting rock stardom from personality to personal expression in "Buying In, Selling Out: From Literary to Musical Celebrity in the United States," *Hedgehog Review* 7, no. 1 (Spring 2005), 29–30. As I have argued, starting with Elvis, rock & roll entailed the idea of the singer being identified with his or her songs regardless of who wrote them.

2. For evidence of this, consider that a Google *n*-gram search shows no usage of the construction "singer-songwriter" prior to the early 1970s.

3. Jewel, "The Immortals—The Greatest Artists of All Time: 60) Joni Mitchell," *Rolling Stone,* Apr. 15, 2004, www.rollingstone.com/news/story/7235480/the_immortals_the_greatest_artists_of_all_time_60_joni_mitchell. That Joni Mitchell was ranked only 60th is shocking and is strong confirmation of DiFranco's point. There are only four women in the top 50, and only Aretha Franklin made it into the top 10. The other three are Madonna, Janis Joplin, and Patti Smith. All told, *Rolling Stone* could find only ten women or female groups deserving a place among the 100 "immortals."

4. David DeVoss, "Rock 'n' Roll's Leading Lady," *Time,* Dec. 16, 1974, www.time.com/time/magazine/article/0,9171,911559,00.html.

5. David Wild, "A Conversation with Joni Mitchell," *Rolling Stone,* May 30, 1991, 66.

6. Sheila Weller, *Girls Like Us: Carole King, Joni Mitchell, Carly Simon—and the Journey of a Generation* (New York: Atria, 2008). Notice that I am discussing the title, which I think is better evidence than the book's content of Mitchell's iconic status. The book makes little effort to explain how the three women represent a generation, and in its treatment of Mitchell could be called a prose version of the *Rolling Stone* chart of Mitchell's love affairs brought up to date. It should be noted that Mitchell has long objected to being grouped with King and Simon.

7. Judy Kutulas, " 'That's the Way I've Always Heard It Should Be': Baby Boomers, 1970s Singer-Songwriters, and Romantic Relationships," *Journal of American History* 97, no. 3 (2010): 690.

8. Wild, "A Conversation with Joni Mitchell," 64.

9. Ani DiFranco, "Ani DiFranco Chats with the Iconic Joni Mitchell," *Los Angeles Times,* Sept. 20, 1998: 20.

10. For a somewhat different take on the emergence of the singer-songwriter, see Kutulas, " 'That's the Way I've Always Heard It Should Be,' " 682–702.

11. Lester Bangs, "James Taylor Marked for Death," in *Psychotic Reactions and Carburetor Dung,* ed. Greil Marcus (New York: Vintage, 1988 [1971]), 53–81.

12. Dave Marsh, *Born to Run: The Bruce Springsteen Story* (Garden City, NY: Doubleday, 1979), 85.

13. Joni Mitchell, interview in *Joni Mitchell: Woman of Heart and Mind,* dir. Susan Lacy (1998; New York: Eagle Vision, 2003), DVD.

14. John Berryman, "Despondency and Madness," in *The Contemporary Poet as Artist and Critic: Eight Symposia,* ed. Anthony Ostroff (Boston: Little, Brown, 1964), 99.

15. M. L. Rosenthal, *The Modern Poets: A Critical Introduction* (New York: Oxford University Press, 1960), 226.

16. Irving Howe, "The Plath Celebration: A Partial Dissent," *The Critical Point: On Literature and Culture* (New York: Dell, 1973), 167.

17. Rosenthal, *The Modern Poets,* 233.

18. Ibid., 232–34.

19. Ibid., 233.

20. Ibid., 237.

21. In this regard, Leonard Cohen's songs remain closer to poetry than do those of Taylor or Mitchell, making him less typical of singer-songwriters in general.

22. Joni Mitchell, quoted in Stephen Holden, "The Ambivalent Hall of Famer," *New York Times,* Dec. 1, 1996, http://www.nytimes.com/1996/12/01/arts/the-ambivalent-hall-of -famer.html?scp=4&sq=Joni+Mitchell&st=nyt.

23. Howe, "The Plath Celebration," 163–64.

24. Mitchell, quoted in Holden, "The Ambivalent Hall of Famer."

25. Joni Mitchell, "The *Rolling Stone* Interview," by Cameron Crowe, *Rolling Stone,* July 26, 1979, 49.

26. Joni Mitchell quoted in Timothy White, "A Portrait of the Artist," *Billboard,* Dec. 9, 1995, 15.

27. Karen O'Brien, *Joni Mitchell: Shadows and Light* (London: Virgin, 2002), 137–38.

28. P. David Marshall, *Celebrity and Power: Fame in Contemporary Culture* (Minneapolis: University of Minnesota Press, 1997), 234.

29. Paul Williams, "The Way We Are Today," in *The Age of Rock,* ed. Jonathan Eisen (New York: Random House, 1969), www.rocksbackpages.com/article_with_login.html?Arti cleID=2272.

30. There is a musical shift as well, as Lloyd Whitesell observes, "By the time of 'The Arrangement' (1969, *Ladies of the Canyon*), reference to folk models is no longer pertinent." He quotes Mitchell herself describing the song as a "forerunner" with "more musical sophistication" than other songs prior to *Blue. The Music of Joni Mitchell* (New York: Oxford University Press, 2008), 19. Cf. Daniel Sonnenberg, who argues that as early as "I Had a King" (1968, *Song to a Seagull*) Mitchell's guitar technique and vocal performance style distinguish "her music from the folk tradition." " 'Who in the World She Might Be': A Contextual and Stylistic Approach to the Early Music of Joni Mitchell." DMA diss., City University of New York, 2003, 24.

31. Rob Mackie, "From Folk Waif to Rock & Roll Lady," *Sounds,* Apr. 27, 1974, rpt. in *The Joni Mitchell Companion: Four Decades of Commentary,* ed. Stacy Luftig (New York: Schirmer, 2000), 63–66.

32. Timothy Crouse, review of *Blue,* by Joni Mitchell, *Rolling Stone,* Aug. 5, 1971, 42.

33. "Joni Mitchell," *Rolling Stone,* May 17, 1969, 10H.

34. Gerald Astor, "Songs for Aging Children," *Look,* Jan. 27, 1970.

35. Sue Gordon Lydon, "In Her House, Love," *New York Times,* Apr. 20, 1969, D19+.

36. Peter Reilly, review of *Blue,* by Joni Mitchell, *Stereo Review,* Oct. 1971, rpt. in *The Joni Mitchell Companion,* 41; Dan Heckman, "Pop: Jim Morrison at the End, Joni at a Crossroads," review of *Blue,* by Joni Mitchell, *New York Times,* Aug. 8, 1971: D15.

37. Crouse, review of *Blue,* 42.

38. Joni Mitchell, interview in *Joni Mitchell: Woman of Heart and Mind.*

39. White, "A Portrait of the Artist," 15.

40. Michael Watts, "Priestess Joni," *Melody Maker,* May 13, 1972, http://jonimitchell.com /library/view.cfm?id=181.

41. Stephen Davis, "Joni Mitchell's *For the Roses:* It's Good for a Hole in the Heart," *Rolling Stone,* Jan. 4, 1973, 60.

42. Sheila Whiteley, "The Lonely Road: Joni Mitchell," in *Women and Popular Music: Sexuality, Identity, and Subjectivity* (London: Routledge, 2000), 78.

43. David DeVoss, "An Evening Spent at Joni's," *Time,* Dec. 16, 1974, www.time.com/time /magazine/article/0,9171,911560,00.html.

44. Loraine Alterman, "Joni's Songs Are for Everyone," *New York Times,* Jan. 6, 1974, 127.

45. DeVoss, "An Evening Spent at Joni's."

46. Wild, "A Conversation with Joni Mitchell," 64.

47. O'Brien, *Joni Mitchell,* 153.

48. "It Happened in 1970," *Rolling Stone,* Feb. 4, 1971, 44; "Hollywood's Hot 100," *Rolling Stone,* Feb. 3, 1972, 27.

49. Alterman, "Joni's Songs Are for Everyone," 127.

50. David Shumway, *Modern Love: Romance, Intimacy, and the Marriage Crisis* (New York: NYU Press, 2003).

51. Mitchell, "The *Rolling Stone* Interview," 50.

52. Malka Morom, interview in *Joni Mitchell: Woman of Heart and Mind.*

53. Joni Mitchell, interview in ibid.

54. DeVoss, "Rock 'n' Roll's Leading Lady"; "Joni Mitchell: Self-Portrait of a Superstar," *McClean's* June 1974, rpt. in *The Joni Mitchell Companion,* 66–74.

55. Perry Meisel, "An End to Innocence: How Joni Mitchell Fails," *Village Voice,* Jan. 1977, http://jonimitchell.com/library/view.cfm?id=412&from=search.

56. John Rockwell, "Joni Mitchell Recaptures Her Gift," *New York Times,* Dec. 12, 1976, D17.

57. Bob Spitz, *Dylan: A Biography* (New York: McGraw-Hill, 1989), 446–47.

58. Ellen Willis, review of *Blood on the Tracks,* by Bob Dylan, *New Yorker,* Apr. 7, 1975, 130–34.

59. Joni Mitchell, interview in "Joni Mitchell," by David Wild, *Rolling Stone,* Oct. 15, 1992, 168.

CHAPTER 8: Bruce Springsteen

1. Jon Landau, "Growing Young with Rock and Roll," *Real Paper,* May 22, 1974.

2. Robert Christgau observed that Springsteen's reputation was heavily dependent on critics as early as 1976, though he limits his focus to rock critics, ignoring the role of *Time* and *Newsweek*: "Yes, There is a Rock-Critic Establishment (But Is That Bad for Rock?)," *Village Voice,* Jan. 26, 1976, http://robertchristgau.com/xg/rock/critics-76.php, accessed July 17, 2003.

3. Peter Knobler with Gregg Mitchell, "Who Is Bruce Springsteen and Why Are We Saying All These Wonderful Things about Him?" *Crawdaddy!,* Mar. 1973, rpt. in *Racing in the Street: The Bruce Springsteen Reader,* ed. June Skinner Sawyers (New York: Penguin, 2004),

29–39; Stuart Werbin, "It's Sign Up a Genius Month," *Rolling Stone,* Apr. 26, 1973, rpt. in *Bruce Springsteen: The "Rolling Stone" Files* (New York: Hyperion, 1996), 29–31.

4. Landau, "Growing Young with Rock and Roll."

5. Landau would become Springsteen's manager and the producer of *Born to Run.*

6. Landau, "Growing Young with Rock and Roll."

7. John Rockwell, "Bruce Springsteen Evolves into a Figure of Rock Expression," *New York Times,* July 16, 1974: 43; Dave Marsh, "A Rock 'Star Is Born' Performance Review," *Rolling Stone,* Sept. 25, 1975, rpt. in *Bruce Springsteen: The "Rolling Stone" Files,* 39–40; John Rockwell, "A New Dylan from New Jersey? It Might as Well be Springsteen," *Rolling Stone,* Oct. 9, 1975, rpt. in *Bruce Springsteen: The "Rolling Stone" Files,* 41–47.

8. Lester Bangs, review of *Greetings from Asbury Park,* by Bruce Springsteen, *Rolling Stone,* July 5, 1973, rpt. in *Bruce Springsteen: The "Rolling Stone" Files,* 32–33; Greil Marcus, review of *Born to Run,* by Bruce Springsteen, *Rolling Stone,* Oct. 9, 1975, rpt. in *Bruce Springsteen: The "Rolling Stone" Files,* 48–51.

9. Jay Cocks, "Rock's New Sensation: The Backstreet Phantom of Rock," *Time,* Oct. 27, 1975, rpt. in *Racing in the Street,* 65.

10. Maureen Orth, Janet Huck, and Peter S. Greenberg, "Making of a Rock Star," *Newsweek,* Oct. 27, 1975, rpt. in *Racing in the Street,* 54.

11. Henry Edwards quoted in Orth, Huck, and Greenberg, "Making of a Rock Star," 55.

12. Mike Appel quoted in ibid., 62, italics in original.

13. Lawrence Grossberg, *We Gotta Get Out of This Place: Popular Conservatism and Postmodern Culture* (New York: Routledge, 1992), 201.

14. Bruce Springsteen, "The *Rolling Stone* Interview," by Kurt Loder, *Rolling Stone,* Dec. 6, 1984, 70.

15. Ibid., 21.

16. Lester Bangs, "Hot Rumble in the Promised Land," *Creem,* Nov. 1975, rpt. in *Racing in the Street,* 76.

17. Robert Beverley Ray, "Bruce Springsteen: Growing Up Is Hard to Do," *Wall Street Journal,* Aug. 4, 1978, 9.

18. Louis P. Masur, *Runaway Dream: "Born to Run" and Bruce Springsteen's American Vision* (New York: Bloomsbury, 2009), 106.

19. Anthony DeCurtis, "What Springsteen Kept to Himself," *New York Times,* Nov. 4, 2010, www.nytimes.com/2010/11/07/arts/music/07darkness.html?pagewanted=all, accessed May 24, 2013.

20. It should be kept in mind that the reviews that greeted *Darkness,* which in the United States were largely positive, did not discuss the record's class identification. That connection has become common only in the 2000s, and especially after Springsteen released the outtakes from the *Darkness* sessions on *The Promise* (2010) in a set that included a video about the making of the album. For the reviews, see Dave Marsh, review of *Darkness on the Edge of Town,* by Bruce Springsteen, *Rolling Stone,* July 27, 1978, http://www.rolling stone.com/music/albumreviews/darkness-on-the-edge-of-town-19780727, accessed May 24, 2013; Mitchell Cohen, review of *Darkness on the Edge of Town,* by Bruce Springsteen, *Creem,* Sept. 1978, www.rocksbackpages.com/Library/Article/bruce-springsteen-darkness-on-the -edge-of-town-columbia, accessed May 24, 2013; John Rockwell, "Jagger, Springsteen and the New Angst," *New York Times,* June 11, 1978, D25+. For more recent readings, see Jefferson Cowie, *Stayin' Alive: The 1970s and the Last Days of the Working Class* (New York: New Press, 2010), 339–42; Dave Marsh, *Bruce Springsteen: Two Hearts* (New York: Routledge, 2004), 193.

21. Marsh, *Bruce Springsteen: Two Hearts,* 281.

22. Bill Barol et al., "He's On Fire," *Newsweek,* Aug. 5, 1985, 51.

23. David Masciotra, *Working on a Dream: The Progressive Political Vision of Bruce Springsteen* (New York: Continuum, 2010), 67.

24. E. Ann Kaplan, *Rocking Around the Clock: Music Television, Postmodernism, and Consumer Culture* (New York: Routledge, 1987), 76–77.

25. Cowie, *Stayin' Alive,* 359. For a more extended reading, see Jefferson Cowie and Lauren Boehm, "Dead Man's Town: 'Born in the U.S.A.,' Social History, and Working Class Identity," *American Quarterly* 28 (June 2006): 353–78.

26. Eric Alterman, *It Ain't No Sin to Be Glad You're Alive: The Promise of Bruce Springsteen* (Boston: Little, Brown, 2001), 163–68.

27. The most well known of such studies is Graham Murdoch and Guy Phelps, "Responding to Popular Music: Criteria of Classification and Choice among English Teenagers," *Popular Music & Society* 1 (1971): 144–51. More recent studies show the same results: J. L. Rosenbaum, Jill Leslie, and Lorraine E. Prinsky, "Sex, Violence and Rock 'n' Roll: Youths' Perceptions of Popular Music," *Popular Music & Society* 11 (1987): 79–89; L. E. Prinsky and J. L. Rosenbaum, "'Leer-ics' or Lyrics: Teenage Impressions of Rock 'n' Roll," *Youth and Society* 18 (1987): 385–97.

28. Dan Cavicchi, *Tramps Like Us: Music and Meaning among Springsteen's Fans* (New York: Oxford University Press, 1998), 122–24.

29. Jack Newfield, "Springsteen: A Spark Starting a Fire," *Village Voice,* Sept. 24, 1985, 27.

30. Alterman, *It Ain't No Sin to Be Glad You're Alive,* 163.

31. Bill Barol et al., "He's On Fire," 48.

32. Fred Goodman, *The Mansion on the Hill: Dylan, Young, Geffen, Springsteen, and the Head-On Collision of Rock and Commerce* (New York: Random House, 1998), 339–42.

33. Robert Christgau, "Journey through the Past," *Village Voice,* Dec. 17, 1979, http://www.robertchristgau.com/xg/rock/decade-79.php.

34. Alterman, *It Ain't No Sin to Be Glad You're Alive,* 161.

35. Ibid.

36. Goodman, *The Mansion on the Hill,* 345–47.

37. James Miller, *Flowers in the Dustbin: The Rise of Rock and Roll, 1947–1977* (New York: Simon & Schuster, 1999), 325.

38. Simon Frith, "The Real Thing—Bruce Springsteen," in *Music for Pleasure: Essays in the Sociology of Pop* (New York: Routledge, 1988), 101.

39. Simon Frith, "Confessions of a Rock Critic," in *Music for Pleasure,* 166.

40. Simon Frith, "The Real Thing—Bruce Springsteen," 97.

41. Ibid., 96.

42. Sawyers, introduction, *Racing in the Street,* 2.

43. The *Seattle Times* quoted in ibid., 13.

44. Christopher Palmer, program notes, *War Requiem,* by Benjamin Britten (London: Decca, 1985), 7.

45. Josh Tyrangiel and Kate Carcaterra, "Bruce Rising," *Time,* Aug. 5, 2002, 52.

46. Patrick Kelly, "'The Rising' of Bruce Springsteen," *America,* Feb. 10, 2003, 8, http://search.proquest.com/docview/209680987?accountid=9902 (accessed Nov. 22, 2013).

47. Noam Chomsky, *9/11* (New York: Seven Stories, 2001).

48. Michael Denning, *The Cultural Front: The Laboring of American Culture in the Twentieth Century* (London: Verso, 1996), 470.

49. Paul Krugman, *End this Depression Now!* (New York: Norton, 2012).

50. For journalistic support for the observation that the Great Recession has been largely unaddressed by popular music, see "Pop Music of the Great Depression vs. the

Great Recession: Seems Bleak," *The Thought Catalog,* Sept. 24, 2010, http://thoughtcatalog .com/2010/pop-music-great-depression-great-recession/; Kathleen Geier, "'The Forgotten Man': The Great Recession in Popular Culture," Political Animal, Apr. 28, 2013, www.wash ingtonmonthly.com/political-animal-a/2012_04/the_forgotten_man_the_great_re036989 .php#.

51. Masciotra, *Working on a Dream,* 16–17.

Conclusion

1. David Goldman, "Music's Lost Decade: Sales Cut in Half," Feb. 3, 2010, CNNMoney. com, http://money.cnn.com/2010/02/02/news/companies/napster_music_industry/.

2. Stan Liebowitz, "Will MP3 Downloads Annihilate the Record Industry? The Evidence So Far," *Advances in the Study of Entrepreneurship, Innovation, and Economic Growth* 15 (2004): 229–60, www.utdallas.edu/~liebowit/.

3. Daniel Kreps, "2010 Album Sales: Way Worse than 2009 Album Sales," Amplifier Blog, Jan. 6, 2011, http://music.yahoo.com/blogs/amplifier/2010-album-sales-way-worse -than-2009-album-sales.html; "2011 Year-End Shipment Statistics," Recording Industry Association of America, www.riaa.com/keystatistics.php?content_selector=2008-2009-U.S -Shipment-Numbers.

4. Ibid.

5. Kreps, "2010 Album Sales."

6. "Stones Rule the Road," *Rolling Stone,* Jan. 25, 2007, 12; "On the Road in 2007," *Rolling Stone,* Feb. 7, 2008, 18; "Bright Spots in the Bad Year," *Rolling Stone,* Feb. 5, 2009, 16; "The Verdict: 2009's Hits and Misses," *Rolling Stone,* Jan. 21, 2010, 12.

7. Elijah Wald, *How the Beatles Destroyed Rock 'n' Roll: An Alternative History of American Popular Music* (New York: Oxford University Press, 2009), 166–229.

8. Max Horkheimer and Theodor W. Adorno, "The Culture Industry," *Dialectic of Enlightenment,* trans. John Cumming (New York: Continuum, 1972), 120–67.

9. Peter Spellman, "Musician 2.0, 3.0. 4.0 . . . Developing Music Careers in Uncertain Times: A Psycho-Spiritual-Musical Manifesto," http://www.mbsolutions.com/articles/. Spellman runs a company called Music Business Solutions and is director of career development at Berklee College of Music.

10. Dave Kusek, *The Future of Music: Manifesto for the Digital Music Revolution,* (Boston: Berklee Press, 2005).

11. Yochai Benkler, "Yochai Benkler: The New, Open-Source Economics," filmed July 2005, posted Apr. 2008, TED video, 17:56, www.ted.com/talks/yochai_benkler_on_the_new _open_source_economics.html; Yochai Benkler, "Yochai Benkler—On Autonomy, Control and Cultural Experience," YouTube video, 7:53, from an interview for Steal this Film 2, New York, Apr. 2007, posted by "stealthisfilm" on July 24, 2011, www.youtube.com/watch ?v=vmiGOQooTNA.

12. Spellman, "Musician 2.0, 3.0. 4.0"; Andrew Ross, *Nice Work If You Can Get It: Life and Labor in Precarious Times* (New York: NYU Press, 2010).

13. "The New Music Biz: Letting Fans Direct the Band," *Time* video, 4:44, n.d., www .time.com/time/video/player/0,32068,114797669001_2025840,00.html.

14. "The New Music Biz: Cracking the Code to Online Success," *Time* video, 5:01, n.d., http://www.time.com/time/video/player/0,32068,114803516001_2027352,00.html.

15. See, e.g., Tricia Rose, *Black Noise: Rap Music and Black Culture in Contemporary America* (London: Wesleyan University Press, 1994), 99–145; Mark Anthony Neal, "Postindustrial Soul: Black Popular Music at the Crossroads," in *That's the Joint!: The Hip-Hop Studies Reader,* ed. Murray Forman and Mark Anthony Neal (New York: Routledge, 2004), 363–87; *Born to*

Use Mics: Reading Nas's "Illmatic," ed. Michael Eric Dyson and Sohail Daulatzi (New York: Basic Civitas Books, 2010), passim.

16. Neal, "Postindustrial Soul," traces this decline all the way back to 1990, and he calls Public Enemy's *It Takes a Nation of Millions to Hold Us Back* (1988) "the apex of politically infused hip-hop," 376.

11/14